Home Networking Survival Guide

About the Author

David Strom is a leading expert on network and Internet technologies. He also runs his own consulting practice in Port Washington, N.Y. and has worked with many of the leading networking vendors on improving their products and refining their marketing strategy.

Mr. Strom began his computing career in 1981 and went to work in Information Technology departments for the U.S. Government and private industry, installing his first local area network in 1984. In 1986 he moved to technology journalism, helping launch *PC Week*'s networking supplement, "Connectivity." In 1990, he created *Network Computing* magazine and was its first editor-in-chief.

He has written extensively on networking for both print and Web publications including *InfoWorld, Network World, Computerworld, cnet.com*, the *Tokyo Daily Yomiuri, Internet.com* and *Techtarget.com*. Since September 1995 he has self-published a weekly series of essays called "Web Informant," sent via e-mail to subscribers around the world, covering topics such as eCommerce, Web advertising, and home networking. You can join this exclusive mailing list by going to his Web site at strom.com.

Mr. Strom is also a frequent speaker, panel moderator, and instructor at industry events and trade shows and at his local high school when he teaches a NetPrep class.

In and around his neighborhood in Port Washington, he has been doing networking and computing troubleshooting house calls.

Home Networking Survival Guide

DAVID **STROM**

Osborne/McGraw-Hill

New York   Chicago   San Francisco
Lisbon   London   Madrid   Mexico City   Milan
New Delhi   San Juan   Seoul   Singapore   Sydney   Toronto

Osborne/**McGraw-Hill**
2600 Tenth Street
Berkeley, California 94710
U.S.A.

To arrange bulk purchase discounts for sales promotions, premiums, or fund-raisers, please contact Osborne/**McGraw-Hill** at the above address. For information on translations or book distributors outside the U.S.A., please see the International Contact Information page immediately following the index of this book.

Home Networking Survival Guide

234567890 CUS CUS 01987654321

ISBN 0-07-219311-5

Publisher
Brandon A. Nordin

Vice President & Associate Publisher
Scott Rogers

Acquisitions Editor
Francis Kelly

Project Editor
Elizabeth Seymour

Acquisitions Coordinator
Alexander Corona

Technical Editor
Tony Ryan

Copy Editor
Jan Jue

Proofreader
Melissa Lynch

Indexer
Valerie Robbins

Computer Designers
Carie Abrew, Lucie Ericksen, Elizabeth Jang

Illustrators
Michael Mueller
Lyssa Wald

Series Design
Lucie Ericksen

Cover Design
Gorska Design

This book was designed and composed with Corel VENTURA™ Publisher.

Contents
at a Glance

Contents

Acknowledgments

No book can be written without the help of many people, and I want to first thank my wife Lisa and daughter Maia for all their patience in putting up with my odd working hours and odd working habits in the preparation of this book. And for their patience in putting up with the changes and ups and downs of our own home network as I tried to test one more product and one other configuration as the book took shape.

I also want to thank the many family members and friends and neighbors who acted as experimental subjects and inadvertent test labs for the numerous products and experiences accounted for in the book. Without their support, this book wouldn't be as useful to you as I know it will be. I'd especially like to thank Tony Ryan, Laura Mogul, and Richard Ford for commenting on early drafts and providing numerous changes and improvements. I'd also like to thank Tony Ryan, Carey Holzman, and Pat and Brownell Chalstrom for providing three great appendices that provide additional technical details.

Finally, I'd like to thank Francis Kelly, Elizabeth Seymour, and the rest of the Osborne/McGraw Hill bicoastal production team for their terrific job in producing this book. Of course, any errors that you find are solely my responsibility, ignorance, or omission.

Introduction

Most of us have a hard enough time dealing with a single, unconnected personal computer (PC) in our homes. We have trouble staying ahead of our kids' knowledge and making unapproved or inappropriate changes to the PC. We are frustrated when we have an important report to finish one evening for a work-related deadline and the computer isn't working because of some game or gremlin or downloaded file that was installed by a family member earlier in the day. We have difficulty keeping the printer stocked with supplies and managing e-mail accounts for everyone in the house.

These challenges pale in comparison to putting together a home network, even a small one involving just two or three PCs. Until recently, you couldn't buy everything that you needed in one box, even if you knew what you needed or could trust the people in your average retail computer store to tell you honestly what to buy. And the "network in a box" doesn't help you if one or more of your computers is running an older version of Windows or Macintosh operating systems (OS), which are notorious for their obscure networking support.

Actually, figuring out what to buy is just the beginning. You have to set up a bunch of different components, and make sure they are wired together. Hooking up a network can be as hard as trying to connect your TV, DVD player and stereo together. It's probably harder, because there are no standard cables and because the software takes more to configure than simple on-screen menus. You might have to drill a few holes in your walls. And you have computers with different equipment configurations and different vintages and versions of operating systems. It is definitely a lot harder!

For those of you new to networking, it can seem overwhelming. You have so many things to consider that you can't distinguish between the PC, the operating system, the network adapter, the adapter's drivers, the cabling, and the protocols connecting everything. One of my neighbors spent the better part of eight hours on the phone with Intel's tech support when he started setting up his network, and others have similar stories to tell. If you are running Windows 95, you almost certainly will run into problems. If you have an older PC that doesn't support PCI or USB adapters, ditto. (If you don't know what these are, we'll explain them later.) If you have a mixture of Macs and PCs, or PCs running various versions of Windows operating systems, you are in for some extended counseling sessions.

After all this is said, don't let the enormous challenge of doing it stop you from considering a home network. The benefits are huge, and worth whatever hassles you go through. Probably the best reason for a home network is to share a high-speed Internet connection among your entire family, so that everyone can benefit from this "fat pipe" and nearly instantaneous downloads. The good news is that surviving your first home network doesn't require a great deal of skill, other than patience and perseverance. That is where this book will prove to be an invaluable guide.

My home network started when I got a cable modem for my home computer. Up until that time, my family shared a single computer; most of the time I was the only one who used the Internet. That changed radically the moment my wife and daughter found out that they could surf the Internet and get e-mail delivered continuously without having to fumble through dial-up commands and wait while the modem did its noisy dance.

All of a sudden, a single shared computer wasn't enough for the family. Once my wife started her own business, and my daughter's homework assignments got more complex, it was clear that two computers weren't going to work, either. Now we needed a network that would enable us to share the high-speed Internet connection as well as the laser and ink-jet printers we had at home. Suddenly, I was doing end-user computing support for my family, and bringing home more and more gear to hook up and to maintain.

I had all sorts of choices to consider. I had to decide how to share files and set up the printers among the computers. I had to choose how to cable everything together, knowing that my wife had ultimate domestic design approval when it came time to run things through the walls and around the rooms. Then there was my cable Internet connection: Sharing that wasn't simple.

Luckily, this is something that I know something about. My background is in corporate end-user support, from those dark ages when networks were coming of age and PCs still had 640 kilobytes of memory. (Yes, that is kilobytes—today you can't even buy memory chips in kilobytes!) I began my professional career in computers just as Apple and IBM were getting into the game, and had set up networks, big and small, for the government and a private insurance company.

Since putting together my own home network I have gone on to set up dozens at friends' and neighbors' homes around Long Island, New York, and have helped numerous others through various articles published in technical trade magazines such as *Byte.com*, *Network World*, and *Computerworld*. (You can read copies of many of my published articles on my Web site, www.strom.com.) I've gained lots of experience setting up a wide variety of products in a wide variety of homes. And I've learned that not everything works as intended.

There are many people I know who, after getting their broadband line for one computer, continue to use dial-up for their remaining computers because they can't deal with the issues surrounding a home network. That is a real shame. In an industry that offers gigabit and terabit speeds for the office, we are still stuck in the slow lane on the home front. This is the real digital divide, and will remain so until the home networking products get better—or if you know a friendly networking expert who is willing to make house calls.

That's where this book comes in. Even if you can't distinguish opening Windows 2000 applications from opening your living room windows, you'll find in here almost everything you'll need to get started with your first home network, and how to survive its quirks and problems. Yes, you are going to have problems along the way, I can promise you that. Networks are full of gremlins, and sometimes figuring out what causes their peculiarities isn't easy. But given that more and more families have multiple PCs in their homes, many of you are going to want to network them and do so successfully. As the number of Internet-connected households continues to increase, there is a compelling reason to get started.

Who this book is for

Writing any book assumes a certain audience and skill level. The goal of this book is to get you running a network with a minimum of fuss and bother, and with just a few inexpensive products. You will have to spend some money to get a network going—how much will depend on how many computers you are connecting together and how difficult it will be to make those connections. My aim is to give you simple advice and, above all, to be practical, with enough detail to guide but not overwhelm you.

If you are an ordinary consumer, with little to no PC or professional Information Technology/computing expertise, then this is the right book for you. I don't assume that you can take apart your PC and put it back together in working order, although I will discuss ways you can add various bits and pieces to your existing computer to make it work over a network. If you have never used a network before, or if you use a network at work but don't really know much about how it works, then you have come to the right place. Even if you have some knowledge, you will still get something out of this book, as you can benefit from my testing and using the various products that I talk about in these pages.

If you have already purchased some networking equipment, but can't seem to make it work, then perhaps this book can help you do some rudimentary troubleshooting, or at least steer you in the right direction to where you can determine that you have bought the right item or need to get something else. There is nothing more frustrating than bringing home a new piece of gear, only to spend hours fooling around with it, while your family stands around, watching you become irate. (Well, you could watch *me* fooling around with some new network gear, and getting aggravated.) That is one of the reasons why I wrote this book: to get even with all the vendors of products that almost, but not quite, work.

This book will also help if you are contemplating doing major renovations on your house and adding a network in the process. After all, the ideal time to add wiring to your walls is when you don't have any walls to deal with, or if you are going to be ripping bigger holes into them than drilling places to run wiring through them. I'll help you figure out where you should locate your PCs, printers, and other devices around your house.

If you already have a bunch of computers, I'll help you figure out which are worth networking, and which aren't. Many books assume that you will rush out and buy the latest PC, fully loaded and running the fastest processor. I don't. I designed this book to cover a mixture of old and new equipment, which is a challenge because every version of Windows (and, to some extent, Macintoshes) has a slightly different way of setting up its networking components.

If you presently own a single PC and are trying to decide whether it is worth it to add a second system to your home, then this book will prepare you for what lies ahead. I will also provide tips on how to incorporate these older computers into your home network.

Rest assured that anything I recommend in these pages is something that I, personally, have tried out in an actual home. Often I have found that something that works in my office, where I have an existing network, won't work quite the same way when I bring it over to a friend's house, where there isn't any network. It isn't that the vendors don't tell you the truth or don't deliver a working product; it's just that every home is different, and these conditions can make it easy or hard to install your network and keep it running.

How this book is organized

Each chapter of this book will focus on a particular task, such as sharing files and printers, and setting up your Internet connection. I assume you are a running a mixture of different computers and operating systems, so I will demonstrate the differences among the versions, including both Windows and Macintoshes, when these differences are important. Given the number of choices involved, I will lay out the advantages and disadvantages of each one and list simple steps you can take to make the appropriate decision.

Each chapter of this book is divided into five sections, so you can read particular ones of interest and follow the discussion when you need it most. Don't feel obligated to read through the entire book if all you are trying to do is get a quick answer to a specific question or solve one problem. The five chapter sections are:

+ An **introduction** to basic concepts

+ **Problems** and issues relevant to that particular topic

✦ **Solutions** to these problems along with recommended products and how to set them up

✦ **Troubleshooting** tips and other suggestions for when things will go wrong or aren't working the way they are supposed to

✦ **Future developments** and directions so this book will still be relevant after it is published

Chapter 1 looks at home wiring choices. Any network requires some kind of connection, and there are many types to choose from, including a new series of wireless products that can avoid drilling holes through your walls and running cables around your floors. I'll discuss where you should locate your computers and printers and how to make sure you pick the right kind of cables.

Chapter 2 examines sharing files and introduces the basic networking concepts that are part of your computer's operating system. I'll also discuss which devices you don't want to share on your home network.

Chapter 3 looks at sharing printers, probably the most obvious device that any home networking user will want to connect to a network. Sharing printers seems obvious, but getting it to work involves choosing the right product and setting it up correctly. By the end of this chapter, you should have a working basic home network set up.

Chapter 4 goes into detail about the single biggest motivation for having a home network: sharing an Internet connection. There are numerous technologies to choose from, and I'll help you decide which one will work best for you and how to make sure you buy the right gear.

Chapter 5 covers e-mail and messaging issues. E-mail, and its close cousin Instant Messaging (IM), are perhaps two universal Internet applications, and probably the most used service by anyone with a computer these days. I'll review how you can set up multiple e-mail accounts on a single computer, make use of AOL IM from your new network, and how to migrate from your existing AOL dial-up accounts.

Chapter 6 looks at how you need to protect your network from intruders and others who want to do damage to your computers. I'll cover setting up your first firewall and installing virus protection on all of your computers, and what to do when someone is trying to break in.

Chapter 7 covers keeping track of your family's surfing habits, and reviews ways that parents can be smart and stay informed about the Web sites, news groups, chat rooms, and other places around the Internet that their children visit. While this is not exclusive to surviving your home network, it is a natural consequence of putting together all this gear and something that every well-intentioned parent should know.

Finally, chapter 8 looks at some of the more advanced applications that you might want to run over your new home network, including connecting your computer to your music and stereo components, using digital video cameras, and controlling your home lighting and appliances.

In addition to this structure, this book uses a series of icons to indicate various special situations throughout the text. The icons are:

SURVIVAL TIP

Survival Tip: A brief pointer to make life easier for you

NOTE

Note: A note to draw attention to something that is important

CAUTION

Caution: Common pitfalls

What this book isn't about

This book isn't going to give you lots of details on how to run large-scale networks; there are plenty of other books that delve into those areas. And this isn't a book that is designed so that someone can get into the guts of their network operating system. Nor is it a way to learn how to set up business-critical functions like backing up files and e-mail list servers. Nor is this book going to go into depth for someone who wants to run a Web server from a home network.

This isn't a book on how to pick the best sites to surf the Internet, or how to run various Internet applications such as newsreaders and chat programs, or where to download the best shareware programs that do the same. You won't find any tips here on how to use search portals or to track down information over the Web (unless of course it is networking information). I don't have many tips on how to select an Internet Service Provider, other than choosing the particular high-speed technology offered by that provider.

I also didn't set out to replace the instruction manuals that came with your computer, or any of the products that I recommend here. (Granted, many of these manuals have gotten skimpier over the years.) My goal is to give you just the right level of detail. If you want something meatier, you can probably find it on the shelf near where you bought this book.

What is on various Web sites

Given that this book covers technologies that are subject to frequent change, the information contained within is probably going to be somewhat out of date. Some of the outdated information isn't that important: Products come and go, and you shouldn't be upset if you try to find something that I recommend but is no longer being made. The important thing is to be able to judge for yourself which products will work for your particular situation, based on the criteria and decisions that I will describe in each chapter.

Having said that, I recommend two Web sites that you can go to for updated information. I have had nothing to do with the content on either Web site, so do take what you find there with several grains of salt.

The first site is called DSLreports.com. It contains lots of information to help you decide on the best provider of Digital Subscriber Line service, one of the major ways that you can obtain a high-speed Internet connection. There are also pointers and links to various home networking technologies on this site.

The second Web site is called PracticallyNetworked.com, which contains copious information about specific networking technologies, reviews of numerous products, and strategies to get your home wired.

From time to time, I'll post updates and suggestions on my own Web site, (http://strom.com/homenet), and provide links to other places around the Web that contain useful information for first-time networkers.

Who I am

In the interest of full disclosure, you should know something about my background and experience. I have always been interested in networking and computer communications, and enjoyed hooking things together to see if they could communicate with each other. I have had my own business since 1992, working for a wide variety of computer hardware and software vendors. My job is to research, test, and write about their products, and explain how to make them work better to the vendors so that you will have an easier time using them, assuming that the vendors take my advice and fix the things that I find wrong.

Product testing comes naturally to me, though I can't tell you why. I certainly don't have any "Mr. Fix It" skills when it comes to getting anything repaired around the house (as my family can attest). I couldn't fix a leaky faucet or change the oil in my car if my life depended on it. But I can fix almost all common PC problems.

Over the years, I have tested hundreds of different products, including Internet software, network operating systems, desktop and network applications, and various networking devices and communications products. In the past decade, I have written over 1000 articles for various computer trade magazines. Before starting my own consulting business, I was the founding editor-in-chief of Network Computing magazine for CMP Media, and hired its first staff of editors and production people. I also ran a new product reviews department for Transamerica Occidental Life Insurance Company, where we put in our first Novell network back in the 1980s. Before that, I was an in-house consultant in Information Technology departments for the U.S. Department of Agriculture and the U.S. Congress Office of Technology Assessment, back when PCs were being created.

This is my second book. My first, written and published in 1998, was called *Internet Messaging* (Prentice Hall, 1998) and written with Marshall T. Rose, one of the inventors of the Internet e-mail protocols. My thanks to Marshall for giving me the courage and teaching me the skills to write a book on my own.

This book grew out of a series of almost weekly essays about Web and Internet technologies, called "Web Informant," that I began writing in the fall of 1995. Some of these essays described my early attempts to set up home networks and document some of the experiences, helping friends and neighbors along the way. Other essays have nothing to do with home networking, and cover issues such as Internet privacy, e-mail security, and more technical topics. If you like what you read here and want a regular dose, you can subscribe to these essays, which are delivered via e-mail, by going to my Web site (http://strom.com/awards).

Chapter 1

Home Wiring Choices

Y
ou are about to embark on a journey whose destination is the connection of two or more of your computers together to share information, printers, Internet access, and more. It is a worthwhile journey and a necessary one (especially if you want to share a high-speed Internet connection), but it can follow a bumpy road. I hope to make it a pleasant journey for you, or at least be your guide and prop you up when you hit the inevitable potholes.

Enough of that metaphor.

If you haven't read the Preface, let me explain my approach in this book. Each of these chapters will first review some of the major issues and obstacles that you will face in assembling various parts of your network. Then I'll tackle what you need to do in terms of picking the right products and setting them up properly. If something isn't working right, I'll give you tips on how to troubleshoot your network. Finally, I'll end on what you can expect to see coming down the pike in the near future.

This chapter covers how you are going to wire your home for a network. Start thinking about this, because your choice of wiring will affect what kind of gear you'll buy and what you'll need to add to your existing PCs to network them properly.

Every network makes use of some kind of connection, and the good news about home networking is that there are some solid products that you can buy to meet your particular needs. The bad news has been that no one really walks you through the decision process so you can carefully match the products and your needs.

I will. That is why you are reading this book.

Networking Vocabulary

I hated those college textbooks that spent the first chapter defining terms. To be effective, however, I need to define a few terms that make up our networking vocabulary, so that when I refer to them later, you'll know what I'm talking about. Knowing these terms will help you interpret what the computer is telling you when you install your network. Since this book can be used by both Windows and Mac people, and since Windows and Macs use slightly different words for the same things, I'll indicate their differences.

✦ **Client**   The client is the piece of software that is used to communicate over your network. It can also be a piece of software that communicates with another program, either on the same computer, or on another computer on your network. Typically, clients connect to servers, which do the heavy lifting and keep track of whatever shared resources (like files and printers) you have. Windows has several client pieces, including the Client for Microsoft Networks. Macs have an AppleShare client. *Clients* and *servers* also refer to the specific computer that is doing the work. The client PC is usually the one on your immediate desktop, connecting to the shared resources on the server. However, these days the notion of client and server is something of a misnomer. They are usually one and the same machine, doing two different tasks: any Windows and Mac PC can easily become both. I can share the files on my desktop with you, and you can share the files on your desktop with me.

NOTE

If you are planning on making every machine a file server[1] in this fashion, realize that a file server is only such when it is powered-on. It doesn't do your home network much good if you turn off your file server PC and then try to grab files from it. Consider this in your design and in how you intend to distribute files around your network.

◆ **Adapter**   The adapter is the physical connection between your computer and the network and is typically an internal Ethernet card that plugs into one of the spare slots inside your PC. (We'll get into other external adapters in this chapter, too.) Windows also refers to modem connections to the Internet as "dial-up adapters," just to confuse things. Most Macs sold today come with built-in Ethernet adapters, and some more enlightened Windows vendors are also including them with their Intel-based PCs.

◆ **Protocol**   A protocol is a communications language that connects two or more programs together. For computers to talk to each other, they must use the same protocol. Most languages use sound, but that doesn't mean that someone who only speaks Japanese can talk with someone who only speaks English just because English and Japanese both use sounds. The same is true for network protocols. Two computers could be hooked to the same network, but if they don't have matching protocols, they can't talk to each other. For networking purposes, we make use of at least one protocol, TCP/IP (Transmission Control Protocol/Internet Protocol). Actually, it is two protocols that are combined for the price of one and are usually considered together. TCP/IP is the language of the Internet, and most modern networking systems use it in some fashion. If you follow my instructions, you will install TCP/IP on every computer in your home network. Windows computers use an additional protocol, called NetBEUI. Macs use their own additional protocol called AppleTalk. Some network-based games use another protocol called IPX. There are plenty of other protocols, but these are the main ones to be concerned about.

---

1   Realize that there are versions of Windows that are explicitly designed as file server operating systems, including Windows 2000 Server versions. Most of you, however, probably don't have these running on your home networks and probably won't want to, either. I don't cover them in this book.

+ **Service**   These are the pieces of software that actually do stuff, such as file and printer sharing. Windows uses "service" in several important ways that we'll get to in Chapter 2, but you can also find Mac-oriented references as well.

+ **User/Owner Name**   This is the identity of the person who is using the computer. Each PC requires you to register who you are when you begin using it on a network. You can have separate and unique user names (and their associated passwords) for every family member, but a better idea is to just use the same user name/password combination on all of your computers. The Mac world calls this the owner name; Windows calls this the user name.

+ **Workgroup and Computer Names**   Microsoft Windows requires each of its computers to be members of a workgroup. The Mac doesn't, but both require you to name each of your computers so you can keep track of them when it comes time to connect to their shared resources.

SURVIVAL TIP

I recommend using descriptive names like UPSTAIRS, DOWNSTRS, JOHNSPC, WIN98, MACG4, and so on. I also recommend keeping all your computer and workgroup names short, fewer than 8 characters. Don't use any embedded spaces or uncommon characters besides letters and numbers.

Each home network comes with three major components, more or less. The *adapter card* is inside or outside each PC, depending on the type of adapter. This provides the actual data to the network and handles all of the physical and logical connections of your computer to the network. The *network cabling* itself is the next component. If you use a wireless network, obviously you don't have to worry about this. (You do, however, have to worry about other things that we'll get to in a moment.) Finally, all of the wires attach to the *hub* or *connector*, and that is used as a central connecting point for your network. Again, not all networks need hubs, and I'll tell you why shortly.

The network adapter cards[2] can take one of four possible shapes. First are two kinds that fit inside your computer, in one of the spare slots. Depending on the kind of slots you have, you'll either want an *ISA* (Industry Standard Architecture) or a *PCI* (Peripheral Component Interconnect) adapter. The other two can be fitted into your computer without having to open up the case.

One is a *PC Card* (also called a PCMCIA card) adapter that fits into a laptop PC Card socket and is about the size of a small deck of playing cards. The other is a *USB* (Universal

---

2   Some people call these Network Interface Cards (NICs). I won't use this term in this book since we all could do with fewer acronyms.

Serial Bus) adapter that attaches to the outside of your computer via a USB port. I'll explain reasons for buying one or the other of these adapters when we come to each situation. Don't worry too much about these three-letter acronyms for now. What is important is understanding why you would need one or the other for your particular situation.

For your network to operate properly, each of these items needs to be correctly configured and must match on all of your computers. A small mistake in a workgroup name or specifying the wrong adapter card will prevent one of your PCs from working on your home network.

Problems

You would think that getting your home networked should be easy. You can quickly decide on the right products to buy, and you can install them without any troubles and have everything up and running within a few hours. Yeah, right. For most of us, this isn't going to happen. It is because of mistakes we make, or configurations on our computers, or how our homes are constructed. You will come across numerous problems in your journey to get your home connected.

If you are new to networking, you probably haven't even thought about some of these issues, and reading this next section might be depressing. As Jessica Rabbit said, "I'm not bad. I'm just drawn that way." The same can be said about your networking experience. The more you know going in, the better your chances are of surviving and overcoming these challenges. Let's take a look at some of the typical problems.

Location Problem

The first issue is where your current computers are or should be located around your house. Depending on a wide variety of circumstances, you will have an easy time to a hard time.

Let's look at the easy situations first and then tackle the problems. If all of your computers are in the same room, or in adjoining rooms, you are in great shape. If all of your computers are near existing telephone jacks, and these jacks are working, and the phone wiring in your home is in good shape, then so are you. If you have access to your attic or basement or crawl space or inside the walls of your home (during a remodeling, for example), then you are going to get through this networking thing reasonably pain-free.

The rest of you are going to have some problems dealing with your computers. If you have or want to have a computer in a room without any phone jacks, or on the opposite side of the room from your jacks, then you will have to figure out how to get wires to that location. You might have to go through the floors, one of the walls, or the ceiling. You might have to drill a few holes and poke some wires around.

Drilling Problem

What if you don't feel comfortable (or don't have spousal design approval for) drilling holes and running wires hither and yon around your house? Even if you did, that still might present more of a challenge for you than you are ready to take on. It isn't just drilling the holes, but understanding how much cabling you'll need, and what kind, and how to attach the right kinds of connectors on either end once you get finished poking it through your walls and floors. Another way is called *wireless networking*. But that isn't a piece of cake, either.

Wireless Problems

If you can't or don't want to wire your home, and you don't have many telephone jacks located in the places where you'd like your computers, choose wireless network products for your home network. They offer the same convenience for hooking up computers that cordless phones offer when you need to reach out and touch someone. The wireless networks make use of radio waves to transmit data to and receive data from one computer and another. Various issues surround the use of wireless networks. Wireless networks may work just fine in your home. They may be impossible to get working. You don't know until you get the products home and start fooling around with them.

Depending on the type of home construction you have and where you locate your computers, you may be in for more trouble than you expected. The radio transmitters and receivers that are part of wireless networking products work relatively well on most homes. You won't be sorry that you suffered through some of their peculiar problems when you take your laptop out by the deck or pool or down the street to surf the Internet and read your e-mails. But when they don't work, they can consume endless hours of fiddling around.

The "S" family residence is a good case in point about wireless hell. Their house is an old stone mansion that has walls several feet thick. They had computers in their basement, which is the hardest place in such a home for radio signals to reach. They weren't able to penetrate their thick walls and establish a connection, even though the overall distance that the signals had to travel was about 25 feet. It didn't help that the basement computer was smack against a wall and under a huge desk. The more mass in between your radios, the less signal will get through.

Wiring Type Problem

If you want to wire your home for networking, you can choose among several major types of cabling that can handle the Ethernet network protocols and products. If you were lucky enough to have your computers near phone jacks, you can make use of a special type of networking called *PhoneLine* that we'll get into in a moment in the solutions section. But if your phone wiring doesn't go where you want your computers to go, then you'll have to consider one of the Ethernet wiring schemes.

Twisted-pair, also called *10BaseT* wiring, is something like your telephone wiring. *Thin Ethernet*, which takes the form of coaxial (coax) cabling, is similar to your cable TV cabling, called *10Base2*. Another wiring scheme is *thick Ethernet*, also called *10Base5* or *attachment unit interface* (AUI) cabling. Finally, *100BaseT* wiring runs at slightly faster speeds than 10BaseT and is supported by most of the Ethernet adapters and hubs available today.

**SURVIVAL
TIP**

Each Ethernet wiring scheme is incompatible with the others, and once you pick the wiring type you must, I repeat, *must*, choose an Ethernet adapter that has that particular type of connector, unless you want to buy additional gear to convert one form into another. The one exception is that category 5 wiring can be used to support both 10BaseT and 100BaseT networks.

The coax connectors look very similar to the kinds of connectors you'll find on the back of your TV set and are called BNCs (for bayonet nut couplers,[3] if you must know). The 10BaseT connectors look similar to the telephone jacks in your walls (although they are different) and are called RJ-45s.[4] The AUI connectors don't look like anything else you'll find on your computer.

Which one do you choose for your home network? I'll give away the answer here (10BaseT), and then explain why in the "Solutions" section.[5]

In addition to the Ethernet choices, another network topology called *token ring* exists. Its popularity, fortunately, is declining, and we can safely ignore it for home networking purposes.[6]

---

3   Some debate exists on what the acronym BNC really stands for. I've heard "British Naval Connector," "Baby Neill Concelman" connector, "Bayonet-Neill-Concelman" connector, and others.

4   The telephone jacks are called RJ-11 and use four wires. The Ethernet jacks for 10BaseT networks are called RJ-45s and have room for eight wires. The "RJ," by the way, means "registered jack."

5   Several additional cabling types for higher-speed Ethernet networks are available, but for simplicity and to make this chapter readable, I don't get into them here. If you want to get into the relative merits of these different Ethernet technologies, I suggest you read a more advanced networking book, such as *Networking: A Beginner's Guide* by Bruce Hallberg (Osborne/McGraw Hill, 2000).

6   In the early days of networking, say, the mid-1980s, token ring networks were all the rage. IBM and numerous other vendors backed them. However, their Ethernet cousins soon outstripped token ring products. Today only a few networks of some large IBM accounts like banks, hospitals, and insurance companies use token ring. A third variety of network, ARCnet, has also come and gone, just to be complete here.

Windows 95 Problem

Wiring isn't your only problem. You are going to have some headaches if you have a Windows 95 computer in your home. Windows 95 is incredibly difficult to network, mainly because it is such an old operating system that much of the networking gear currently sold doesn't really work with it. If you can upgrade your PC to a more recent version of Windows, even Windows 98, you will be much better off. If you can't, prepare to have some major headaches.

How can you tell which version of Windows you are running? Bring up the Control Panel, go to System, and compare what is shown in the upper-right corner with Table 1-1.

CAUTION

If you have the original Windows 95 (the 4.00.950 version), you are likely to have some problems with at least one of the products recommended in this book, and probably more. Think about upgrading to a newer version, if you can. If you have the later version, Windows 95B, you might be able to squeak by.

Why will you have problems? Mainly because the latest network adapters don't always support Win95, and when they do, they have all sorts of quirks that you must deal with to get them installed properly. The later versions of Windows do a much better job of automatically detecting and handling the variety of network adapters you'll fit inside your machine. Note that there are two versions of Win95: a more recent version, sometimes called Win95B, has networking improvements, but still isn't as capable as later versions, such as Win98.

SURVIVAL TIP

If your computer has at least a 400-MHz Pentium and 128MB of RAM and a 6GB hard disk, then it should be able to handle a new operating system such as Windows XP or Windows ME. If you don't have this kind of machine, try to find a copy of Win98.

Windows Operating System	Version Number Reported in System Control Panel
Windows 95 (original)	4.00.950
Windows 95B	4.00.950b or 4.00.1111
Windows 98 (original)	4.10.1998
Windows 98 Second Edition	4.10.2222 A
Windows ME	4.90.3000
Windows 2000 Professional	5.00.2195
Windows XP Home/Professional	2002

Table 1-1.   Windows Version Information

Old Mac Problem

All newer Macs, like the iMac or the G4, come with built-in 10BaseT Ethernet adapters.[7]
You may have an older Macintosh that doesn't come with a built-in network adapter.
Macintoshes are incredibly easy to network, provided that you have a Mac that comes
with an Ethernet or wireless adapter. If it doesn't, then you will face the same problems
that the Windows folks have to deal with as a matter of course. You'll have to locate the
special slots for your adapter and make sure you purchase the right kind for your particular
Mac. This isn't insurmountable, just one more thing to deal with while you are trying to
get things working.

You could have problems with your new Macs as well. If you want to mix old and new
Macs on your network, you might have trouble finding a common wiring scheme that will
work for both without buying some additional pieces to connect them. While the newer
Macs come with Ethernet built in, they also do *not* come with LocalTalk, the system used for
the older Macs, built in. If you want to take advantage of using PhoneLine wiring instead of
ordinary Ethernet, you'll have to purchase network adapters for this system.

Under-the-Hood Problem

I have some bad news. Not all adapter cards will fit in all slots of all computers. In an ideal
world, every PCI-type adapter card would work in every PCI-type slot, but that isn't the
case. There are various subspecies of PCI slots, and, unfortunately, you don't know if
you've picked the wrong one until you open up the machine, put your adapter card in the
slot, and then try to get everything working.

To make matters more troubling, some PCs have different types of PCI slots in the
same machine. This means you could get your network card working if you moved it over
one or two positions. Why do vendors make this stuff so complicated? I won't go into the
differences between PCI slots here. But you have been warned.

Some of you may not have the skills necessary to be comfortable opening up your
computer's case and fiddling around with its innards. In that case, you have to purchase
a special adapter that connects to its USB port.

CAUTION

If you are running Windows 95, you are out of luck, because Windows 95 doesn't support USB
connectors. If you have a computer made before 1997, probably no USB ports came with it.

---

7   Some of the newest Macs have built-in 10/100/1000=megabit Ethernet ports and work on all
     three speeds.

Other solutions besides USB have thankfully fallen by the wayside, or as my Internet friends say, have been "eclipsed by events." These products attached to your computer's parallel printer port and connected to either a wired 10BaseT Ethernet or to the AC power lines of your home. Neither was appropriate for home networks—parallel port adapters because they were too expensive, and AC power lines because they were unreliable. If you have come across either of these products, and you have a computer that is too old to make use of USB, and you are desperate and too cheap to buy a new PC, then by all means try them. Just don't call me if they don't work, and don't expect much from them when they do.

I have confined my discussions of networking to the process of physically connecting all of your computers around your home. Many challenges lie ahead, even once you get the wires (or wireless) products that you need. We will get to these issues in subsequent chapters. First, let's figure out what you need to purchase to solve these problems and match up the right kind of gear with your situation.

Solutions

Before we can attempt to solve any of these problems, you need to answer a few basic questions posed in Table 1-2. Start at the top row, work your way down until you get to a situation number, and then read the text under that situation. If you have more than one situation that applies to your home, read several, or heck, read the entire section here to get a good overview of what is in store for you.

NOTE   In this chapter I don't actually cover installing anything in your computers, other than the wires that you may need for your network. You'll have to wait until you get to Chapter 2 for that. You have your hands full with wiring issues right now—focus on those.

Here's some general advice before we discuss each of the situations. Your circumstances may include more than one solution. If so, always pick the wired over the wireless solution. Network wiring is inherently more predictable and stable than wireless, if you compare products of similar features and quality. The nature of wireless communications means wireless is always a dicey proposition. You may have all sorts of radio noise in your home that could make it difficult to get a wireless network established properly. The wireless networks use the same frequencies that a lot of things around your home use. For example, your cordless phones and your network could interfere with each other. It's best to use the wired choices when you can.

Question	If the Answer Is Yes	If the Answer Is No
Are your PCs located near existing (and working) telephone jacks?	Situation #1 (PhoneLine networking)	Continue below
Do you have the carpentry skills and spousal design approval to run wires and drill holes around your house?	Continue below	Situation #2 (wireless USB)
Are you running Windows 95?	Situation #3 (replace with new PC)	Continue below
Do you have any Macs?	Situation #4 (Mac networks)	Continue below
Are you brave and talented enough to open up the PC and install a network card and its drivers?	Situation #5 (ordinary Ethernet)	Either Situation #6 (wired USB) or #2 (wireless USB)

Table 1-2.   Wiring Solutions Matrix

You might know someone who is handy with home wiring, whether it is alarm systems, telephones, or cable TV wiring. If you don't mind paying this person to do the job for you, then use standard Ethernet cabling and hook up your computers that way. This will always be a superior solution, and if your Cable Guy understands how to assemble a proper Ethernet cable, then it is well worth your while to pay for this kind of service.

To see how one family solved their wiring needs, check out Appendix C and the case study of the Chalstroms' Annapolis home. They took advantage when building their new house to specify locations for wiring. It's a good example of what is involved if you wish to wire your home for more than computer networking, to include telephones and cable TV.

NOTE

Earlier, I mentioned that network adapters come in three basic varieties. So what do you buy? Refer to Figure 1-1 for an illustration of how each adapter fits into the overall scheme.

✦ **PC Cards**   Use this if you have a laptop. Just about every modern laptop computer sold over the past decade contains slots for one or two PC Cards. This is probably the best solution, but it is also the most expensive adapter you can purchase.

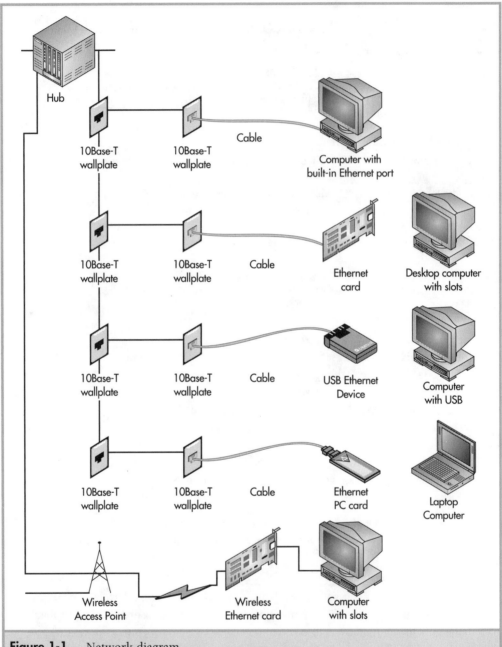

Figure 1-1. Network diagram

✦ **USB adapter**   If you don't want to open up your computer, or if you want a somewhat less expensive solution for your laptop, consider a USB adapter. You can't use any of the USB adapters if you are running the original version of Windows 95, unfortunately. These are somewhat less expensive than PC Cards.

✦ **PCI/ISA card**   This is the way to go if you feel comfortable opening up your computer, and your computer has a spare slot that can handle one of these cards. This is the usual recommendation for most Windows PCs and those Mac desktop computers that don't already come with built-in adapters. It's also the cheapest of the three choices. Network cards can be had for about $25–$50, and less if you look hard and long enough for some bargains.

The two types of internal cards differ. What you purchase will depend on the vintage of your computer, whether you have anything else occupying the slots inside the case that will conflict with the ISA cards, and whether you have empty slots that you can fit one of the network adapters in. Buy a PCI adapter, with the possible exception of a machine made before 1997. I would choose an ISA adapter for this kind of machine.

Whatever product you purchase should state clearly whether it is PCI or ISA, and if it doesn't, assume that it is ISA. PCI cards used to cost more than ISA, but that price differential has all but vanished. Finally, PCI cards are used in both Windows and most modern Macintoshes, making them something of an advantage. (Although you'll need drivers for the Mac side of things because most PCI adapters don't come with support for Macintoshes. Adapters from Farallon are noteworthy exceptions that support both types.)

I have used adapters from Netgear, Linksys, 3Com, Farallon, Asante, Intel, and D-Link and can recommend them all for most purposes. Does this mean that every adapter that I have tried works on every machine? Far from it. In general, the newer the machine, the less trouble I have had in installing an adapter. In some ancient machines, none of the newer adapters I have used have worked, and some new machines can confuse just about anything that I have put in them.

Of course, not every vendor makes adapters for all nine possible types of situations. Table 1-3 covers the major vendors for both Windows and Macintoshes. (Some special considerations for deciding on the best networking solution for Macs will be covered in the Situation #4 section.)

SURVIVAL TIP

Netgear, Linksys, and Farallon have the widest selection of products available. You should probably start with those three vendors' products when supplying your network.

As mentioned earlier, don't buy anything until you finish reading Chapter 2 and have a good idea of what is in store for you. Table 1-3 gets you started assembling your parts list.

Product Type	Wireless	PhoneLine	Ethernet
Windows PC Card adapters	Netgear, Linksys, Orinoco	Linksys	3Com, Linksys, Netgear
PCI/ISA Windows adapters	Netgear, Linksys, Orinoco	3Com, Intel, Linksys, Netgear, Farallon, Diamond	3Com, Netgear, Linksys
USB Windows adapters	D-Link, Linksys, Orinoco	Intel, 2Wire, Linksys, Netgear	3Com, Linksys, Netgear
Mac PC Cards	Apple, Farallon, Orinoco	None available	Asante
PCI/Internal Mac adapters	Apple, Farallon	Farallon	Built-in, Asante, Farallon
USB Mac adapters	None available	Farallon, Diamond	None available

Table 1-3. Network Adapter Recommendations

We'll discuss the specific circumstances for wireless, PhoneLine, and ordinary Ethernet in the sections that follow.

Web sites for more information on these products include:

Apple   http://www.apple.com

Asante   http://www.asante.com

3Com   http://www.3com.com

2Wire   http://www.2wire.com

Intel   http://www.intel.com

D-Link   http://www.dlink.com

Netgear   http://www.netgear.com

Linksys   http://www.linksys.com

Farallon   http://www.farallon.com

Diamond   http://www.diamondhome.com

Orinoco/Agere/Lucent   http://www.wavelan.com

Situation #1: PhoneLine Networking

Let's look at the specific parts you need, summarized in Table 1-4.

As you can see, choosing PhoneLine makes things very simple: once you buy your adapters and connect them to your telephone jacks, you are essentially done. Since phone

Adapter	Cabling	Hub
PhoneLine adapter	Uses existing telephone home wiring	None needed, except for Internet sharing

Table 1-4. PhoneLine Parts List

wiring is in every home, chances are this is a good place to start when considering how you are going to hook up your computers.

Phone wiring typically has two separate wires to connect your telephones, one red and one green. Take off the faceplate of one of your phone jacks, and you'll likely see the little wires covered in red and green insulation plastic. The colors are important, as we'll find out later. The nice thing about PhoneLine networks is that you can carry both data and voice conversations over the same set of wires, and the two don't usually interfere with each other. Your telephone still rings when you receive a voice call, and your computers are happily chatting away with each other, sending their data packets to and fro.

With the exception of some early Macintosh-only networks,[8] before the invention of PhoneLine networking, you needed more than these two wires to hook up your computers— four, in fact. This is the standard Ethernet wiring that we'll get to in a moment. Most of us don't have lots of spare wires running around our homes, so the PhoneLine solution is the one to start with if you can. If you are going to use PhoneLine products, you must have the following circumstances:

First, the same phone line is wired to every room of your home that you want to place a computer in. For homes that have every telephone connected to the same line (or phone number), this isn't a problem. But if you have a second (or third) phone number in your home, and this number only rings in your den, then you might have problems. If you have multiple phone numbers, you need to find the one set of phone wires that goes throughout most rooms of your home, and make sure that these are the rooms that you intend to hook up all your computers. If not, then you either will have to add additional phone wiring, or use standard Ethernet cabling.

You can purchase the right PhoneLine network adapter for each of your computers and install the adapter properly. We'll get into that in the next chapter.

---

8   Early Macs used LocalTalk, which made use of two wires and could work over telephone-grade wiring. However, they required their own wiring system and could not operate over the same wiring that carried voice conversations.

**SURVIVAL
TIP**

Use PhoneLine networking components when you can. This will work if your existing PCs are located near working telephone jacks and if your new PCs can be connected to a phone jack. The obvious advantage is that, for the most part, you won't need to install any new wiring around your home.

Two exceptions to these circumstances are as follows:

✦ **You intend to connect your home network to the Internet.** If you skip ahead to Chapter 4, you'll see that you'll need a special hub/router device that will connect your PhoneLine network to the standard Ethernet that is used by all cable modems and other high-speed broadband connections. You might need to connect one of your phone jacks to a bridge device (that has both PhoneLine and Ethernet connectors) or to connect one of your phone jacks to one of these special hub/router devices.

✦ **Your phone wiring isn't up to snuff.** How do you know this going into the project? Unfortunately, you don't. You might have very old phone wire in your walls that is good enough for voice conversations but not good enough for supporting your data networking needs. Sadly, you only find this out when you hook up everything. If you live in an old house and you have had trouble with your phones in the past, this is not a good sign. If you have very long runs of phone wiring (several hundred feet) or live in a very big house, chances are the PhoneLine products won't work well.

If you have a fair number of new Macs with built-in Ethernet adapters, they won't work with PhoneLine networks, and you will have to buy a USB or internal PCI PhoneLine adapter for these units. That might be more costly than just running standard Ethernet wiring around your home, depending on how many machines you have and where they are. If you have mostly Windows PCs that didn't come with any built-in networking adapter, this isn't an issue.

Situation #2: Wireless Networking

Let's look at the specific parts you need, summarized in Table 1-5.

If your phone wiring is held together with chewing gum and duct tape, and you can't run any new wires around your home for whatever reason, then you need to think about one of the wireless network solutions for your home. You have a lot to consider, so bear with me as I present an overall introduction to the genre and recommend specific products for you to purchase.

Wireless networks sound easier because you don't need wires to connect everything. Many subtleties, however, affect installing a wireless network correctly. Because you don't

Adapter	Cabling	Hub
Wireless adapter	None needed	Wireless access point

Table 1-5. Wireless Parts List

see the actual connection, everything happens with software, and configuration of your equipment becomes critical.

Wireless networking gear used to cost several hundred dollars, had lots of problems interoperating across vendors, and was difficult to set up and configure. Each of these issues is thankfully past, although getting a wireless network put together is still more an art form than anything else. In this section, I'll introduce you to the various bits and pieces of a wireless network and review the products available.

Wireless networking products are getting better, cheaper, faster, and easier to use. That is the good news. But before you get excited that you can hook up any computer anywhere in your house, let's first review some terms. (This won't happen again. Really, I promise to stick to the practical stuff after this.)

Any wireless network is composed of two basic elements, an *access point* and a *wireless network adapter card.* The access point is a bridge between the wired and wireless parts of your network. You can think of it as a transmitter that keeps all of your wireless adapters communicating—although each wireless adapter has both a transmitter and receiver.

CAUTION   Some vendors make access points that are nothing more than a hollow shell of plastic; you might need to purchase a wireless adapter PC Card to fit inside these units. (I wish I could be more definitive here, but a lot depends on how these items are packaged. Be aware.)

Some vendors, such as Apple, make access points that do more than bridge between wireless and wired Ethernet. The Apple ones (called AirPort Base Stations) also include a wired modem that you can connect to your telephone line. This makes their access point a dial-up router for your home network, so that you are able to share one telephone line amongst your entire collection of home PCs, even ones that aren't Macintoshes.

Some vendors have begun to incorporate access points into firewall/router/hub devices as well, making them useful if you intend to connect your wireless network to a broadband cable or DSL wired network. I'll cover these units in Chapter 4, so don't worry about them for now. If you are considering hooking up your home to the Internet, you'll need to consider these type of devices when you are purchasing your gear, so don't buy anything until you read that chapter thoroughly.

Besides the access point, you need a wireless network adapter in each of your PCs. What you get depends on the kind of PC you have, just like in the wired world.

◆ **PC Cards** The better PC Card adapters have small antennas sticking out the side of the card, and thus out of the side of your computer. This could be an issue, depending on where the PC Card slots are located on your laptop. Hopefully, the wireless adapter's antenna doesn't get in the way of anything that is permanently attached to your laptop. Depending on the vendor, the antenna can be anything from a short tab, to something like a cell phone antenna that has a telescoping extension, to something that is integrated into the laptop. Toshiba and IBM sell several of their laptops with these built-in wireless adapters. Nothing further needs to be added to the computer to have it make a wireless connection. Models include the Toshiba Satellite Pro 4600 and IBM ThinkPad i-series models, among others.

Apple has taken a middle ground in terms of integration. Their latest laptops come with built-in antennas, but still need an additional $100 AirPort card to function on wireless networks. For example, in the iBook portables, you need to install the card underneath the removable keyboard to provide a complete wireless setup.

To make matters more confusing, Compaq sells its Evo line of laptops that come with a special wireless network slot called a Multiport. Of course, you have to purchase these special wireless adapters from Compaq or one of their resellers to fit in this spot, although you could use standard PC Card adapters as well.

◆ **PCI adapter cards** Some of the wireless PCI adapter cards have room for a PC Card adapter that sits inside the computer housing and attaches directly to the PCI adapter itself. This is the case with products from 3Com, Cisco, SMC, and D-Link. When you buy the PCI adapter, you also get the PC Card adapter. Some products, such as Netgear's NetBlaster, have externally mounted antennas with a short cable, which can help improve reception and increase overall network throughput when compared with those products that come with fixed, internal antennas.

SURVIVAL TIP

You can choose from a few ISA wireless adapter solutions as well, but if you have the slots to spare for a PCI card, go with that.

+ **USB adapters**   If you don't feel comfortable opening up your computer or if you don't have any spare slots, some vendors provide USB wireless adapters as well.

In addition to these terms, let's also review the three basic types of wireless networks:

+ **A mixture of wired and wireless computers**   You have some people using wireless connections and some using fixed wired network connections. You'll need to figure out which household members will roam about your home and property and whether you can get by with a single access point to handle the signals to reach these places. Placing more than one access point around your home requires some understanding of the obstacles that will block the radio waves. The thicker your walls or the more steel inside them, the shorter the range your users can roam. Just as cellular phones can find "dead spots" as you travel around your neighborhood, the same is true with wireless networks. The radio signals may be unable to reach places such as a basement room. You can't easily tell this ahead of time, unfortunately. For most of you who are going to consider wireless networks, this is probably the configuration you are going to end up with.

+ **Peer-to-peer wireless networks**   Every desktop or laptop user is wireless and connects to others with wireless LAN adapters installed in each computer. Essentially no wired parts exist on the network, and you don't make use of an access point. This is useful for just sharing files and printers with your various computers, but isn't as useful for sharing Internet access. It is a good place to start any wireless experiments, but you probably are going to move fairly quickly from the peering model to the first wireless/wired model.

+ **Two wired networks bridged with a wireless connection**   You have two different wired network segments, separated by a street or a short distance that would be difficult to wire. If you have several outbuildings on your property, or if you want to connect your home to one of your neighbor's (I have seen this happen, don't laugh), then this is the model for you. You will need to purchase two access points and install them in each building. You might also need to purchase extended antenna options to increase the wireless range between the two access points, depending on how far apart they are.

Apple's AirPort Base Stations don't support this last mode, unfortunately.

Another dimension to the wireless networking world concerns the actual radio frequency that these networks operate at. When you start shopping around for your wireless gear, you'll see designations such as 802.11b and 2.4 GHz: both terms refer to the same kind of wireless networks.

Products with these specifications are the only type of wireless networks that you should be considering for now.[9]

All of the products that I recommend are the 802.11b specification. You might see some others, most notably from Intel under the AnyPoint label, but I wouldn't recommend their wireless products because they aren't 802.11b. AnyPoint products run a whole other system that is less capable, slower, and more trouble.[10]

These 802.11b wireless products are especially useful if you have a laptop and frequently travel. A number of American and European airports have begun to install wireless networks around their terminals, making it easier for you to get connected when waiting for your flight.[11] See Table 1-3 earlier for my specific recommendation of products. Purchase the adapter and wireless access point from the same vendor if you want to keep your life easier. This means if you have a mixture of Windows and Macs, you should buy your access point from either Apple or Farallon's NetLine Wireless Broadband Gateway. The Apple Base Station needs to be configured with a Mac. The Farallon, along with similar products such as the SMC Barricade and the 2Wire, makes use of a web browser to set it up.

A combination PhoneLine/wireless access point/firewall/router is the 2Wire Home Portal 100W. It only has one wired network port, however. If you want your access point to connect to more than one wired device, such as a print server, wired Ethernet PCs, or possibly a cable modem, then look into products such as SMC's Barricade Wireless router, 7004WBR. It has a three-port hub in addition to the wireless access point, and firewall features.

Don't worry if you don't know what a firewall is yet. We'll cover these features in Chapter 4. Don't buy anything for your wireless network until you read that far and understand how your wireless access point will interact with the rest of your network. Chapter 4 also describes Internet access issues, which can be important in determining which access point you end up purchasing. Windows XP versions offer improved support for wireless networks, so if you are looking to upgrade to XP, that might be a good reason to consider this operating system.

---

9   As you can imagine, a wide range of radio frequencies and wireless network types besides the 802.11b/2.4-GHz products are available. Some 802.11a products operate at 5 GHz and won't necessarily work with the 802.11b ones. Some products that go by the name "HomeRF" are an entirely different world. A good reference source for more details can be found here: http://www.proxim.com/wireless/whiteppr/wlangde.shtml

10   The Intel products use HomeRF specifications, which aren't compatible with 802.11b. A third home wireless specification, called Bluetooth, doesn't really apply to network situations, but I mention it just for completeness here.

11   If you need to find a wireless Internet connection when you are on the road, check out this resource. For a small monthly fee, you can subscribe to MobileStar's publicly available wireless Internet locations at many airports and hotels: http://www.laptoptravel.com/wireless

Don't think that because you are designing a wireless network, you should plan on all of your PCs to hook together wirelessly. I would advise against this approach, since if something goes wrong with your wireless network, you have no other recourse. A better idea would be to locate the wireless access point near one of your computers, so that you can connect them via a wired Ethernet cable and make use of this computer for troubleshooting purposes if something should go wrong with the wireless network.

Each wireless access point has at least one wired Ethernet 10BaseT port on it. (The SMC unit has four ports, and the Farallon device has two.) This means that the access point acts like a bridge between the wired and wireless devices on your network. If you want to hook up more than this number of wired devices, you'll need to connect your access point to a standard wired Ethernet hub.

Apple's Base Station also includes a wired modem, as mentioned earlier. This means you can connect your home network to the outside world without having to make use of a cable modem or other higher-speed service. If you have several family members who do lots of file downloading and game playing, however, they will quickly become dissatisfied with sharing any dial-up service. If you want to use America Online, you can't with this setup.

Situation #3: Buying a New PC with a Network Adapter Preinstalled

Let's look at the specific parts you need, summarized in Table 1-6.

If you read the computer trade and enthusiast magazines, you get the feeling that you are the last person on the planet who is running an older operating system version. Yet you are not alone and indeed are probably in very good company. Most of us don't like messing around with our computers. As long as they continue to work and run the programs we have on them, without crashing too frequently, we will continue to run whatever version of operating system originally came with it.

When it comes to networking, running an old OS can be trouble, particularly if the version predates Windows 95 or MacOS version 8.5. These older versions don't hold up well when it comes time to mix and match with the current stuff available from Microsoft and Apple.

Adapter	Cabling	Hub
Comes included with new computer	Depends on the situation	Depends on the situation

Table 1-6. New PC Parts List

If you have one of these moldy oldies, consider buying something new to start your network or to augment other more recent machines at home. If you do buy something new, consider buying a machine that comes with a networking adapter built in. All new Macintoshes come this way, with a 10/100/1000BaseT wired Ethernet connector, and some of the Mac laptops come with half of the wireless Ethernet adapter already fitted inside the machine as well. Most of the Sony desktops come with wired 10/100BaseT Ethernet adapters, and all laptops either come with Ethernet connectors or can be easily upgraded to include an Ethernet PC Card adapter, too.

If you order your PC online, from Dell, IBM, Gateway, and other major vendors, you can choose your particular kind of networking adapter, such as a standard 10BaseT adapter, wireless, or PhoneLine adapter. Whatever it is, the moral of this story is to try to purchase a new PC with the appropriate networking hardware included, so you don't have to mess with it later on.

Situation #4: Mac Networks

Let's look at the specific parts you need, summarized in Table 1-7.

In this book, I attempt to cover both Windows and Macintosh computers, because I believe that many of our homes contain a mixture of both computers, especially as Macs become more popular for home-based video and graphic arts functions. So if you already have an older Mac and want to hook it up to your network, or if you want to get a new Mac, then this approach is for you.

The older Macs may or may not have a built-in 10BaseT adapter, depending on the particular model you have. So many variations and shapes and sizes exist that it is difficult to provide any general direction. First, read the information about older Mac models and what Ethernet adapters are available for them at http://www-commeng.cso.uiuc.edu/nas/nash/mac/ethernet.mac.html

Adapter	Cabling	Hub
New Mac: 10/100/1000BaseT comes included Older Mac: separate purchase required	Depends on situation	Depends on situation

Table 1-7.   Mac Parts List

If you want to hook up older Macs to a wired Ethernet network, you have a good chance of finding an adapter that will work. Asante's Mac Products Guide on their web site covers the various models and which of their adapters will work inside of which Macs (http://www.asante.com/products/adapters). You might have to take out an internal modem card and replace it with your Ethernet card in some models. (This means you will lose the ability to have any dial-up access to the Internet, as well as to use this modem for faxes, but you can replace the internal modem with an external modem if this is an issue for you. If you intend to connect your home network to the Internet anyway, the lack of dial-up access isn't really a problem.)

Some of the older desktop Macs used a different internal circuit card standard called NuBus, various Ethernet adapters are still available for these computers. Other older Macs came with a built-in Ethernet connector, although it wasn't a 10BaseT connector. You'll have to get an adapter cable (called Apple AUI) to convert this into 10BaseT, available from Asante and others.

If you have more than one old Mac that doesn't have any Ethernet connector, then you can purchase a bridge device from Farallon and others that will go from LocalTalk (the older networking scheme used by these computers) into wired Ethernet.

If you are designing a wireless network, you are going to have problems, unless your Mac can use a PC Card wireless adapter. If it isn't a model of Mac laptop that comes with a PC Card slot, you are out of luck if you want a completely wireless network. You can still use the LocalTalk/Ethernet bridge mentioned earlier, but that involves some wiring.

Finally, if you desire a PhoneLine network, you will need to have either a USB or PCI slot to connect one of the Farallon PhoneLine products. If your Mac doesn't have one of these (which is likely, given that most Macs with these requirements are the newer models that also have built-in Ethernet connectors), you'll have to outfit your Macs with Ethernet adapters and then buy an Ethernet-to-PhoneLine bridge, like the Netgear PE102 model or Farallon's HomeLine Ethernet Adapter.

As I mentioned in the previous situation, all current Macs come with built-in network adapters for wired Ethernet. That makes your job a lot easier, especially when you turn to Chapter 2 and have to install the software to network these computers. You have almost nothing to do at this point.

If you want to connect these newer Macs to a PhoneLine or wireless network, you have to buy some extra parts. Most of these modern Macs come with USB and PCI slots, or both. Your best choices are from Apple, if they sell the particular part you need, or from Farallon or Asante.

SURVIVAL TIP

With additional adapters, I recommend upgrading your operating system to at least Mac OS 8.6. Apple recommends OS 9.0.4 for using AirPorts and other wireless products. Older versions of Mac OS used a less-capable networking schema called MacTCP. Newer versions have TCP/IP built into the operating system and are a lot easier to deal with. (You'll see how in the next chapter.)

Situation #5: Standard Ethernet Adapters

Let's look at the specific parts you need, summarized in Table 1-8.

As I mentioned earlier, the type of Ethernet cabling that you are going to install in your home is going to be 10BaseT, otherwise known as twisted-pair Ethernet. This is the most flexible, the easiest to troubleshoot, and the least costly of the three cabling types. It is not the easiest of the three to install, but is the most reliable once you get it going.

Yet if you are reading this section, you have had problems with your phone wiring, or you are reluctant to get involved with wireless networks, you are just conservative and want the best possible wiring system, no matter the cost or the hassles. Perhaps all of your computers are located in one room, or so close together, that it makes sense to use standard Ethernet wiring.

NOTE

Having run networks for years on Ethernet, I am most comfortable using it—with good reason. Once you take care of wiring issues, the typical Ethernet network will give you years of trouble-free service. Though the networking protocols and schemes were developed decades ago, Ethernet is still robust and useful enough that it will probably be around for several more decades. It is rare to find something in the world of computers with such staying power, so it's worth considering.

Earlier in the chapter I mentioned the various wiring choices for Ethernet and came down very solidly behind 10BaseT wiring. Here's why I don't recommend the others for your network. Coaxial cabling is very easy to hook up a few computers if they are located in the same room or adjoining rooms of your house. But the moment you want to run this across several floors, you are asking for trouble. Coaxial (coax) cabling also is fairly dicey when it

Adapter	Cabling	Hub
10BaseT Ethernet adapter	10BaseT category 5 cables	Required

Table 1-8. Ethernet Parts List

breaks and can bring your entire network down at once, making it difficult to troubleshoot a problem.

Think of those strings of holiday lights you see at the end of the year. With some of the cheaper versions, if one bulb on the chain goes out, the entire chain is dark. That is what having coax Ethernet is all about. 10BaseT Ethernet doesn't have this problem, because each computer is connected to a central hub with its own wire. If one wire breaks, only that computer is affected.[12] Also, the thick Ethernet cabling is too unwieldy and expensive for most people to work with.

Many network adapter vendors sell products that come with multiple connectors, usually called "combo" cards. These generally cost a bit more than cards with just the 10BaseT connector on them, but if you feel you want to hedge your bets and buy something that can be used in a variety of circumstances, go ahead.

SURVIVAL TIP

Coax Ethernet is actually useful in one circumstance: hooking up two parts of your home together, where you can't or don't want to run multiple cables between the two. In this case, you would need to buy two hubs that have a coax port and put each hub in the separate wing of your house. You would wire each computer to the hub still with 10BaseT, but then connect the hubs with 10Base2 coax.

There are two types of twisted-pair wiring: 10BaseT and 100BaseT. What is the difference? About 90BaseTs—only kidding. The "10" or "100" refers to the overall speed of the network in megabits per second, a number that is just about useless in our daily lives, like an erg.100BaseT networks do operate faster than 10BaseT ones, but not ten times faster, and usually not more than twice as fast. In actual practice, you would be hard pressed to tell the difference.

All 100BaseT products sold today also operate at 10BaseT speeds. Chances are if you wanted to buy just a 10BaseT Ethernet adapter, you probably couldn't, unless you found a used one for sale on eBay. The same isn't true for hubs, and you can buy just 10-megabit hubs or 10/100 hubs for slightly more money. By all means buy the 10/100 hubs when you can afford to do so, even if the extra speed is more imaginary than real. They are usually better products, and when you do large file transfers, you'll want the extra speed available with these hubs.

For the purposes of this book, I'll treat the two as the same when I refer to 10BaseT networks.[13]

---

12   A good illustration of the problems with coax wiring and the advantages of twisted-pair Ethernet, can be found at http://www.wown.com/j_helmig/tpvcoax.htm

13   Not to complicate things, but there is actually a third network speed: 1000BaseT, or *gigabit Ethernet*. The current crop of Macintoshes supports these speeds, and some of the Windows adapters do as well.

You need to know about two types of 10BaseT Ethernet cabling: *straight-through* and *crossover*. Each 10BaseT category 5 cable is composed of four or eight individual wires, each with a special color code. The wires are wrapped together in pairs, which is why they are referred to as twisted pairs. The twist enhances the electrical properties of the cabling. To keep track of the pairs, one of the wire strands is covered in solid color insulation, while the other has that color alternating with white. Unlike our telephone wiring, the colors are mixed together on the same wire in an alternating pattern (such as orange/white for one wire and blue/white for another) because the people who think of these things couldn't come up with eight different colors that most of us could easily distinguish.[14]

The difference between the two types is easy to explain, but difficult to determine just by looking at the cabling. You use straight-through cables on almost every connection between computer and hub. The only time you would use crossed-over cables is when you want a network of two PCs without any hub between them. How do you know you have the right kind of cable? When everything works fine, you have the right cable configuration. Usually, you can only buy straight-through ones, and those are the only ones you can use.

Why four or eight wires per cable? Ethernet only uses four of the wires to do its business, but most of the time you buy a cable that contains all eight wires. That is just the way things are.

Don't try to save some bucks by paying for a four-wire cable. It isn't worth it.

CAUTION

A final note: Hundreds of different Ethernet cards are available. Some come with just the 10/100BaseT connectors; some come with all three connectors (and cost more). The reputable brands are Linksys, Netgear, and 3Com, with 3Com costing more than the others. In my opinion, the 3Com cards are usually worth the extra money. They have given me years of trouble-free service, and the company is very good about providing updated drivers for various operating systems.

---

14   For more detailed information about the color codes and some other discussion about wiring technologies, see John's Closet (at http://www.johnscloset.net/wiring). You can find another concise source on wiring basics, including a good explanation of the various color codes and cable types, on Linksys' web site: (http://www.linksys.com/faqs/default.asp?fqid=20). Finally, if you want to get more detailed information about the various cabling standards for 10-, 100-, and 1000-megabit Ethernet networks, see Siemon's web site (http://www.siemon.com/white_papers/ 99-12-17-demystifying.asp).

Also, in this situation you'll definitely need to purchase a hub for your network. You'll want to review Chapter 4 and make a decision on the type of hub you need. Base your decision on the number of computers you'll eventually have on your network and whether you will be connecting your network to the Internet and need some kind of protection that comes built into your hub. For most home uses, hubs are a commodity that you can comfortably select based on number of ports and price, and not worry about the variability of other features. Current products can use 10-Mbps or 100-Mbps speeds, older products only support 10 Mbps.

Once you have figured out the right adapters, it is time to do the actual wiring. Skip ahead to the "Wiring Your Home" section, and we'll go through what you need to do.

Situation #6: Wired USB Adapters

Let's look at the specific parts you need, summarized in Table 1-9.

If you don't want to open up your computer and are running at least Windows 98, then buying a USB adapter makes the most sense. In Table 1-9, I mention the three different types of USB adapters: for standard 10BaseT Ethernet, for PhoneLine networks, and for wireless networks. I covered the last two situations earlier; in this section, I focus on wired Ethernet USB adapters.

The single difference between your standard wired Ethernet situation #5 and this one is that you will buy a different part for each of your PCs. Other than that, you proceed to run the wires around your home and connect them to a hub. With USB gear you never have to open up your computer case and be confronted with the mass of wires and mess inside it. Be prepared to pay additional money for this advantage.

Adapter	Cabling	Hub
(1) USB Ethernet adapter	10BaseT category 5 cables	Required
(2) USB PhoneLine adapter	Uses existing telephone home wiring	None needed
(3) USB wireless adapter	None required	Wireless access point required

Table 1-9.   USB Parts List

Wiring Your Home

Now is the moment of truth for those of you willing to wire up your homes. You first need to decide whether you are going to buy prefabricated and terminated cables or make your own.

Up to this point, our discussions about cabling have assumed that you will use the same cable all over your house. If you want to do a professional-quality job, you want to use two different kinds of cabling for your network. If you go back to Figure 1-1, you'll see icons for cables that connect the PCs to wall plates. Also, runs of wire connect wall plates to each other, and other cables go from the wall plate to the hub. This is how businesses connect their computers and, while it may seem like overkill, it will prevent problems down the road, such as when someone pulls the PC out from the wall and pops the connector off your Ethernet cable. If you have designed your wiring system in the fashion illustrated in the diagram in Figure 1-1, you will just have to replace the short *patch cord* that connects the PC to the wall plate.[15]

Buy prefabricated cables whenever possible. Realize that you will have two issues. First, you must make sure that the length of cable matches where you intend to put them in your house. If they are too short by a few inches, you are going to have some major headaches. Second, the *terminated cables* (meaning that they come with the connectors already installed) are going to require you to drill bigger holes through your walls to push them through. That design approval that you thought you had received earlier could quickly evaporate as your household sees the gigantic holes you need to get your cables around the house.

Maybe you are handy enough to make your own cables. In that case, you should definitely use the dual architecture mentioned earlier. Use wall plates and run wires between them, and then use preterminated patch cords to connect the wall plates to either your hub or your computers. Some of the network wall plates that are sold make it relatively easy to do this connection. You don't need any special tools or expertise and don't even have to strip off the insulation from the wires to hook up everything.

Supplying instructions on how to do this is outside the scope of this book. A number of sites around the Internet can help, and I'd start with this one, which has detailed instructions, along with a parts list and pictures showing you the steps required:
http://www.homepcnetwork.com/wireintro.htm

This is basically what the telephone company does when they wire your home for phone wiring: The bare end goes into a phone jack, and you plug in a RJ-11 cord that connects your

---

15   The patch cable conductors are stranded (so the cables flex well), and the wall plate–to–wall plate
      cables have solid conductors (which have better electrical properties, especially at higher frequencies
      and for faster network speeds like gigabit Ethernet).

phone to the jack. While you are crawling about your basement, your crawl space, your attic, and anywhere else that you can get to run your cables, consider the tips set forth in the following table, taken from the Web site John's Closet about crawling under your house.

Wear a pair of good old coveralls. They not only keep you a bit cleaner, they are also easy to slip on and off as you switch from crawling under the house to going in to get a cold beer.
Wear one of those dust masks or you'll be picking black boogers out of your nose for a week.
It is really hard to carry stuff around with you under there. Limit yourself to the absolute bare minimum of tools—nothing if possible. If you have to carry some tools, try to use cheap stuff. You are highly likely to leave something under there and you really won't want to go back to get it.
I have best luck with a drop-light on a long extension cord. A flashlight is just awful, unless it's small enough to hold in your mouth.
Try to keep the dogs from following you in, as they are likely to find dead rats. Be careful to avoid the skeletal remains of the cat that found the dead rats.

—From www.johnscloset.net

Recap: Buying the Right Hub

Since hubs seem mysterious, I'd like to review what you need to buy. If you have chosen PhoneLine networking, then you don't need to buy a hub—for now. You still need to connect your PhoneLine adapters in your PCs together to the outside world, and to do this you'll have to either get a PhoneLine bridge to regular Ethernet, or obtain a device that bridges the two networks in combination with other uses. But that's for Chapter 4, where we talk about getting hooked up to the Internet.

The same is true for wireless networks. You don't have to worry about a hub for now, but you will have to worry about how to connect it to the Internet.

The rest of you will buy a hub to hook everything together. Many books and networking consultants will tell you that you don't need a hub if all you are going to do is network two computers. You can save about $40 if you don't buy a hub. But why bother? Let's just dispense with this bad advice quickly. It's bad advice because no sooner do you go through all the trouble of getting your two-computer network set up than you find out you have more than two devices to connect. What about that cable modem? That's three. And the printer server? That's four. Suddenly, your little network isn't so little.

SURVIVAL TIP I hope you have followed my advice and brought all your wires into your basement or wherever the nearest phone/cable termination point is located in your house. This is where you locate your hub.

What should you buy? You have two basic choices: the cheapest thing possible or something with an eye toward the future high-speed Internet connection that you most likely will end up installing in your home. If you don't ever, and I mean ever, plan on having an Internet connection shared among your household, go out and get the cheapest four- or eight-port hub you can find. (The difference in price for the extra four ports isn't worth arguing about, but if it will make you feel better to save a few dollars, go ahead.)

Hubs come in all shapes and sizes.[16] Apart from the number of ports, some come with a special "uplink" button or port that allows you to connect one hub to another. In case you run out of ports, you can expand your network easily. You can do this without the special uplink port, but it takes some effort and the right cables.

Hubs also come with switched or nonswitched ports and support for both 100-megabit and 10-megabit networks. This doesn't amount to anything more than marketing. Any network running faster than 10 megabits isn't going to make much difference to you, mainly because the speed that you connect outside of your humble home is going to be much slower than 10 megabits. The only reasons that justify a more expensive and capable hub are if your household members are playing lots of network games among themselves and if you plan on making copies of large amounts of data around your home network. For the average household that is sending e-mail and viewing web pages and writing documents, these features don't much matter.[17]

However, if you plan on connecting your home to the Internet, a cheap hub is a waste of money. You are better off getting one of the combination firewall/router/hub devices that I recommend in Chapter 4. So you might want to flip over there and read through that chapter before continuing here. Just so that we are clear: these devices, which I call "frhubs," include more than just the physical connection of all of your Ethernet cables. They include software to protect your home network from the outside world. If all that you are looking for is the physical connection of your Ethernet, then buy whatever hub is convenient and in your price range.

---

16   Hubs just for USB devices are different from the networking hubs that we are talking about here.

17   If you want to read more about hubs and understand the various differences, go to Practically Networked site (at http://www.practicallynetworked.com/networking/hubinfo.htm). They go into much more detail and give you lots of buying and configuration advice.

Troubleshooting

Back when I worked in the Information Systems department for Transamerica Occidental Life Insurance Company in downtown Los Angeles, doing technical support usually meant having an audience when you arrived at some user's cubicle. This experience did not prepare me for the kind of audience that I have when doing home networking support: namely, my friends and family. At the insurance company, a user in distress would be interested in getting his or her computer working properly, but the process by which I would do so wasn't as important as when they could get back to work.

With home networking support calls, the process is everything. This audience would question why I was doing something to the computer or the phones or drilling those holes in the wall.

At this point in your own networking process, you don't have much to troubleshoot. Nothing is really hooked up to anything. So let's review some basic guidelines for when you do get going.

When Do I Troubleshoot My Network?

Two rules of thumb apply when it comes to doing troubleshooting or any networking activity:

✦ **Do any networking assembly <u>and</u> troubleshooting when nobody is home, or when all of your household members are asleep.**   The less they know about your activities, the better off you are. That doesn't mean that you should schedule nightly upgrades and intensive learning sessions. Just understand that your household will quickly become used to having their computers working; they'll be unhappy about anything that you do that will interfere with their computer activities. (For example, when you bring down a network server or fool around with some new piece of software that takes out your protocol configuration.)

I strongly suggest doing the larger tasks, such as wiring and installing a new version of your computer operating system, when all of your family is off at the movies. Better yet, send them away for a few days to visit your in-laws, so you can have some quality time home alone: just you, your network, and a few hours of frustration while you try to figure out why something doesn't work. There is nothing like trying to debug a network problem when your family is bugging you to get it working so they can finish their homework, check their e-mail, or send a quick message to their friends. If you can't send your family away for an extended vacation, then I strongly suggest that you do not attempt to do any installation right before the dinner hour, unless you want to further raise the emotional stakes involved.

✦ **Remember that your voice telephone service is a critical application for your family.** Anything that you do that will mess up your phone service will create all sorts of bad news and create it quickly. This includes connecting any PhoneLine devices. While they are supposed to work and not interfere with your voice service, I have seen situations where they don't and do.

I Can't Get My Cables Fabricated

While detailed instructions on what to do about making your cables and getting them tested are beyond the scope of this book, I strongly recommend Leviton's troubleshooting guide, which can be found at http://www.levitonvoicedata.com/learning/wiring.asp

Also, numerous places will sell you lengths of cables, either preterminated or bare end, to your own specifications, including different colors.

SURVIVAL TIP

BlackBox.com, 877-877-2269, is a good source for information about making cables; DataCommWarehouse.com, 800-397-8508, is another. They both will send you thick printed catalogs for free that describe their many products, including hubs, network adapters, cable crimping tools, and other odds and ends. I strongly recommend using prefabricated patch cables for connecting your computers to the wall outlets whenever possible.

Futures

The good news is that USB and PhoneLine products are getting better and more mature, making it easier for just about everyone to install a network without having to deal with a traditional internal Ethernet adapter. The bad news is that there will continue to be a confoundingly long list of various choices for buyers of Ethernet adapters. Also good news is that both Windows and Mac OSes are getting better at recognizing a wider range of networking products and making it easier for you to install the network because it is now part of the operating system (more recently for Windows than Macs).

Wireless products are also becoming cheaper in price and better in quality, and the price gap between wired and wireless will continue to drop. I continue to hope that more PC vendors will include networking adapters with their Windows machines, something that can only help you as the new home network grows.

But you don't really have a home network yet. All you have is a bunch of wire in your walls (or a wireless design plan). Let's move to the next chapter, start to hook up things, and get your network fired up.

Chapter 2

Sharing Files

Now that you've taken care of the house wiring, it's time to hook up your computers so you can begin to share files around your network. Isn't that why you poked holes in your walls and connected all those cables?

In this chapter, you'll learn the basic operating system changes that you'll need to perform to get your PCs talking to each other. This is the first step toward creating your network. In subsequent chapters, you'll find out how to get printers on the network and how to obtain Internet access. Don't skip ahead: If you don't take the time to master the rules set forth in this chapter, you are liable to have problems down the road, which will force you to come back to these pages to fix your mistakes.

Let's look at some of the problems you might encounter as you set to work.

Problems

Networks can vex the most experienced computer user. There are times when even I get frustrated because I have overlooked a small intermediate step or mistyped a key configuration parameter. Or I just plain don't know why computer A can't see computer B, even though everything else seems to be working. There is a lot to think about when your home network is up and running. Making sure that you didn't break something while trying to fix something else can be a challenge. It would be easy if you could throw a "networking" switch and turn it on with one command, but the process isn't that simple. That's why I wrote this book.

What Do I Have to Install?

From the decision matrix in the last chapter, you already know what kind of equipment you need: an internal, USB, or wireless Ethernet adapter, and either a PhoneLine or ordinary Ethernet adapter. You'll also have already set up your hub and hooked the wires to it.

At this point in our narrative, you have my permission to go out and buy the rest of your gear. If you are planning on connecting just the computers you own, then buy the appropriate network adapters for them.

SURVIVAL TIP   If you are buying a new computer, make sure it is fitted with the appropriate adapter at the time you buy it.

Ideally, you want the same brand of adapter in all of your computers. If you own a variety of laptops and desktops, or Windows and Macs, then obviously this isn't possible. You will have to mix and match products. The more you can standardize your equipment, however, the fewer troubles you'll encounter when something goes wrong and you're wondering what's inside your machine.

I speak from experience: Wherever possible, I now have the same Ethernet adapter in my machines. It is true that different brands of Ethernet adapters will work together on the same network. But if you have to replace or repair a nonworking adapter, it will be easier to locate and install the right set of driver files if you know that each of your PCs has the same one.[1]

Applications Aren't for Sharing

An early misconception about having a home network is that it means installing software on one computer and then running it all over your home. Sorry to break the news, but this isn't possible, nor is it desirable. While a few software programs allow you to do this, the vast majority of them, including just about all the commercial products that you will be using, don't work this way.

Let's say you want to share a Microsoft Word document between your upstairs and downstairs computers. Meaning, one day you make changes to the document downstairs, and the next day you happen to be upstairs and want to jot down a few notes on the same document. To make this possible, you need to purchase a separate copy of Word and install it on each machine first. Otherwise, you won't be able to work on your documents on both machines.

So why bother with a network if you have to purchase and install all of your applications separately? You do get to share your data files, Internet connection, and printers—all compelling reasons.

Other Things You Don't Want to Share on Your Network

Just because you have a network doesn't mean that everything needs to be connected to it. While some interesting devices can be connected (I'll get into that in Chapter 8), some things you shouldn't even attempt to connect to your network.

The first and foremost thing is your *PC fax* application. While it is possible to share your fax application, it is messy, complex, and fraught with problems. It is far easier to save your documents to a shared folder on one computer with the fax modem and to send your fax directly from it. Some networked fax devices work reasonably well. They are expensive and quirky, however, and you need to get the basics nailed down first.

I'd also say any *dial-up modem* is going to be problematic if you want to share it over the network. Microsoft has included tools for this in later Windows versions, and they also have

---

1   Not every network adapter will work the same way with every hub or router on your network.
      Buying the same products at least gives you some experience with the quirks of that product.

an Internet Connection Sharing wizard and routines to allow you to share a single modem across a network. However, I wouldn't recommend going down this route unless you have a lot of time on your hands. Modems are cheap these days, and most PCs come equipped with one, whether or not you intend to use it. There are other ways to share a dial-up Internet connection.[2]

Next are *scanners*. Network-attached scanners are available, and if your scanner comes with a USB port, you might be tempted to hook it up to more than one machine via USB connections. That may or may not work, depending on the scanner and the version of your operating system. Hewlett-Packard (HP) sells a scanner that is designed to work with its print server product line, but I haven't tested it to see how easy it is to work over a network. Most scanners are inexpensive, but you don't really use them all that much anyway. Plus, you need to be close to your scanner to operate it, so having several of your computers share it isn't really that useful.

Other *USB devices,* including music players and Palm Pilots, are best hooked up to a single machine in your home, unless you want to load the synchronization/docking software on each of your home machines. Then things can get confusing when it comes time to dock the device. Finally, if you have a *mixed Mac and Windows network,* you may not want to share any files between them. You could just leverage a shared printer and a shared Internet connection. Depending on the applications loaded on each kind of machine, that could be an acceptable situation; it is indeed the situation in my own home. (In case you want to share files between the two worlds, I will discuss how to do this in the next chapter.)

Solutions

You recall our discussion of the various networking components in the last chapter, including adapters, clients, protocols, and such. Let's get to work. There are five steps involved in configuring all of these components properly:

1. Install the appropriate network adapter and operating system drivers.

2. Install the networking components you need.

3. Get your IP network configured.

4. Enable file sharing on each of your computers.

5. Make any adjustments for mixed Mac and Windows networks.

---

2   The Netopia R2020 is my recommended choice for a great way to share a dial-up connection across your home network. (I'll have more to say about this in Chapter 4.) There used to be other products in this market, most notably from Ramp Networks but, sadly, their product line has been discontinued. A shame, really.

At this point, you have decided how to network your home. You have a plan for installing new wiring, using existing phone wiring, or buying one of the wireless networking solutions. You also have purchased your networking adapters and a hub, if necessary.

Install the Appropriate Network Adapter and Operating System Drivers

If you have a Mac, chances are you already have an Ethernet adapter that comes with the computer. If you have a really old Mac, like a Performa, you'll need to purchase the right kind of Ethernet adapter that will fit inside the machine. A good site to figure out what product to buy is maintained by Asante, which just so happens to sell the lion's share of Ethernet adapters for various Macs. Go to http://www.asante.com/products/adapters, and then click on the Mac Products Guide link.

The Mac world is relatively easy to work in. You open the case, put in the adapter, and screw everything back together. (For some of the older Macs, you might be replacing a modem card with the Ethernet adapter, but you are about to get connected on the fast lane and won't need that slowpoke modem anyway.) Start up the Mac, put the floppy disk in the driver, and launch the installer application that came with your network adapter. Also, connect your Ethernet cable to the network adapter. It should go in a socket that looks similar to a telephone connector, but is a bit bigger. You might have to reboot your computer, but other than that, you are set. Move on to the section on making changes to your operating system, unless you have to do some work on your Windows PCs.

Ah, Windows. I could write pages and pages of material on how to install network adapters. I'll try to keep my comments as brief, yet helpful, as possible. If all else fails and you can't seem to get things working, go to the "Troubleshooting" section and pore over those details.

How you install this adapter depends on the type I recommended for you in the last chapter. If you purchased a USB adapter, you merely hook it up to the USB port on your PC with its supplied cable. The good news about USB is that how to fit the cables between the adapter and your PC is very obvious, and you can't mess this up. You can even do this while your PC is powered-on. In a few seconds the computer should recognize something new has been added to its configuration. It will ask you to insert the floppy disk or CD-ROM that came with the adapter and will copy the necessary driver files from this disk. You might have to reboot your machine, depending on the version of Windows you are running.

Now comes the hard part if you've purchased an internal network adapter. Turn off the computer, unplug the power cable from the back of the system unit, and remove the cover. First, find the empty slots where the circuit cards fit. Then remove the screw for that particular slot cover, take the cover out of your machine, and insert your adapter in that slot.

Ensure that you're grounded (tap your finger on a metal part of the computer case to make sure you don't discharge any static electricity to the network adapter). Be sure to insert the card straight down into the slot. Leaning on one edge or another of an adapter card to insert it has sliced my palms more than once. Now replace the screw, replace the cover, and hook up your power cords.

If you feel uncomfortable taking apart your computer and want more detailed illustrations and step-by-step pictures about how to do this, go to the HomePC Network site (http://www.homepcnetwork.com/ethernet.htm).

You have one more step with the Ethernet adapter (unless it was a wireless adapter) that you installed. Connect your Ethernet cable to the adapter, putting it in the socket that looks slightly bigger than a telephone connector. You now should turn your computer back on and get ready to install the drivers and operating system software to support your network adapter. The lights on your hub should light up when you turn on your computer, indicating that there is a working connection between your PC and the hub. If not, continue reading the installation instructions before heading over to the "Troubleshooting" section.

If you are using a wireless adapter, go through the installation depending on the type of product (internal, USB, or PC Card adapter) you have. Also set up your wireless access point first. Some models must be attached via a special USB or serial cable for their initial configuration. Some products, like Apple's AirPort Base Station, can only be configured from a Mac, while others can only be configured from a Windows PC. Also read through the "Troubleshooting" section about wireless products now.

Install the Networking Components You Need

For *Windows PCs,* you should see a screen that says you have installed new hardware and asks how you want to continue. Choose Disk From Manufacturer, and insert this floppy or CD-ROM. Pick the correct location of this disk for the new hardware wizard to copy the drivers. You may have to specify a directory on your floppy, depending on the version of Windows that you are running, because manufacturers have different versions of their drivers.

When this routine is done, reboot your machine, and it will ask you for a user name and password. As I suggested earlier, you might want to use the same pair for all your Windows computers to make it easier to log into your network and share resources. When would you not want to do this? Say, if you wanted to give access to a particular set of shared files that only the parents could see, or if one child wants to keep his or her files from being shared across the network. For now, let's keep things simple.

NOTE

All versions of Windows after Win95 install the TCP/IP protocols as part of installing a new network adapter. For Windows 95, you'll have to add this protocol to your network configuration before you can proceed. Bring up the Network control panel, select Add | Protocols | Add, and click on "Microsoft" in the left pane. Then choose TCP/IP and click OK. Skip to the next section to configure the TCP/IP arrangement.

For *Macintoshes,* you will typically configure both AppleTalk and TCP/IP. To configure AppleTalk, go to the AppleTalk control panel. Choose Connect Via Ethernet or Wireless, depending on which adapter you are using to network your computers. The window should look like the one in Figure 2-1. If it does, close the window and save your configuration. Do this on every Mac you wish to connect. We'll get to naming your Macs in a moment.

IP Network Setup

Okay, you have a hub, you have wires, and you have your network adapters installed in your computers. Now let's get everything together.

Each machine must have a unique address if it is going to use TCP/IP protocols. An IP address is composed of four numbers separated by periods, like this: 1.2.3.4.

Most addresses are assigned to Internet providers or businesses, who then assign them to their users. Several groups of addresses are reserved for private networks such as your home

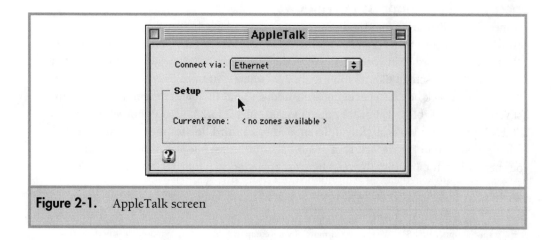

Figure 2-1. AppleTalk screen

network. One of the reserved groups of addresses is from 10.0.0.1 through 10.255.255.255. We'll use that range for our examples since the addresses are guaranteed not to conflict with addresses used by popular Web sites or other places you might want to connect with.

If you have more than one computer with the same address, you'll find out really quickly. Either Windows or your Macs will start complaining, saying that someone else is hogging that address. You can automatically assign TCP/IP addresses if you have a firewall/router/ hub, but for now I'll show you a simple way to set up everything.[3]

Make sure that all of your computers are on the same IP subnetwork (subnet). This is a way to divide and conquer large enterprise networks. Since you have a small network, you want everyone to talk to everyone else. You accomplish that by making sure that the first three numbers of the address are the same for each of your home computers, regardless of whether they are Windows, Macs, or anything else. Even print servers and other devices have to have these same three numbers.[4] Our examples will keep the first three numbers as 10.0.0 and use the last number for each device we hook to our network. You'll see the examples use numbers 10.0.0.1, 10.0.0.2, and so on…up through a maximum of 10.0.0.253. Since most home networks won't have more than a few devices, plenty of addresses are available.

Address ranges can be more involved than this, but for now let's just stick with this simple numbering scheme because you have a few other things to do. Make a list like the one in Table 2-1 so that you will remember which computer has which address. Assign them in any order, as long as the first three numbers match.

Specifying the IP Address in Windows

To specify the IP address for Windows computers, you have to bring up the Network control panel, whose name depends on the version of Windows you are running, but does at least have the word "Network" in it. Go to the listing for TCP/IP, right-click on Properties, and you will see a screen like that in Figure 2-2, where you need to enter the IP address.

Select the check box for specifying an IP address, and then enter the number from the list you based on Table 2-1. For the subnet mask, enter **255.255.255.0**. For Windows 2000/XP, this screen looks slightly different and has a third line for the gateway/router address, as shown in Figure 2-3. Don't worry about this last address until you connect your network to the Internet. If you'd like, for now you can enter **10.0.0.1** or the address

---

3   Windows 98 and later versions come with a way to automatically configure TCP/IP without having a special router/hub. However, if one or more of your computers is running Windows 95, this is not going to work. You can read more details at Helmig's Web site (http://www.wown.com/j_helmig/ w98tcpip.htm), but I recommend using the method described earlier to specify an IP address, unless you are planning on buying a router/hub for your Internet connection.

4   If you are interested in learning more about TCP/IP networking, you can obtain more information from many places. One of the more concise Web sources is Howard Gilbert's PC Lube and Tune at http://pclt.cis.yale.edu/pclt/COMM/TCPIP.HTM

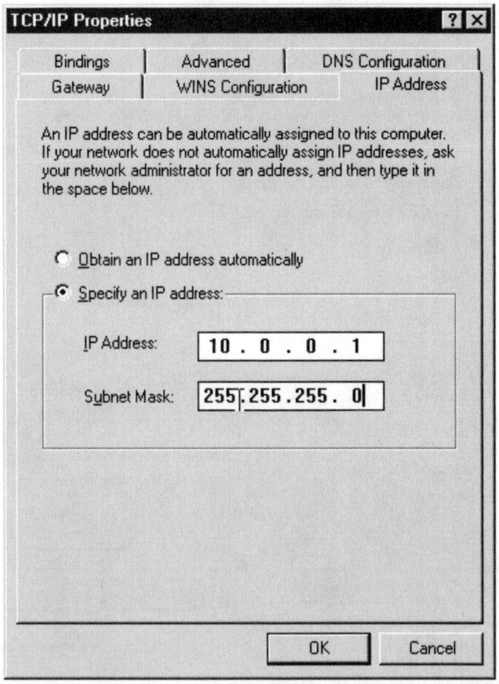

Figure 2-2.   IP address for Windows 95/98/Me

of one of your other machines. Leave the DNS information blank until it's time to connect to the Internet.

The next step in Windows is to specify the name of your computer and to make sure that file sharing is supported on the machine. While you are in the Network control panel,

Computer Name, Description	IP Address Assignment
David's office computer, Windows 2000	10.0.0.2
Lisa's office computer, Macintosh	10.0.0.3
Mary's computer, Windows Me	10.0.0.4
John's computer, Windows 98	10.0.0.5

Table 2-1.   IP Address Assignment

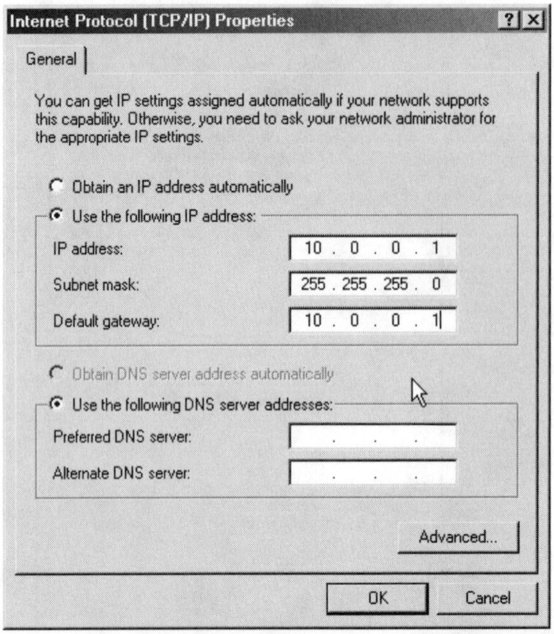

Figure 2-3. Windows 2000/XP IP address screen

go to the Identification tab, and enter a unique name for each of your computers. Choose something that you'll remember them by, such as "Upstairs" and "Downstairs" or "JennyWin98." You can't have spaces and other odd characters, and the names each have to be fewer than 15 characters. Make sure that you enter *exactly* the same workgroup name for each computer here, as shown in Figure 2-4.

The screen is in a different location for Windows 2000 and XP. Bring up Control Panels | System | Network Identification | Properties, and you'll find it. For Windows XP, it lurks on the Control Panels | System | Computer Name screen.

To finish specifying your network, you must ensure that you have file-sharing services installed on each computer. Again, this is usually found in the Network control panel. When you first bring up this control panel, your screen should look like Figure 2-5 if you are running Windows 95/98/Me. Click the File And Print Sharing button, and select both boxes to enable file sharing and print sharing from this computer.

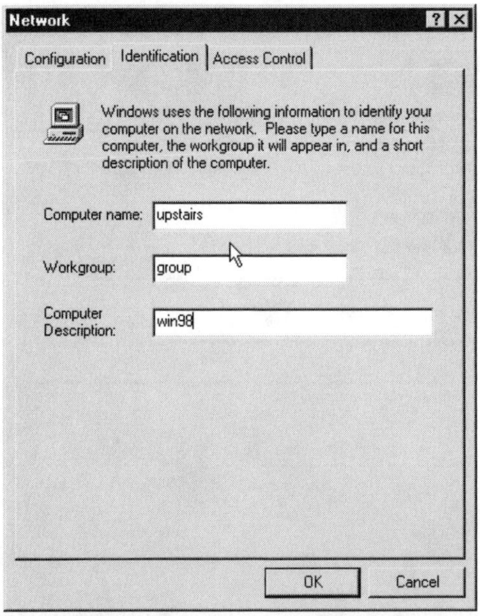

Figure 2-4.   Windows network identification screen

You'll notice in Figure 2-5 that both File And Printer Sharing For Microsoft Networks and Client For Microsoft Networks are in the list of installed components. This is the case for Windows 95/98/Me. If they aren't present in your configuration, you'll have to add them. (Click the Add button shown in Figure 2-5, go to Clients | Client For Microsoft Networks And Services | File And Printer Sharing For Microsoft Networks, and add both components.)

Windows 2000/XP has a slightly different components screen, similar to the one in Figure 2-6. Go to Settings | Control Panel | Network And Dial-Up Connections[5] | Local Area Connection, and then right-click and choose Properties. Again, to add components that aren't showing up here, click the Install button, and choose the appropriate service or client piece.

If you have more listed components showing up in your components screen, review the "Troubleshooting" section for how to get rid of them.

---

5   Windows XP calls this Network Connections, but otherwise the process is the same.

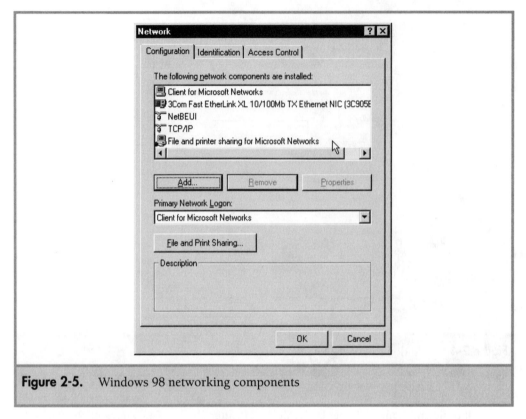

Figure 2-5.   Windows 98 networking components

Specifying the IP Address for Macs

To specify the IP address for Macs, go to the TCP/IP control panel. Choose Connect Via Ethernet at the top, and then select Configure Manually. Enter the number from your handy table (Table 2-1) for the computer's IP address, enter **255.255.255.0** for the subnet mask box, and leave the Router Address box blank. The screen should look like Figure 2-7. Then close this window, and save the configuration. Do this on each Mac on your network (of course, giving each of them a unique number). If you are using something other than Ethernet to connect them, such as a wireless adapter, you should have another entry to choose from in the TCP/IP control panel. If not, then either your adapter isn't installed properly, or you need to find a more recent match of drivers.

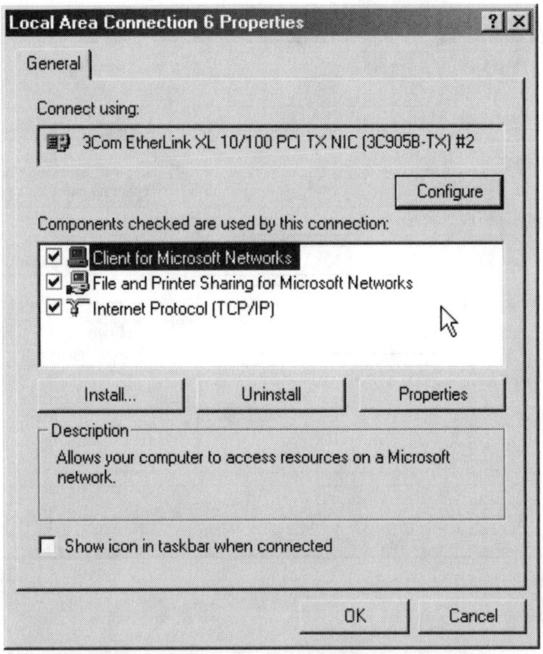

Figure 2-6.   Windows 2000 networking components

If these choices are unavailable, your machine may have been previously configured and some choices locked. Figure 2-7 was taken in Advanced user mode. You can lock a configuration item in the Administrator user mode. Then it is not editable in the Basic or Advanced modes. Under the Edit menu, select User Modes, and choose Advanced or Administrator.

If your Mac is a laptop, you may have a configuration that was set up by the network administrator at your office. In that case you may want to take advantage of the Mac's ability to store and save multiple configurations. Go to Edit | Configurations, and then duplicate your current configuration, giving it a new name, for your experiments with home networking. That way you can later go to Edit | Configurations and switch back to the configuration that was set up by your work network administrator.

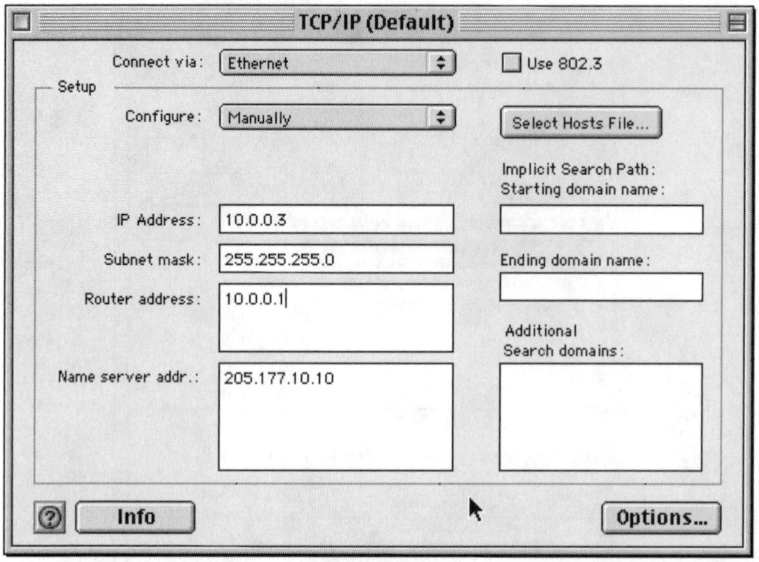

Figure 2-7. IP address for Macintosh

Enable File Sharing on Each of Your Computers

Now we need to enable file sharing on your computers. This is the easy part. Make that two easy parts, because you first have to set up the shared folder on your computer that will act as the server. Then you must connect to it from the computer that will act as a client. A single machine can be both: you can set up your downstairs computer with a shared folder "DOWN" and an upstairs computer with the shared folder "UP." This way, your files are available to you no matter which machine you're using, provided that the server machine is powered-on when you are trying to access the shared files.

On Windows 95/98, bring up Windows Explorer. On Windows Me/2000/XP, bring up Internet Explorer and then choose View | Explorer Bar | Folders. In either case you'll see a tree with branches for the various folders and files on your hard disk.

Create a new folder, call it "DOWN" or "UP" or "DATA" or something of the sort. Then right-click on its name in the Explorer tree, and scroll over to the Sharing command. Enable sharing for this folder, and give it the same name as the folder's name so you can remember what you are doing later. You also will have to specify the kind of access you want your network users to have to this shared folder. I suggest for now that you choose the Full access type and give it a password that is the same as the user login passwords for all your machines. See Figure 2-8 for what to expect.

SURVIVAL TIP

For security reasons, you'll want to give your shared folders a password. Without this, and without the protective measures discussed in Chapter 6, you leave your home network wide open to hackers, once you have an Internet connection.

Close this screen and you are all set. The icon next to the folder name in the Explorer tree has changed to an outstretched hand, indicating that this folder is now sharable across your network. Do the same on each of your machines as desired: It is probably a good idea

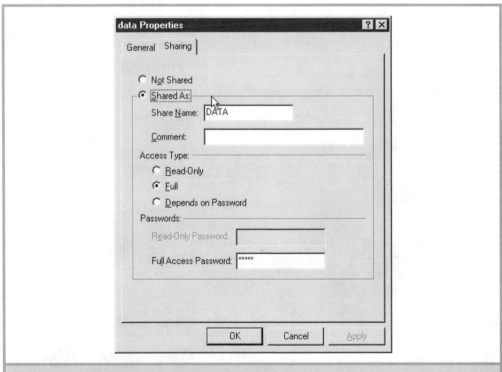

Figure 2-8.   Enabling file share names for Windows

to have at least one sharable folder on each machine. You could share your entire C: drive, but that probably is not a good idea. Files that Windows needs to operate are scattered throughout the drive. If one of your family members accidentally deletes these files, your machine won't boot.

Now, how do you see this shared folder[6] and get the files that you want to be available on all of your PCs? You could bring up Windows Explorer or Internet Explorer (choosing again View | Explorer Bar | Folders to get it to show you your files on your hard disk). You have two choices here. One is to go to the Network Neighborhood or My Network Places and see if the shared folders are displayed in the list.

I prefer to go to Tools | Map Network Drive, provide the computer name and the shared folder name, and choose a drive letter that this folder will correspond to. Fill out the information similar to that in Figure 2-9.

What is going on here? Basically, you are extending the reach of your computer over the network to include this shared folder as if it were just another hard disk sitting inside your machine. You have a C: drive and probably a D: drive for your CD-ROM (and other drive letters for other devices like Zip drives and possibly a DVD drive and other hard disk partitions). Any other drive letters that aren't being used for your local disk resources are

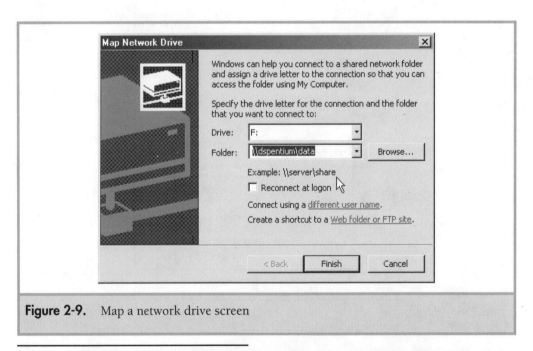

Figure 2-9.   Map a network drive screen

---

6   Windows Me has the ability, called *Net Crawling,* to search automatically for shared network folders.
     To set this up requires making changes to the Windows registry, which is not for the casual user.
     For more details, go to Helmig's Web site (http://www.wown.com/j_helmig/wmecrawl.htm).

available to be "mapped" to your network file shares, which is probably more letters than you know what to do with.

Now you can have the Z: drive for your shared folder on one machine, a W: drive for another, and an Y: drive for a third. I hope you can contain your excitement, because right now you have a working network in your home. Be proud of yourself.

What, something isn't working? Start reading the "Troubleshooting" section, and see if you can figure out what went wrong.

If you have any Macs, first go to the File Sharing control panel, and turn on File Sharing (see Figure 2-10). It might take a few minutes to bring it up. Once it is running, double-click on the hard disk icon on your desktop, and create a new folder inside it that you intend to share. Let's call it **data** just for now. Next, highlight this folder, go to the Apple menu, go to Automated Tasks | Share A Folder, and start that process. (Or you could click on that folder, and bring up File | Get Info | Sharing, and your Mac will ask you if you want to start the File Sharing service for you. Say yes.) Also, fill out the Network Identity section of this screen, to include your name and password and the name of each of your Macs. As I said earlier, create a different computer name, but use the same owner name and password to keep things simple for now.

Your data folder is ready to be shared on your network. To make sure, click again on the folder, and bring up File | Get Info | Sharing. You'll see a screen like that in Figure 2-11.

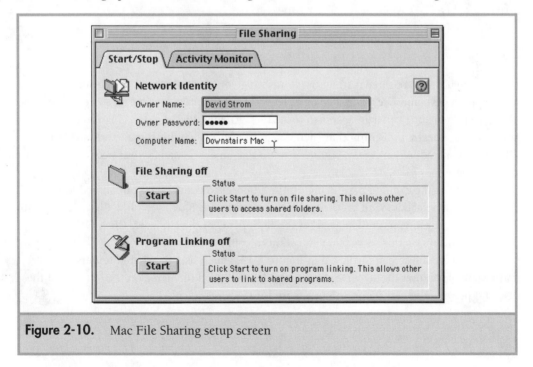

Figure 2-10. Mac File Sharing setup screen

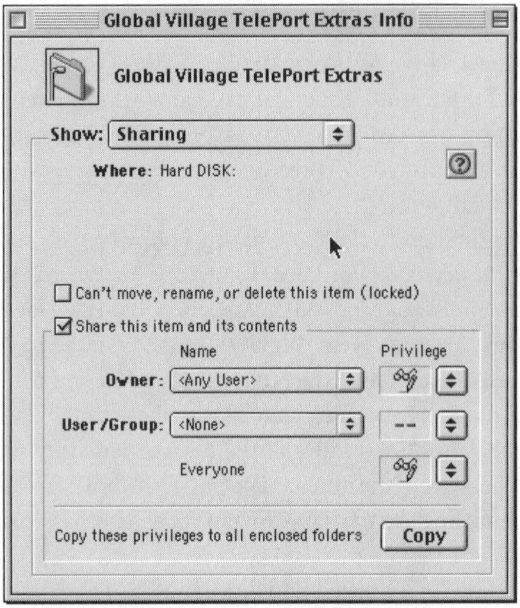

Figure 2-11. Mac options for file sharing

Note that there are three distinct user categories for Macs: Owner, User/Group (specific group privileges), and Everyone. For now, let's just set the privileges for all three to the same thing, so that anyone can gain access to these files. An icon that is a combination of a pencil and glasses appears, indicating that each category of users can both read and write to the files in this shared folder. Again, you need to do this on every Mac in your network that you want to share files from.

Now comes the exciting part. Bring up the Chooser to connect to your shared folders. Click on the AppleShare icon on the top left, and your screen will look like Figure 2-12, with the name of your file server displayed on the right panel of the Chooser. Click OK to choose the shared folders on this server that you want to connect to.

You will see the screen displayed in Figure 2-13, which lists the shared folders that you have available on that file server. Select the folders, click on the name on the left side of the list, and provide the user name and password for these resources.

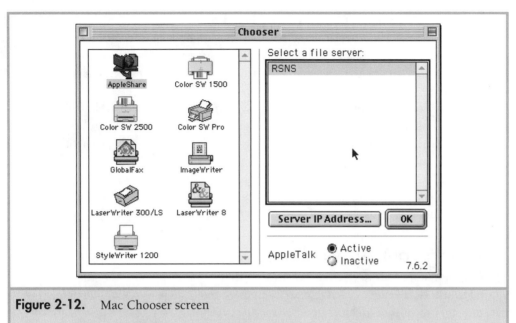

Figure 2-12. Mac Chooser screen

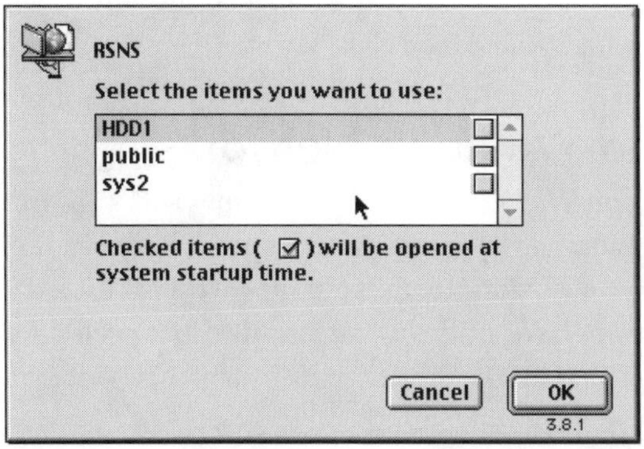

Figure 2-13. Mac Chooser shared folders

Once everything is done properly, your desktop will have a new icon of a disk drive that indicates the name of the network share. You can click on it, open it, and start saving files there for all your family to share. Sorry, Mac owners don't get the excitement of having a bunch of disk drive letters, they just get pretty icons on their desktops. But it amounts to the same thing.

Finally, newer versions of the Mac operating system have options for enabling file sharing and program linking over IP connections. Do *not* enable these options, as they create an increased security risk for your home Macs. With these options turned on, someone from across the Internet could access your files.

You'll notice in our discussions that we only describe sharing files among like kinds of computers. If you want to share files between your Macs and Windows PCs, you'll have to do some additional work, see "Mixed Mac and Windows Networks" shortly.

Adjusting Your Applications

The final step in this odyssey is to make it easier to find your files once they are stored on your network. Go around to each of your computers and change the default document or data directory to your shared folders, so that whenever someone creates a new Word file, Excel spreadsheet, or whatever, they will be able to find it again. Moreover, once they save it to this shared folder, you will be able to retrieve it from any computer in your house.

For example, let's say that your mapped drive of your downstairs file server's shared document directory is the Q: drive. To change Word to automatically go looking for documents in Q:, go to Tools | Options | File Locations | Documents, click the Change button, replace whatever is listed there with Q:\, and then click Save.

Mixed Mac and Windows Networks

If you have both Macs and Windows PCs, you probably will want to share files between the two worlds. If you are running the same applications on both kinds of machines (such as Microsoft Office) and have versions that match the format of their data files,[7] then there will come a time when you have a file on one machine, but need it on another.

---

7   The catch is "versions that match." Microsoft Office is very particular about the version of the
     documents you create in one and view in another, and sometimes your formatting gets messed up
     even though it looks like the entire document was parsed by the software just fine. All I can say is,
     sorry about this, try to keep your versions of various applications in synch, and write Microsoft a
     nasty letter. For editing Web pages and other text files, the Mac doesn't like the Windows line-ending
     character, or maybe it is the other way around. So you might have some cleaning up to do when
     moving things back and forth. A good book that goes into more detail than I do here is *Crossing
     Platforms* by Adam Engst and David Pogue (O'Reilly, 1999).

You have several choices, depending on how often you intend to share files between the two systems.

If you don't have that many times where you need a common file, the easiest thing to do is to send the file as an e-mail attachment from one computer to another. Of course, this means you'll have to set up separate e-mail addresses for the family members on these two computers, and you'll also have to read Chapter 5, which covers how to set up your e-mail applications.[8]

Sending e-mail back and forth gets tiring once you do it a few times and realize that your packets have traveled probably halfway around the world to get the 10 or 20 feet from one side of your house to the other. A better solution would be to give both machines common access to the files. You can do this via floppies or Zip disks (if both machines have the same kind of drives. (Some of the more recent Macs don't come with a floppy drive, for example.) You must format the floppy or Zip in Windows format on your Windows machine. The Mac can read them. (There is also a program for the PC that can read Mac formatted disks, but it isn't as good.) Finally, VirtualPC, a program that runs Windows on your Mac, is a good solution if you have mostly Macs and still want to run some Windows software on them.

Since this is a networking book, let me suggest a few network-based solutions for sharing common files between Macs and Windows. If you want to spend as little money as possible, you can make use of the built-in Web servers[9] that come with Windows and Macintoshes. This is a bit cumbersome since you need to know exactly where you have put the file and how to bring up your Web browser and find the file. But it can work in a pinch, and there is no additional software to buy, other than dealing with setting up the Web server utility.

Finding whether you have this utility installed can be a challenge. In Windows, this is called the Personal Web Server and can be found in various places depending on the version of Windows you are running. If you have Windows 98 Second Edition (SE), find your CD-ROM, go to Start | Run, and then type *x:\add-ons\pws\setup*, where *x* is the location of your CD drive. If you have Windows 2000 Professional, go to Settings | Control Panel | Add Or Remove Programs | Internet Information Services | Details, and then select the box at the bottom of the list next to "World Wide Web Server."

---

8   You can do this by using the same e-mail address, meaning that you can send yourself the file from machine A to machine B, but it is somewhat tricky, since you have to configure machine A's e-mail account to just send and not receive messages.

9   Another alternative to using a Web server is to set up on either the Windows or the Mac a File Transfer Protocol (FTP) server and to use the built-in Windows FTP client or one of the Mac FTP clients like Fetch to move files back and forth between the two worlds. I don't recommend this method unless you have lots of experience with FTP and understand what you are doing. You could easily replace a current version of your file with an older one by mistake. One of the easier FTP server programs to use is from Rhino Software and can be downloaded at www.serv-u.com.

For the Mac, this is called Web Sharing and is found under Control Panels. Mac OS 8 and later versions come with Web Sharing.

If you want to share files without using a Web server, you can buy Dave on the Mac, or PCMACLAN on the PC. They do similar things, but from different perspectives. It depends how many of each computer you have. If you have fewer Macs, use Dave. If fewer PCs, use PCMACLAN.

+ **Dave** http://www.miramarsys.com/products/

+ **PCMACLAN** http://www.thursby.com/

If you need to have more or less constant interchange between the two worlds, the best solution is to use Microsoft's NT/2000 Server versions (but not the workstation or professional versions). If you are in the market for a new computer and constant interchange is going to be important for you, it makes sense to buy one with 2000 Server preinstalled. If you want to upgrade one of your existing Windows machines to the server versions, go ahead, but it could be tricky. Have a machine with at least 256MB of RAM and 10GB of a hard disk along with at least a 500-MHz Pentium processor.

If you have a less capable machine and can get your hands on NT Server 4.0, you should be able to get things working with this operating system as well. Realize that the server operating systems of these products can cost about $1,000, depending on where you buy them. You may want to reevaluate whether you really need to have the cross-system interchange. If you are interested in having a Windows server to run your own Web site from your home, or to use other Windows services (such as playing streaming audio or running a database server), you can obtain the Macintosh pieces for essentially no additional charge.

All server versions come with support for Macintosh file and print services, but you need to install these modules. For Windows 2000 Server, these services can be found under Settings | Control Panel | Add Or Remove Programs | Other Network File And Print Services | Details. Once you install the Mac file and print services, you'll need to follow the Macintosh networking checklist items (under Configure Your Server | Advanced | Checklists) to set up a network share and enable Mac users to see it. Then connect from the Mac with the standard Chooser process.

More detail than I give you here is involved with doing this, and if you are really interested in getting more information, I would recommend that you take a look at the HomePC Network Web site (http://www.homepcnetwork.com/pcmacovr.htm). They have lots of pictures of how to open up your computers and install the appropriate adapters, and more instructions on the various choices just mentioned.

Troubleshooting

There are many places where things could go wrong in these early stages of setting up your network. Let me try to cover the major issues and provide some tips and tricks to resolve your problems.

If you are feeling adventurous, take a look at the suggestions to troubleshoot your network from consultant Carey Holzman. (See Appendix A.) While going through numerous steps might be overkill, this is probably as complete a checklist as you can find if you are stumped for why you can't get something working on your network.[10]

Your Windows PC Won't Recognize Your Network Adapter

You bring home your network adapters, eagerly awaiting the moment you can have the house to yourself and install them in your computers. You follow my preceding directions, and after you install the driver disk and reboot your computer, something goes wrong. You can't seem to get your PC to recognize your adapter.

First, try to install the same adapter into another PC, perhaps with a more recent version of Windows on it. If it is recognized and works properly, you have at least narrowed down your problem to the first PC. Perhaps the version of Windows isn't supported for that particular adapter. Perhaps the slot that you placed the adapter in is not working. (Not all slots on all PCs are created equally.) Or something else installed in that first PC could be preventing the adapter from working, such as a modem or a sound card that is interfering.

How do you know that something isn't being recognized by Windows? Go to Control Panel | System | Device Manager, and look for your adapter with a small exclamation point in a yellow circle next to it. That means that Windows knows something about the adapter, but it isn't completely installed. It may be set up wrong or have a conflict with another device or some other problem. Double-click on that device, look at its properties, determine if it is having a resource conflict with another device, and if so, change one of the settings on the device to parameters unused by the conflicting device. This is very general information, but a lot depends on the type of adapter you have, what else is in your system, and whether the adapter is a PCI or ISA model. To make any changes, look for the setup program on a floppy or CD-ROM that came with your adapter.

---

10   An updated copy of this appendix can be found on Carey's Web site
      (http://www.users.qwest.net/~careyh/netfixes.htm).

Another situation that I came across is a mismatch between the network adapter and your hub port. Some network cards don't work at faster than 10 megabits per second (Mbps), and you might have to go into the Network configuration screens and explicitly set up your card to operate at 10 Mbps so that the drivers you have will work with the adapter. I wish I could give you more detailed instructions here, but much depends on your specific equipment.

If all else fails, you have limited choices. You could try to purchase a different variety of network adapter and see if that works in your computer. You could try to remove the various plug-in cards one at a time to see if one of them is interfering. If you purchased a PCI-style network adapter, see if there is room inside your PC to install an ISA-style adapter. These are usually more trouble to install, but they could be your only hope. If you are running Windows 95, upgrade to a more recent version, such as Win98. Or, you could donate your computer to a local school and buy something new, which, while expensive, is probably the quickest way to get network enabled.

The Lights on Your Hub Aren't Lit

Almost all hubs include indicator lights that tell you when a PC is connected to one of their ports. One of your first clues when you turn on your PC is if this indicator light doesn't come on, meaning one of several situations. Most likely your cable is defective, hasn't been wired properly, or the connectors aren't completely seated inside the adapter and hub receptacles. Jiggle everything to make sure you have a solid connection.

One suggestion is to obtain a short length of Ethernet cable, bring your hub next to your PC, and see if you can connect the hub to the PC with this piece of Ethernet. If the light comes on, you know it is your cable that needs further work.

Another possibility is that you are using the wrong kind of Ethernet cable. Remember, there are two kinds, and you might have installed the "other" one. Without more expensive test tools, it is difficult to track down further cabling issues, however.

Something Is Wrong with Your IP Network

Another problem could be that you set up your IP network incorrectly. If you are going to troubleshoot IP problems, you are in for some rough times. There are several different places to check, including using Ping/WhatRoute, taking a look at WINIPCFG/IPCONFIG, and bringing up the Network Neighborhood/Chooser. Let's review what you can learn from each of these tools as you try to figure out what is going on with your network. See Table 2-2 to find out which tool works with which type of system.

Type of System	Tool Available
Windows 95/98/Me	WINIPCFG, PING
Windows 2000/XP	IPCONFIG, PING
Macintosh	WhatRoute

Table 2-2. Rudimentary IP Tools

WhatRoute doesn't come with the Macintosh operating system software; you'll need to download it first from the programmer's Web site (http://homepages.ihug.co.nz/~bryanc).

IPCONFIG and PING are command-line utilities that are included with every version of Windows. To invoke them, bring up a MS-DOS command-line window, type **IPCONFIG** or **PING YAHOO.COM** at the command prompt, and press ENTER. You'll see a display of information. If you have a choice and can use WINIPCFG, try that instead of IPCONFIG. It will give you a better sense of what is going on, and you won't have to deal with command-line parameters. To run this, go to Start | Run, enter **WINIPCFG**, and press ENTER. Your screen should look like Figure 2-14.

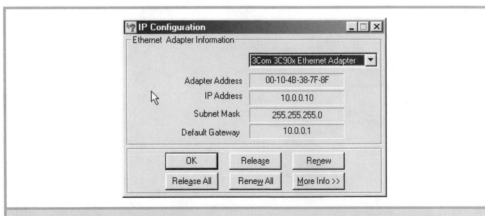

Figure 2-14. WINIPCFG screen

For WhatRoute, find where you saved the copy of the software on your hard disk, and then double-click on the icon to bring it up. You have several tools at your disposal, including the Ping utility, as shown in Figure 2-15.

The Ping utility sends out a series of packets to the particular server and tells you whether the server can respond. It is very useful for figuring out if there is a path between your computer and the outside world, as well as between two computers in your home. But before you can use Ping, you first need to know the IP address of all your computers. That is where the other tools come in handy. Go to each of your PCs, bring up this tool, and copy down the IP address that it reports. If you did everything correctly, it should show something in the 10.0.0.*x* range of addresses or the range of your hub's DHCP server if you purchased one of the devices mentioned in Chapter 4.

CAUTION What happens when you find out that your IP address is something like 169.254.*x.x*? Your computer actually hasn't found the DHCP server, and either your Mac or Windows has helpfully given you some random IP address from this sequence. This is called *autoconfiguration,* and it means that your network connection isn't working for the moment. You'll have to troubleshoot your cable as the most likely source of your problem.

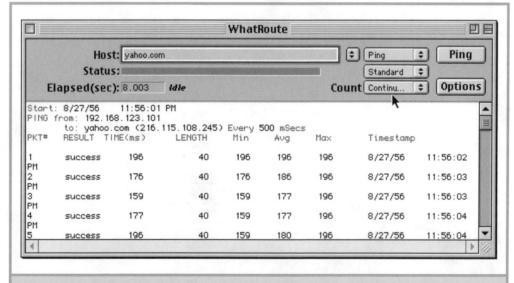

Figure 2-15. WhatRoute Ping utility

You Have Too Many Networking Components

Windows can be maddening when it comes to the various bits and pieces of networking support you need. Your Network control panel might contain more than the neat short lists that you saw on the previous screen shots. Here are a couple of examples of multiple listings that need some pruning.

In Figure 2-16, you see that we have two 3Com Ethernet adapters listed.On our machine, however, we actually have only a single adapter. Somehow we installed it twice. Delete one of these adapters, and you probably will have to reboot your machine. Hopefully, this will fix any problem you are having. You might have to delete everything from the Network control panel and start from scratch to get things working properly.

Figure 2-17 shows another case of an overgrown Network control panel.

With this computer, we have too much TCP/IP support. If you are planning to give up your dial-up access and use a broadband cable or DSL connection for your Internet connection, eliminate both of the TCP/IP entries associated with the Dial-up adapter, leaving just the one associated with the 3Com network card, as shown in Figure 2-17.

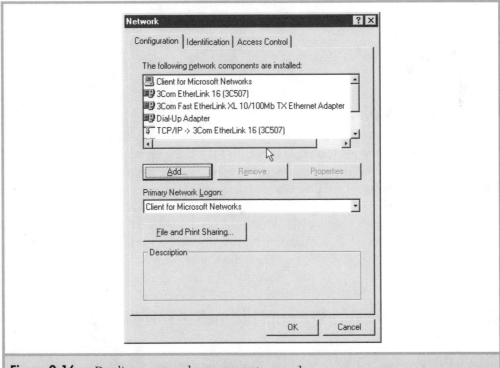

Figure 2-16. Duplicate network components, case 1

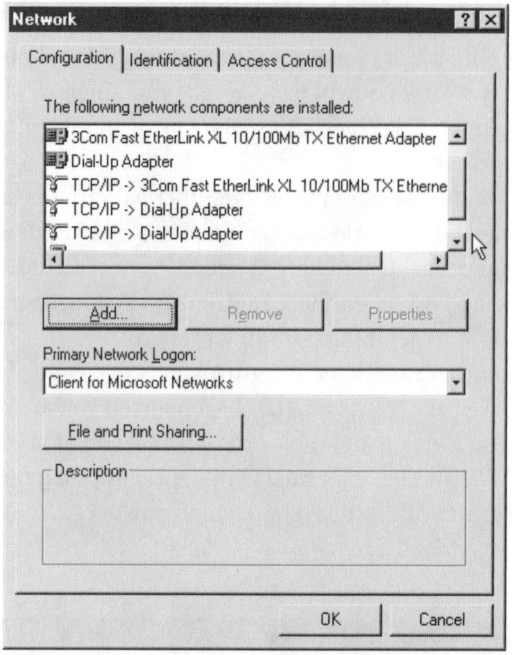

Figure 2-17. Duplicate network components, case 2

Disappearing Networked Drive

Sometimes your networked drives will disappear from your Windows Explorer listing or from your Mac desktop. What can you do? For the Mac, bring up your Chooser and again try to connect to the file server and the shared folders. You might have had a network problem, or someone might have disconnected the power from your hub or removed a cable when you weren't looking.

For Windows, bring up your copy of Windows Explorer or Internet Explorer, and try to map the network drive again. You might have to first disconnect the mapped drive before you can connect to it again. (Windows is sometimes stupid when it comes to disappearing networked drives.)

Your Login and Workgroup Names Aren't the Same on All Computers

One of Windows' many quirks is that if you haven't correctly specified the workgroup name on all of your computers, you won't be able to view their shared folders. Go to the

Networking control panel, and make sure that the workgroup name is consistent across all of your machines.

Next, make sure that the user name and password combination is the same for all of your Windows machines. You may have to reboot your machine for these changes to take effect.

NOTE

Windows 95/98 use the term "Network Neighborhood." Windows 2000/Me/XP use the term "My Network Places." They both refer to the availability of shared folders and file servers on your network.

Locking Down Your Network for Specific Family Members

In some circumstances you may want to provide limited access to shared files for certain family members. To do this properly, you will need to enable user-level security and set up a more complex network than the simple network that I describe in this chapter. This is outside the scope of this book, but I recommend that you read the chapters in *Networking: A Beginner's Guide* by Bruce Hallberg (Osborne/McGraw Hill, 2000) on security to get the specifics.

The Servers Don't Appear in the Mac Chooser

It could be that your servers are using AppleTalk over IP, rather than pure AppleTalk. An alternative is to enter the IP address of your server in the Chooser dialog box, and see if you can connect to it and view its shared folders. Remember, to find out what this value is, go to the Control Panel | TCP/IP screen, and the IP address should be displayed.

Troubles with Wireless Networks

Setting up wireless networks with components from more than one vendor is possible, thanks to better implementations of the 802.11b standards. But it isn't always easy. There are several things to consider if you do intend to mix and match components from different vendors. Here are some pointers as you go about testing the various products.

1. **Make sure that you have a working setup.** Try connecting an access point and a wireless adapter from the same vendor to make sure that both products function as intended.

2. **Turn off any encryption.** Wireless network products have implemented encryption in many different mechanisms, with multiple parameters to adjust to get it working properly. To increase your chances of getting things to work, turn off encryption at

both the access point and in the wireless adapter settings. Once you get everything working, you can try to turn it back on for increased network security.

3. **Ensure that each network uses the same ID number.** Make sure that you have specified these consistently and correctly among the access point and adapter settings. Different products call this ID number different things, such as an SSID, a Network Name, an ESS ID, or a Wireless LAN ID number. The trick is to find the right number (usually printed on the bottom of the access point) and to enter it correctly (allowing for possible case sensitivity) in the right place in the configuration screen.

4. **Keep things close together for testing.** Don't try to set up your wireless computer too far away from your access point. Indeed, try setting them up initially side-by-side on the same desk to facilitate the entire configuration. Otherwise, you may be running around your home with little to show for it.

5. **Adjust the channel/frequency settings and transmission rates when in doubt.** Most products allow you to specify one of the 11 radio channels that are used in these products. If you are having trouble communicating between access points and adapters, try to set them to the same frequency, and see if you get a signal. If not, adjust the data transmission rate downward. Most products allow you to set the data transmission rate as well, and it could be that the products are too far apart to maintain a signal that can support 11 Mbps.

6. **Make sure you have the right network setting.** Wireless network adapter cards can be set up in one of two modes: ad hoc or infrastructure. *Ad hoc* refers to peer-to-peer networks without any access points; *infrastructure* refers to networks that make use of access points. This seems obvious, but if you have chosen the wrong setting, your network won't work.

7. **When in doubt, try to install the product on Windows 98 Second Edition.** Other versions of Windows don't have the best support for drivers for wireless networks, but most support Windows 98. If you are running Windows Me, make sure you have special drivers for that operating system, as Windows Me is very particular about what it supports.

Setting Up Your Access Point

Let's see how to set up a wireless access point using the Farallon NetLine Wireless Broadband Gateway access point as an example of what is involved and then go through the steps to get it working.

The best procedure is to connect the access point via standard Ethernet cabling to one of your computers to set its configuration parameters. Since the Farallon unit uses a Web-based system, you can use either a Mac or a Windows PC, as long as your browser version is recent. I recommend Internet Explorer 4.01 or, better, version 5 or 6.

The Farallon access point comes in three parts: a power transformer, the unit itself, and a PC Card wireless network adapter that fits inside the unit. Connect everything together. The unit has three RJ-45s on the back: two are for your local network, and one is to connect the access point to your cable or DSL modem. Don't worry about the latter for now, but do hook up your PC to one of the local network ports.

Now go to your PC. Instead of following the instructions about a manual IP address in this chapter, change the setting in the TCP/IP properties to obtain a dynamic IP address. You may have to reboot your machine to make this work. Bring up a Web browser, and type in the address **192.168.0.1**, which is the default IP address for the Farallon unit.

If all goes well, you should see the configuration screen on your Web browser. Click on Configure | Wireless Setup, and you should see the screen in Figure 2-18.

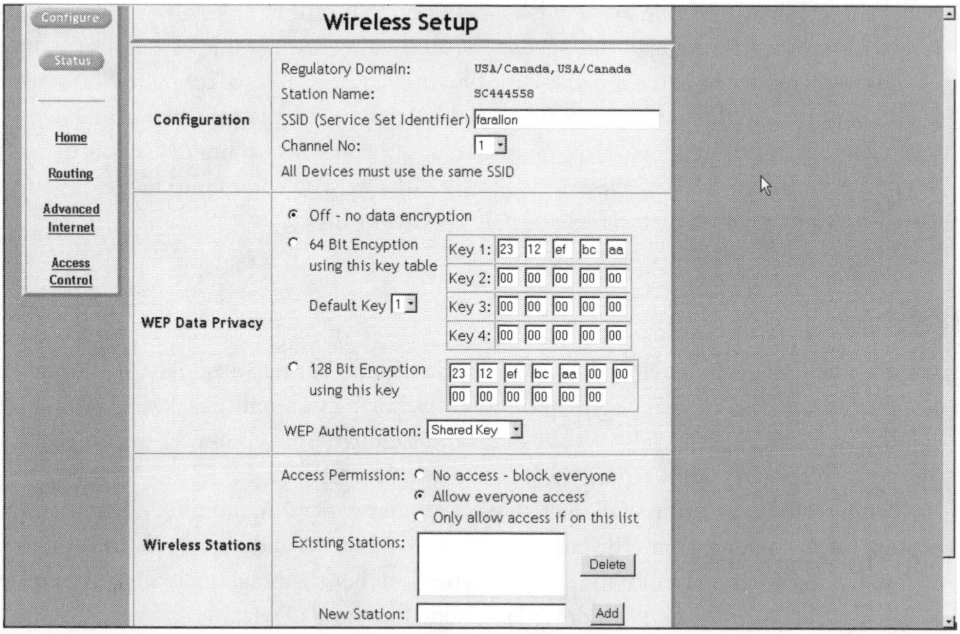

Figure 2-18.   Farallon wireless gateway setup screen

There are several critical parameters that need adjusting here. First, the SSID should be something that you can easily remember, such as "Stromhome." Once you enter it here, you'll have to use the same name on all of your PCs when the time comes to set up their individual wireless adapters. Set the channel number to channel 1 for now; again, you'll want to use that channel in each of your PCs so they can communicate with the access point.

Next, turn off WEP Data Privacy for now. When you get everything working, you can turn on encryption and protect your network from people driving by your home. (I guess this will be the new form of drive-by shooting, but let's not get into that right now.) Also, under Wireless Stations, select the Allow Everyone Access option. Again, once you have a working connection, you can tighten up your network. Save your settings.

Now go to one of your PCs that you want to wirelessly connect to. Install the Farallon wireless adapter (or whatever wireless network adapter you decided to use) in that computer. Remember to go through the configuration screens and provide the same SSID and channel number for that card. You should be able to see a connection between the card and the wireless access point, and lights should start flashing on the tops of the wireless antennas, indicating that they are talking to each other. With luck, data should start moving between the two, and you should be able to establish a network connection.

If not, reread the beginning of this section. Try adjusting one parameter at a time, going back and forth between the two computers: the one that has the browser configuration screen of the access point and the one that has the actual wireless network adapter installed.

Once you have everything working, enable encryption and set up limited access to particular users on your network. If you forget this, anyone who comes into range of your access point can grab a connection and possibly copy your files.

Futures

What started out as a simple request, to share files around your network, isn't so simple to implement. While there are many steps and obstacles, having this ability makes a lot of sense for your home network, especially if your kids tend to move from computer to computer and not remember where they stored their files.

We can hope that the future will make it easier to network your computers together, but I don't see this happening soon. The latest versions of Windows and Mac operating systems have more complexities and more things to go wrong, rather than making it any easier to set up your network. Both Mac and Windows have added all sorts of wizards and routines that complicate the networking picture and will require some patience on your part to understand what is going on.

The good news is that Microsoft is finally focused on networking as an intrinsic part of Windows, which is something that Apple and the UNIX communities have accepted and dealt with for many years. Some of the leading computer vendors have begun to build their computers with built-in Ethernet and wireless adapters, accepting that these machines will become part of networks from the moment they are taken out of the box. Major computer retail stores now sell two-PC-network-in-a-box kits, complete with cabling and everything you need to get a small network going. These are all encouraging signs.

But your chores aren't done yet. Your next step is to get your printers to work on your network, and that is the subject of our next chapter.

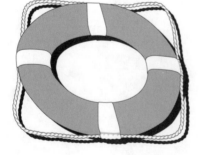

Chapter 3

Sharing Printers

When networks were first invented, their most popular use was to share printers. It makes a lot of sense: Printers take up lots of desktop real estate, and even the busiest household uses a printer occasionally, at best. Just about every application involves printing at some point, however. We print Web pages for reference or to read offline, we print e-mail messages that are important, and we create documents and spreadsheets that are designed to be printed.

If your household has three or more computers, running around with documents on floppies to find a computer with an available printer can get tiresome and stressful. Sometimes it seems as if every household member has to print something at the same time, and everyone's document is critical and has to be done Right Now. Sharing your printers on the home network can help reduce these conflicts. By networking them, everyone has access to a printer.

In the early days of networking, laser printers could cost several thousand dollars and network adapters several hundred. Prices have dropped, but it still is cheaper to install a network adapter than to buy a new printer. When you factor in the convenience and savings in desktop space, the thought of networking printers in your home becomes enticing.

Sharing a printer also limits the number of toner cartridges or other model-specific supplies you have to buy, meaning users with limited knowledge don't have to worry about determining which cartridge goes into which printer. It also means that the user doesn't have to worry about going to multiple vendors to obtain replacements.

Plus, sharing a printer is an obvious way that you can point out your networking prowess and brag to your friends and household that you have a *real* network at home. A printer is something that we can all understand and touch—no mysterious protocols and under-the-covers stuff going on here. That's the theory, anyway.

Problems

Just because the reasons are compelling doesn't mean that it is going to be easy to set up your networked printers. Begin by figuring out where the printers are going to be. Depending on the type of connection and your home layout, you may or may not be able to find a cable long enough to connect the printer properly. (Don't laugh—I am serious. Many networking sessions have stopped abruptly because of a too-short cable and no place to readily buy a longer one.)

You might want to locate the printers in more public areas if computers are in your children's bedrooms, so you can monitor what they are printing (or at least appear to monitor their work; more on this in Chapter 7). You may want to put the printer someplace that makes it easy for household members to grab their printouts without having to disturb the person sitting at the nearby computer. (Keeping the printer off the floor is probably a good idea.) You may have some laptops in the house that will make it harder to connect printers directly to them, unless the laptops aren't going to be moved around much.

What if you only have one printer and need to share it among two or more computers? Designating who "owns" the printer can be difficult, and can often precipitate a political struggle for control. I suggest using psychology here, particularly among your children, to convince them that having the printer nearby may not always be desirable. Alternatively, you could just declare the location as parental prerogative and leave it at that!

SURVIVAL TIP

If one of your printers is attached to your downstairs computer, then both that computer and the printer have to be powered-on if you are going to send printouts to it from your upstairs computer. This seems obvious, but it is an important issue.

Next you need to figure out what kinds of printers you want to use. This, of course, depends on what you already have in your household and what kinds of print jobs you anticipate from your family. It also depends on how much money you want to part with for a new printer. You can choose among basically three types of printers:

✦ **Laser printers** typically print in black and white. They cost more initially, but then cost less to operate per page. They use expensive toner cartridges, but these cartridges usually last for several thousand pages. Lasers are also the fastest printers: they print from four to 12 pages per minute, which is helpful if you have a long report to finish late at night. There are some brands of laser printers that handle color, but these cost several thousand dollars and are targeted at people, such as graphics artists, who demand high-quality prints.

✦ **Ink-jet printers** typically can handle color printing and are cheap to buy, but cost more than laser printers to operate per page. Ink cartridges are cheaper than the laser toner ones (and a lot smaller), but the cartridges only last for several hundred pages at most. The initial cost of the printer can be equivalent to about three cartridges, and some printers use two or more ink cartridges at a time. Many ink-jet printers are bundled for free or for a reduced price when you purchase a new PC, but they are usually the most expensive printers to operate. There are many ink-jets that can do a credible job printing digital photographs, but these require expensive papers to produce the best results.

✦ **Multifunction printers** typically combine printing, scanning, and faxing in one single unit. These are usually ink-jets, and they can cost about as much as buying a separate fax machine and printer. I haven't had much luck with them and wouldn't recommend them, unless you are really crunched for space, don't mind making compromises in terms of print quality or ease of use, and don't expect to need a laser printer soon. For networking purposes, you can consider these similar to ink-jets in how they are going to be attached to your network.

**SURVIVAL
TIP**

Many resources can help you select a printer. Two of the best Web sites are http://cnet.com and http://www.zdnet.com/pcmag. PC World Magazine's Web site (http://www.pcworld.com, searching for printer reviews) provides a thorough analysis of the cost per page for producing both black-and-white and color prints on its top recommended ink-jets, which can be helpful when you need to consider the overall operating cost and are lured by the low prices on these printers.

Most likely, you will want to have one of each variety to cover the changing demands of your household's printing needs. If you are buying a new printer, it makes sense to buy a laser if you only have ink-jets, or vice versa. Typical brands include Hewlett-Packard, Lexmark, Brother, and Epson. When it comes to laser printers, I am partial to HP and Lexmark. The two printers that I have had for years keep working, and many others that I have seen from these companies are still printing after long years of service.

Another issue is figuring ways you can connect your printer to your computer and then determining how to extend this connection to your network. Printers can attach to your computer in one of four ways: via a parallel port, a serial port, a USB port, or a LocalTalk port. Each port has its own kind of cable that will fit only in that particular port; the cables are manufactured in different lengths, depending on how far apart your printer and computer are.

Some printers include multiple ports, which makes them easier to network (more on that in a moment). LocalTalk ports were found on all Macintoshes sold up until a few years ago, when the iMac and G3/G4 brands came out and eliminated these ports. If you have a household with older Macs with LocalTalk ports and a multiple-port printer, you are in luck; they are the easiest to network. If you have a household with some new and some old Macs, you will need some additional gear to network these printers.

Most printers sold today have parallel ports, which have been found on the earliest PCs and still are supported on most Windows/Intel machines. (There is an exception: A few years ago, vendors began selling computers that did not include parallel ports, called "legacy-free PCs." If you have one of these, you won't have a parallel port, although you will have several USB ports to choose from. You could purchase a special plug-in card that adds a parallel port if you need to connect an older printer.)

**SURVIVAL
TIP**

Be aware of a technological limitation with regard to the length of your parallel cables. If you have a cable longer than six feet, you may not be able to communicate with your printer, especially on dot-matrix printers. So keep those cables as short as you can.

Another and probably better way of connecting a printer is via standard Ethernet cabling. Some printers, particularly more expensive ones that are geared toward offices, come with Ethernet connections built in or available as a separate plug-in card. These cards typically go inside your printer, and you usually have to unscrew a small panel or open the printer to find out where they go. If you are brave enough to open up your PC, then there shouldn't be any challenge to installing such a card. Of course, this means you have to figure out which plug-in card will actually work in your printer.

An Ethernet-connected printer makes it easier to share, since all you have to do is connect the Ethernet cable to a hub and set up the printer on your network. Two situations, however, might prove difficult.

First, if you don't have a pure Ethernet network in your home, you won't be able to connect these printers. If you are using wireless connections, you'll have trouble locating and hooking up Ethernet-attached printers and might have to move them closer to your hub or cable modem connection where you have a wired Ethernet port to hook them up.

If you took my advice in the first chapter and located your hub in your basement or near where the cable/telephone wires come into your house, then you'll see that is probably the least convenient location to put a printer. If you are using a PhoneLine network, then you will have to purchase a special printer server that is compatible with this protocol and wiring scheme. For both wireless and PhoneLine networks, you might need to run a special Ethernet cable from your hub to your printer, or else make use of a printer that is attached to one of your PCs directly.

Second, if you have Macintoshes, you'll need to make sure that your printers support EtherTalk protocols. Otherwise the Macs won't be able to print to them.

A final issue is how to share a printer among different operating systems, particularly Windows and Mac OSes. The different Windows versions themselves aren't always easy to figure out how to set up and how to share printers, particularly if your printer is connected just to the network or to another computer on your network. If one of your computers is still running Windows 95, it will be more difficult to connect to the network (as you found out in Chapter 1) and more difficult to set up as a print server. If you have a mixture of Windows operating systems, you'll have to spend some time understanding their differences and figuring out the appropriate software and drivers for each machine. You'll also probably have a somewhat different setup routine to get a printer working on each computer.

Solutions

Before I can recommend any solutions and describe how to share your printer(s) on your network, look at the following solutions matrix, and pick the situation that matches your current and planned conditions. Read the questions along the top row, and then pick the right cell of Table 3-1 based on the kinds of equipment you have. If I am asking questions to which you don't yet know the answers, or if you are unsure, then just pick one of the cells of the table for now to get a better feel for how to proceed.

Situation 1: Only Windows PCs, Keeping Printers in Present Locations

This is the simplest and least costly situation, so let's start here. Let's assume you are concerned with networking Windows PCs and are able to share your printer that is currently attached to one of your computers. For this situation, you'll make use of the built-in tools that are part of the operating system to make the printer available on the network. You don't need any additional hardware, and other than setting the appropriate configuration screens, you don't have much to worry about. You do have to keep the computer on all the time, or at least on all the times that you will want to print. That may or may not be convenient depending on where your computers are.

Of course, with the advent of high-speed Internet connections, many of us leave our computers always powered-on, so that may not be as much of an issue as you first think. (I have a friend, however, who likes to turn her computer off after using it. You don't really save anything by doing this because most modern PCs don't consume all that much power when they are idle. If you want to conserve power, by all means turn the monitor and your printers off at night when you are finished with the machine and everyone is going to be asleep anyway. Or turn off your PC if you are going away for a long weekend or several days. Otherwise, keeping your PC on all the time is fine.)

Computer Types	Present Location	New Location
What **kinds of computers** do you currently have on or are you planning to buy for your network?	Do you plan on keeping the printers in their **present location(s)**?	Do you plan on **moving them around** to new location(s) to share on your network?
Only Macintoshes	Situation 2	Situation 2
Only Windows	Situation 1	Situation 3
A mixture of both	You won't be networking your printers.	Situation 4

Table 3-1.   Network Printing Solutions

Consider the consequences if you don't have your printer's PC powered-on, and you need to get something printed in a hurry: You first have to boot up that PC and then run back to your original location and fire off the print job.

Many modern printers include both USB and parallel ports. This makes them easy to share with two computers. You don't need to connect them to your network directly, or even have any network at all in your home if all you are interested in is sharing the printer between these two computers. This works well if the two computers you want to hook up to your printer are located in the same room and are located near enough to each other, and to the printer, that you can stretch the cables between everything. (You might have to buy longer cables, and given what longer cables cost, you might be better off with one of the less expensive print servers if you ever plan on adding a third PC to the mix.) This is the way we currently operate here at Chez Strom: the parallel port goes to my Windows PC, while the USB port goes to my Mac. It isn't really a network, but I won't tell anyone if you won't.

What if you have more than two computers? If all of your computers are in the same room, you can buy a USB hub and share them that way. I don't particularly recommend this approach. For about the same amount of money, you are better off buying a printer server. (See Situation 3 later in this chapter.) Using a USB hub means that only your USB-capable printers are connected together. If you want to share files or share your Internet connection, you still need a "real" network to hook everything up. And if you have non-USB printers, you will still need a real network.

Okay, so we have run out of choices, and it's time to bite the bullet and install a networked printer. What to do?

To share a directly connected printer under Windows, follow three basic steps:

1. Pick the PC that you are going to connect to your printer, what I'll call the "print server computer," and enable printer sharing through the Windows operating system commands.

2. Turn on sharing for that particular printer, and give it a name to identify it to your network.

3. Set up each computer on your network to connect to this printer.

All of this assumes that you have correctly installed the printer on your print server computer to begin with and that you can send printouts from this computer to the printer without any problems. If you are getting a new printer and want to share it in this fashion, you still need to install it first to the computer that you will use as the print server machine. The good news about a new printer is that you usually haven't yet lost the CD with all the printer software on it.

For the first step, you need to go to the Settings | Control Panel | Network in Windows 95/98/Me and click the button for File And Print Sharing. Next, select the option "I want to be able to allow others to print to my printer(s)," as shown in the illustration. Now reboot your computer.

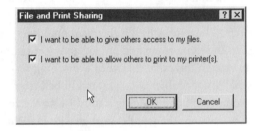

For Windows 2000/XP, if you have already set up your computer to share files and printers under the instructions in Chapter 1, then you are all set. If not, then go to the Settings | Control Panel | Networking And Dial-Up Connections for Windows 2000 (or Network Connections for Windows XP), right-click your mouse on Local Area Connection, choose Install | Service | Add, select File And Print Sharing For Microsoft Networks, and then click OK.

For the second step, make sure the printer attached to this computer is sharable. Go to Settings | Printers and right-click on the printer, and then choose Sharing.

Choose a name for your shared printer, say, "Lexmark," if you have a Lexmark printer, as shown in Figure 3-1. Don't fill out the Password or Comment box. Then click on the Apply and then OK buttons, and your printer is ready to be used by others on your network.

Once you do this correctly, you'll notice that the icon in your Printers folder changes slightly. An outstretched hand now appears underneath the printer icon, as shown in the following illustration. The check mark above the printer icon is to show that the printer is the default one used by that computer.

The third and final step is to set up the printer on each of your remaining networked computers. You'll need the driver disc that came with the printer, unless you are lucky and

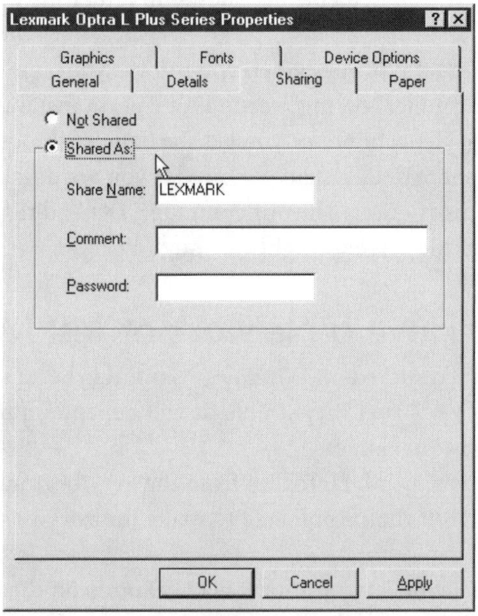

Figure 3-1. Naming a shared printer

the drivers come included with your Windows operating system CD. You can instead download the drivers from the Internet Web site of your printer manufacturer if you have lost these CDs and you have a working Internet connection. This assumes the vendor has a competent Web site where you can find the drivers for their printers and particular operating system. Sound like a lot of trouble? Maybe you should take a few minutes and look for that CD that has the drivers on it.

The easiest way to execute this last step is to use the Add A Printer wizard that comes with Windows. Go to Settings | Printers and click on the Add Printer icon to start the wizard. You'll be asked whether the new printer is local or networked, and naturally you'll choose networked. Then you will bring up another window and begin to browse your network. With luck you'll be able to see the printer's name underneath the computer name on your network. You might be asked to install some driver files, and depending on the version of Windows, you might need to dig up that printer software CD disc.

If you don't see the printer name listed, first click on the small plus sign to the left of the computer name. That will expand the outline view of your network list and hopefully show

the printer there. See how the Okidata printer shows up under the computer name Mebox in Figure 3-2.

Sometimes you can't find the printer when you browse your network. Don't give up hope; see the following "Troubleshooting" section for tips on installing it.

This seems like a lot of steps, but once you get the hang of things, it isn't that hard to do. I probably have provided more details than you need if you are diligent about following the various dialog boxes and instructions on your computer. Depending on the version of Windows you are running, the screens might vary slightly.

Situation 2: You Have a Network of Just Macintoshes

So far our discussions have centered on Windows computers because sharing a directly connected printer among Macs isn't very simple. It will depend on the vintages of printer and Macs that you have in your home.

It didn't used to be this way. Macintoshes from the very beginning were designed to share networked printers. But then Apple had to make improvements and made it harder for everyone.

Macs have two ways to connect to printers: via USB ports on the newer models, and via LocalTalk ports on the older models. By definition, if your printer came with a LocalTalk

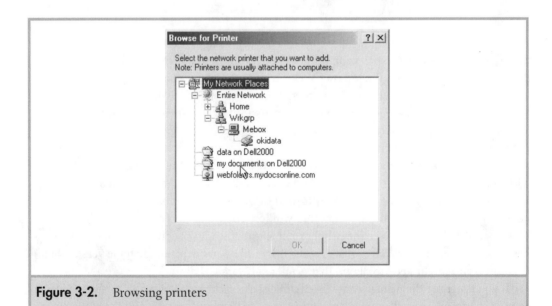

Figure 3-2.   Browsing printers

port, it was Mac-ready and has the necessary drivers to work with your older Macs. If your printer has a USB port, chances are good that it has a Mac printer driver, and you can hook it up to a single newer Mac just fine. But you won't be able to network it without another piece of software from Apple or someone else.

There are several possibilities. My first recommendation is to use the free USB Printer Sharing software, available from Apple. This only works on more recent Macs and on printers with a USB port. If you have an older Apple StyleWriter or ImageWriter printer, you can share it with a free piece of software from Apple called Printer Share Extension that goes in your control panel. (For both of these tools, go to http://asu.info.apple.com and enter the name of the tool in the search box to find the appropriate page to download the software.)

If you have an Epson laser or ink-jet printer, you can use a piece of shareware called Epson Share (http://www.ses.fr/epsonshare/). To use Epson Share, you have to install two pieces of software: one that goes on the Mac that is connected to the printer (and turns it into a print server) and another that goes on each Mac that is on your network to communicate with the shared printer. For everything else, you might be able to use a free piece of software called SharePrint (http://www.akua.com/Software/AppleScript/) from Akua Interactive Media, although I haven't tried it.

If your printer is an older LocalTalk model, and you have a mixture of old and new Macs (or are about to buy a new Mac, and, of course, it doesn't come with any LocalTalk ports), then you'll need to bridge the old with the new. There are two ways to do this: with hardware or with software. Hardware devices that come with both LocalTalk and Ethernet ports are sold by Farallon and Asante. You connect the former to your printer and the latter to your network hub. To use software, you'll need Apple's LocalTalk Bridge program running on a Mac that has both LocalTalk and Ethernet ports, meaning a pre-iMac model. (Search Apple's software site as mentioned earlier.)

With any of this software, if you are running pre–Mac OS 9.0 operating system software, you might have to upgrade to a newer version of the operating system. Some of the products require software to be installed on just the Mac that will share the printer. Others require software on all Macs on your network. When you download the software, read the instructions carefully.

Situation 3: Moving a Printer to a New Location, Windows PCs Only

Directly connected printers have their drawbacks. If you have computers in more than one room of your house, you'll need to keep all of your computers with printers connected to them turned on all the time. That may be inconvenient. Maybe you don't want to turn every room of your home into a mini-office and want to consolidate all of your printers in one place, along with their associated supplies and mess. Maybe you have to move the printer to a new location in your house.

A bigger issue with directly connected printers is that they decrease the performance of the PC they are connected to. You don't get something for nothing. In this case, the advantage of setting up your printer without any added cost will mean that household members using that computer might find it takes longer to do their work. As they are typing away on that machine, their computer may be busy taking care of the print jobs coming to it from elsewhere on the network.

Why is this the case? Every time you send a print job to that printer, the PC that it is connected to first makes a copy of the file on its own hard disk, then sends that information to the printer. While this isn't a big deal for your average word processing document, if you are printing lots of graphics or photographs, you'll definitely see a big decrease in performance during these print sessions. If your home network grows to include four or more PCs, sharing printers in this fashion can really burden the computer acting as the print server.

For these situations, you'll want to either purchase a printer with an internal Ethernet connection or buy a separate print server box. If you are in the market for a new laser printer, then it might make sense to consider one with the networking built in. While they cost a few hundred dollars more than printers with just a standard parallel port, they usually are also more rugged and will last longer and print pages faster than their cheaper relations. Printers from Lexmark and HP are good choices for those that include built-in network adapters.

Before you congratulate yourself on thinking so far ahead, realize that picking the right internal networking adapter can be difficult. Take as an example the HP printer line. HP actually has made printers that accept two different kinds of plug-in cards: one is called EIO and one called MIO. (These aren't acronyms, they are the names of the cards.) Of course, they are incompatible with each other. Table 3-2 shows which printers use which plug-in card.

Don't freak out yet. All of the JetDirect products have an RJ45 connector that can be connected to a standard Ethernet network, and the 600N also includes a LocalTalk connector to hook it up to older Macs. Expect to pay about $200–$300 for one of these adapters. They're expensive, but they cost about the same as a separate printer server and don't require a separate power supply and one more cable behind your desk.

The internal network adapter is limited to those printers that can accept them and to those who are willing to wade through all the mumbo jumbo mentioned earlier to buy the right product. Perhaps a better choice is to use an external print server box. It can turn just about any printer into something that will work on your network. This is a separate piece of hardware that comes with several different connectors and its own power supply. What you buy will depend on how many printers you want to hook up to your network, how much

Printer	Compatible Plug-In Cards
EIO printers (use either the JetDirect 600N or 610N adapter)	LaserJet 2100, 4000, 4050, 4500, 5000, 8000, 8100, and 8500
MIO printers (use JetDirect 400 adapter)	LaserJet 5Si, 5Si MX, 5Si NX, 5, 5M, 5N, 4Si, 4Si MX, 4V, 4MV, 4M Plus, 4, and 4M; HP Color LaserJet 5, 5N, and 5M; HP DeskJet 1200C, 1200C/PS, and 1600 CM; HP DesignJet 600, 650C, 650C/PS, 700, 750C, 750C Plus, 755CM, 2000CP, 2500, 3000CP, and 3500CP

Table 3-2. HP JetDirect Printer Plug-In Cards by Model Number

you want to spend, and whether you want to support just Windows or both Windows and Macs. (See Situation 4 later in this chapter.)

The cheapest alternative is called a *pocket print server* and is about the size of a deck of playing cards. Think of these units as converter boxes that take the parallel port of the printer and turn it into an RJ45 Ethernet connector. These attach directly to the parallel port in the back of the printer, and most avoid the need for a separate power supply or parallel cable. Typical vendors include D-Link and Extended Systems, and these devices sell for about $100. The advantage is that they are small and don't add yet another cable to the mess behind your desk because they draw their power from the printer's parallel port.

The disadvantage with the pocket devices is that they only work with a single printer: if you want to hook up more than one printer, you'll have to spend a bit more for a device that has more than one parallel port. Products from HP, Intel, Linksys, and D-Link include two or three ports—a great solution if you want to consolidate all of your printers in one room. Of course, you'll need to cable each printer to the print server and provide an outlet for the print server's power supply.

Before I go into details about how to set up a print server, here's an additional wrinkle. Until recently, print servers were available only if you were using standard Ethernet cabling for your network. However, some products, including the HP JetDirect 70x print server (which costs about $100), now support PhoneLine networks. This means that you can plug in your printer to the 70x's parallel port and plug the 70x into your home telephone jack. Your printer is now on your home network. You can locate the printer in your kitchen or someplace where you don't have a computer, if that will work out better. The only proviso is that your print server must be connected on the same phone line as the rest of your network.

While this sounds promising, the JetDirect 70x is not a product that I can recommend. In my tests it was quirky. It only supports networks of less than 100 feet of phone cabling[1], which means if you have rather convoluted wiring for your telephones, or a large house, you will have problems getting it to work. I ran into some other software glitches when I tried it in Family M's house and couldn't communicate between the print server and the attic computer, but could connect to it just fine from another computer on a lower floor that was closer to the print server. Based on these experiences, I would be cautious about buying this product, look around for PhoneLine print servers from other vendors, or wait for HP to improve their product.

Setting up a print server will take some effort. Let's demonstrate what is involved setting up the HP JetDirect print servers on Windows so you get some idea of what is involved. It is harder than setting up a printer in Situation 1, but we aren't talking about lifting a heavy object here (unless you are moving your printer several times as you try various locations around your home). What if you don't have an HP JetDirect box? This should give you a good idea of what you have to do.

You'll need to install two pieces of software on your Windows machine: first is the configuration and administration software that sets up the print server's IP address and enables the various protocols and ports. HP calls this Web JetAdmin[2].

SURVIVAL TIP Note that Web JetAdmin will work across all HP print servers, whether they are internal MIO or EIO units or external boxes. So in case you lose the software CD that came with your server, you can download a copy from HP's Web site. You need to install Web JetAdmin on only one of your Windows computers.

Web JetAdmin is a complex piece of software engineering that only an HP engineer could love, and probably only the engineers who wrote the code at that. If you are just buying an HP print server for the first time, you should install and run it and with luck it will work. I had problems using it on an older print server, and if you run into problems too, you'll probably want to skip over my description and go straight to the "Troubleshooting" section on how to configure your HP server for an alternate strategy.

---

1   How do you know the total length of your home phone wiring? I am sure 99 percent of you haven't the foggiest idea. You could buy one of these devices and get it home and find out like I did that it worked in some places but not others. Such is the life of a home networker.

2   HP used to offer two different JetAdmin tools: one that was tailored for specific operating systems, and one that was tailored for specific operating systems but that created a Web server on the monitoring computer. However, in mid-2001 they discontinued the former series of tools. You need to download the version of Web JetAdmin that is designed for your OS. Unfortunately, they only work with Windows NT and Windows 2000. If you have another version of Windows, or if you are running an all-Macintosh network, you are out of luck here because HP does not have a version of its JetAdmin software that you can use to set up your print server. You'll have to borrow a friend's Windows computer to set it up, or see the "Troubleshooting" section for more details on how to set up the server's IP address on your network.

Basically, you need Web JetAdmin to do two things: first, to give your print server an appropriate IP address so it matches up with the rest of the computers on your network. (Remember our warnings from Chapter 2: Your IP addresses have to match up, but they also have to be unique. If you skipped that chapter, now would be a good time to go back and read that section before you proceed.) Second, you need to tell the Web JetAdmin software what kinds of printers are attached to the print server's parallel ports (if you purchased a model with more than one parallel port and have more than one printer to connect to your network using this device). Then you can keep track of these when you set up the shared printers on your networked PCs.

Enough of the chitchat. Let's get down to business. First, install Web JetAdmin software, making sure that you have the right Windows version. (Only Windows 2000 and NT are supported, along with a bunch of UNIX OSes.) If you don't have either of these versions on any of your home PCs, skip ahead to the "Troubleshooting" section. Now bring up the

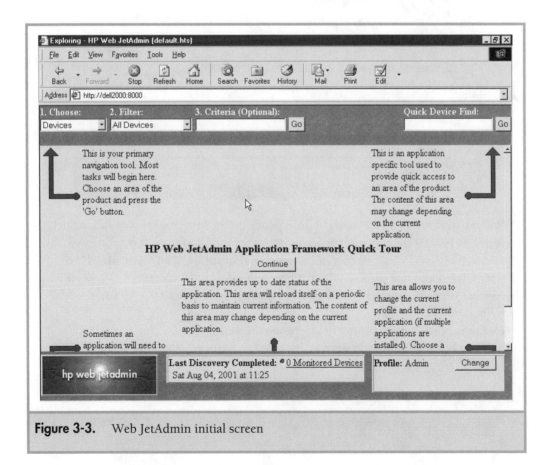

Figure 3-3. Web JetAdmin initial screen

program by opening Internet Explorer (or a Web browser of your choice, but I would recommend IE), typing in **http://*computer-name*:8000/** at the address bar.

The *computer-name* should be the name of the machine where you installed Web JetAdmin; the slash at the end of the line is very important; otherwise the software won't load. Once you do this, you should see a screen asking you to agree to let HP download its Java applets needed to run the program. After you click OK, you'll see a screen like the one in Figure 3-3 (on the preceding page).

Click the Go button on the top middle portion of the screen, and it should find your printer server sitting somewhere on your network, as shown in the illustration.

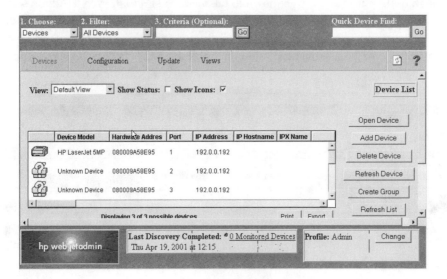

Notice that it shows my HP LaserJet 5MP sitting on the first parallel port and the default IP address of 192.0.0.192. Depending on the make and model of the printer you have attached to the server, it may or may not know this information. Don't be alarmed. The JetDirect server that I had comes out of the box with a default IP address of 192.0.0.192. That doesn't match my recommended network configuration of 10.0.0.x, so you need to change the address.

To do this, click on that printer listing inside the device window, and then click the Open Device button. You should get a screen that will allow you to set up a new IP address for the print server. Use the following information:

```
IP: 10.0.0.100
Subnet-mask: 255.255.255.0
Default-gateway: 10.0.0.1
```

Click Save and it should reset your printer server to the IP address of 10.0.0.100. If you decided to use some other IP address range on your network, substitute the first three numbers for 10.0.0. in both the IP address and default gateway entries.

Finally, you might have to fool around with setting up the right kind of printer that is attached to your server. Now is a good time to track down the drivers CD or download them from the Internet.

Once you get your server configured, you need a second piece of software that allows each Windows computer to find the print server and send its print jobs to it. HP calls this JetDirect, not to be confused with the name of the print server device itself. Unfortunately, if you are using 95, 98, NT, or Me, you'll have to install the software and set up your printer port accordingly. Chances are, depending on the version you used to install Web JetAdmin, you might have already installed the JetDirect software on that computer. For the remaining computers on your network, you'll have to install JetDirect and usually reboot your computer before you can finish setting up your printers.

JetDirect may have installed a menu option called Add An HP JetDirect Printer to your Windows menus. If so, choose that and follow the easy Setup path, using the IP address that you specified earlier for the print server, as shown in Figure 3-4.

Click Next and JetDirect should create the printer port on that computer, after asking you which port your printer is connected to on the print server. Then it asks you for the make and model of your printer, and it installs the printer and sets it up correctly. If all goes well, you should be able to start printing to that printer. Congratulations! It's a lot of work, but once you get the hang of it, you should be fine setting up the other computers around your house.

SURVIVAL TIP

Remember, you'll have to go to all of your computers and install first the port and then the particular printer model.

Some Windows versions, such as Windows 2000 and XP, don't need this additional piece of JetDirect software. They can recognize the IP address of the print server directly, without having to mess around with additional drivers. Setting them up is easier.

Figure 3-4. JetDirect easy setup

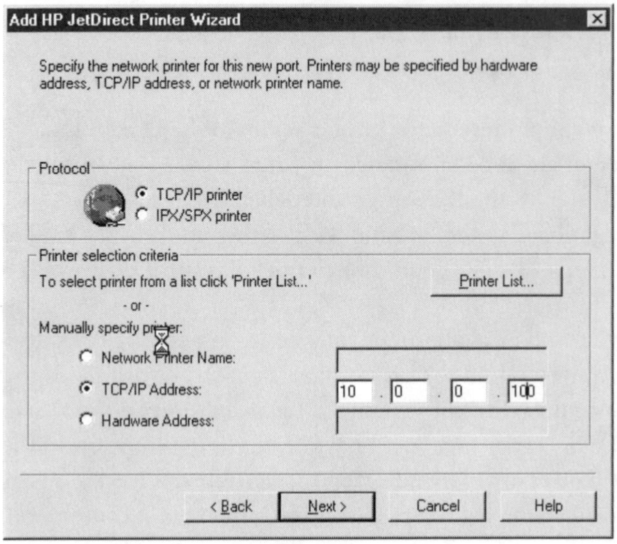

When you start the Add A Printer wizard, it asks you which type of printer you want to install, a local or network (or in the case of Windows XP, local or printer connection). Choose local. (Yes, I know, it really isn't local, but that is the correct choice here.) On the next screen, choose Create A New Port, using a standard IP port selection if that is offered to you, as shown in Figure 3-5. That will bring up the Add TCP/IP Printer Port wizard.

Click Next and then type in the IP address of the print server (10.0.0.100 in our examples), select which parallel port if you have multiple parallel ports on your server, and then proceed through the various screens selecting your make and model of printer. This should work with both XP and 2000 in pretty much the same way. At the end of this process, you should have a new printer icon showing up in your Printers folder.

Of course, the preceding explanation is only for one particular print server—the HP JetDirect models. You might have something else, but you should be able to follow the instructions that came with your product and go through an equivalent series of steps to install your networked printers. If you don't find the JetDirect software, or HP has made some changes and this doesn't work as described, then see the "Troubleshooting" section for faking out—and finishing—your print server installations.

Add Printer Wizard

Select the Printer Port
Computers communicate with printers through ports.

Select the port you want your printer to use. If the port is not listed, you can create a
new port.

○ Use the following port:

Port	Description	Printer
LPT1:	Printer Port	
LPT2:	Printer Port	
LPT3:	Printer Port	
COM1:	Serial Port	
COM2:	Serial Port	
COM3:	Serial Port	

Note: Most computers use the LPT1: port to communicate with a local printer.

● Create a new port:
Type: Standard TCP/IP Port

< Back   Next >   Cancel

Figure 3-5. Windows 2000 TCP/IP port setup

Situation 4: Sharing a Printer on a Mixed Windows/Mac Network

If you have a mixed Mac/Windows network and want to share your printer between both
types of computers, the best solution is to use an external print server. An exception to this
is if you have only two computers side by side and can use the two different printer ports
on the back of the printer and hook them to each computer separately.

To share a printer on a Mac/Windows network, you'll need to make sure that your print
server supports AppleTalk protocols. HP, Intel, and D-Link all sell multiple-port print server
and pocket servers that support Macs, but make sure of this before you buy a specific model.

Be aware that to set up these print servers, you begin with your Windows computer.
None of the products can be set up on Macs, although once they are set up, you can print
from Macs just fine. That means trouble for all-Mac home networks. If you do have an

all-Mac network, I would recommend buying one of the Lexmark Optra Lasers with an internal print server interface built in or following one of the suggestions mentioned in Situation 2.

Once you get your server configured under Windows, the Macintosh story is actually pretty easy. Install the Mac printer drivers on each of your Macs for the appropriate model of your printer. If you don't have a driver disc and are willing to take some chances, then install an Apple LaserWriter IINTX as your printer. Next, go to the Chooser, shown in Figure 3-6, and select the printer that should show up in the list as your default printer.

Another solution is to pick up a copy of Thursby Software Systems' Dave. Dave (at thursby.com) allows your Mac to access Windows file servers and printers through the Mac's Chooser, just like any other Mac-oriented printer. But the price of Dave is about the same as an external print server box, and the hardware is more expandable in case you add additional PCs in the future.

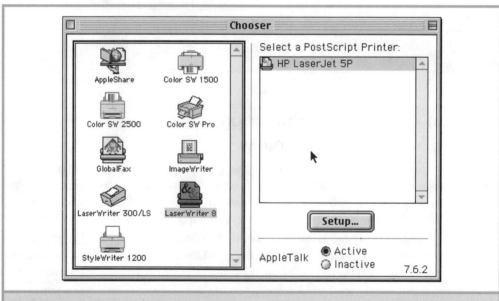

Figure 3-6.   Mac Chooser printer listing

Troubleshooting

Here's a list of some of the things that can go awry when setting up your shared printer.

Can't Find a Printer

If you can't locate the shared printer on your network, you can try something else. The strategy is to first install the printer on each of your networked computers as if it were locally attached to that computer's parallel port, called LPT1. You can use the Add A Printer wizard and do everything except saying yes to printing a test page (because that won't yet work). You need to know the manufacturer and model number of the printer to set up the right drivers.

Once the printer driver software is installed, go to Settings | Control Panel | Printers, and right-click on the printer's icon. Choose Properties and change the port setting to the network name that you picked in step 2 in Situation #1 earlier. You'll also need the network name of your PC that is acting as the print server. If you have forgotten it, go to My Network Places, and you should see it in the list.

Understanding Networked Printer Names

Shared printer names follow the same conventions as shared Windows computer names: a double back-slash, followed by the name of the computer, another back-slash, and the printer name. So if you know that the computer name is UPSTAIRS and the shared printer name is LEXMARK, then the full name to reach the printer would be

```
\\UPSTAIRS\LEXMARK
```

You can enter this information where Windows asks you for the name of the shared printer. If the computer is on and connected to the network, Windows should be able to find it.

Macintosh Printing Problems

See http://www.threemacs.com for helpful information. They have lots of troubleshooting tips and suggestions on how to try to connect various printer models together. They also have updated information as new Mac network printing products become available.

Trouble Getting Your HP Print Server's IP Address Configured

You can try an easier way than slogging through the Web JetAdmin stuff. First, change the IP address of one of your Windows computers to 192.0.0.1, with a subnet mask of

255.255.255.0. (This is usually done by going to Settings | Control Panels | Networks, clicking on the listing for your Ethernet card/IP protocol pair, and then clicking on Properties.) You might have to reboot, depending on which version of Windows you are using. Next, go to your Start menu, select Run, type in **Telnet 192.0.0.192**, and press ENTER.

This will bring up a command-line window, and if all is working as planned, you will be talking directly to the JetDirect server. Press ENTER a few times, and you should see it respond with a few commands of text.

Now type in the following commands, ending with pressing ENTER:

```
IP: 10.0.0.100
Subnet-mask: 255.255.255.0
Default-gw: 10.0.0.1
Quit
```

This should reset your server's IP address to 10.0.0.100, which hopefully is on the same subnet as the rest of your computers. If you have chosen a different subnet from my instructions in Chapter 1, substitute the first three numbers instead of "10.0.0." Make sure you type this stuff exactly as I have shown you, or you'll set up the IP address to something else. Now change your PC's IP address back to its original setting, reboot your PC if necessary, and the JetDirect should be ready for you to set it up properly.

Faking Out Print Server Installations

My description of HP JetDirect installation of the printer drivers for each computer on your network may not work as intended because HP tends to make changes to its software without notifying me—can you believe it? So here is another way to install your printers, what I call the "fake-out" method. You might have to install the software that came with your print server first, to make sure that you have the appropriate port for Windows to recognize.

Bring up the standard Windows Add A Printer wizard, and proceed to add the printer of your choice (using the CD-ROM driver disc that came with it, if you can track it down). Start by telling the wizard that you are adding a local printer. I know, you aren't telling the whole truth, but we'll come back and make it right by the time you are done reading the next paragraph.

When you are done, *don't* click on printing a test page, but just click OK. Now go to Settings | Printers, and right-click on the printer icon that should be showing up on your screen, select Properties, and then choose Details | Add Port. Change the port from LPT1 (the standard parallel port) to your JetDirect (or whatever your printer server is called) port name. (See Figure 3-7.)

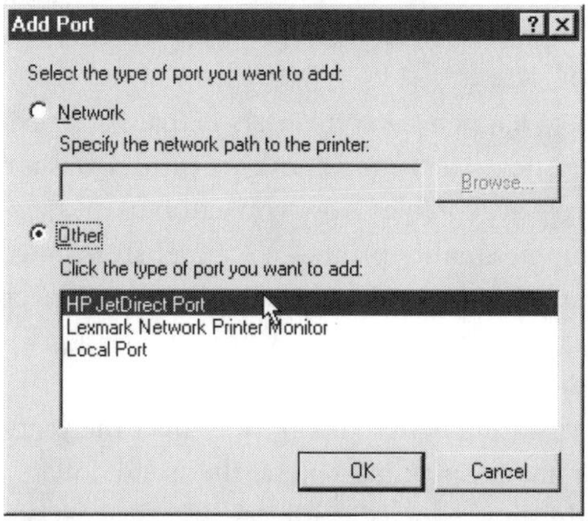

Figure 3-7.   New JetDirect port

Power Cycling Everything As a Last Resort

My Lexmark laser printer only recognizes ports if they are active when the printer is powered-up. That means that I need to connect the printer to my Ethernet and parallel port devices before turning it on. I had a situation as I was writing this chapter where my print server wouldn't find the printer, despite everything else seeming to be fine. Once I turned the printer off and on, it found the print server and activated the port, and pages started spewing out of the machine.

Futures

Printer prices will continue to come down, and it won't be long before we see ink-jets given away when you buy a box of cereal or something similar on the consumer level. As PhoneLine networks increase in popularity, expect to see more printers incorporate this kind of network attachment as part of their basic package. If the HP PhoneLine print server is any indication, prices will continue to drop, making them more and more attractive to home users. (Hopefully, HP will make its PhoneLine network installations easier.)

As wireless networks become more popular, it makes sense to create wireless print servers that can be placed anywhere in your home. I would expect to see such products within a few years, particularly as wireless networking chipsets continue to drop in price and as more vendors become interoperable with each other due to better standards implementations. One of the first indications of this is D-Link's DI-713P Wireless Broadband Router, which includes a print server along with support for wireless networks. Others are available from Asante, Linksys, MaxGate, and SMC Networks.

One of the best things to happen for consumers is that the price of obtaining higher print quality continues to drop. A few years ago, an ink-jet printer was a messy, dreary affair, with print quality that was barely acceptable. Now you can buy ink-jets for less than $200 that can print almost photographic-quality prints—on expensive coated papers—but still, the quality is exceptional given what you pay for the equipment. Expect this trend to continue as prices drop and print quality improves. Thus, if you own a printer that cost you more than $300 and it breaks down, it may not be worth repairing.

Laser printers also have gotten better and cheaper over the years. It used to be that finding a fast laser printer meant spending several thousand dollars. Now you can find them for not much more than the most expensive ink-jet, and the cost per page to operate a laser continues to drop as they are made with better components that last longer.

Microsoft made it easier for users of Windows 2000 to share printers, but then took a step backward with Windows Me. Hopefully, future versions of Windows will continue to make it easier to share printers and to connect to networkable printers. While you certainly wouldn't want to choose your operating system based on its printer support, at least you can do something easier in Windows 2000, even something as small as sharing a printer around your network.

However, not all the news will be good. If you have a mixture of Macs and Windows PCs at home, expect to spend more time and more money investigating and integrating printers. Print server vendors who care about Macintoshes are few and far between. Despite the rise in popularity of Macintoshes, most print server vendors still consider this a niche market and gear most of their corporate and higher-priced line of servers toward Mac users.

Finally, expect to see print servers showing up on more different kinds of devices. For example, Linksys makes a network-attached disk drive that also includes a print server and a parallel port that can be shared among Windows and Macs. Umax, Asante and others all make firewall/router/hub devices (more on these in the next chapter) that also include a parallel port print server. As more and more printers make use of USB connectors, expect to see more devices that allow you to connect USB printers in this fashion.

Chapter 4

Sharing your Internet Connection

N ow that you have a working network, it is time to put it to good use. Most of us are interested in making a faster connection to the Internet that we can share among all of our home computers. It is a lot easier and cheaper to share your high-speed Internet connection than to buy everyone a big screen. If Internet-based games ever progress beyond the shoot-em-up stage, that could be a big reason to have everyone home at night, typing away. The family that connects together stays together, or something like that.

As you can't be too rich or too thin, you can't have too fast an Internet connection. Seconds count when you're bringing up a page of graphics-heavy goo from the Web, or downloading a humongous file. If you are currently using your modem and a phone line to get to the Net, you are traveling in the slow lane.

Sometimes Internet slowdowns aren't under your control: When popular sites such as Victoria's Secret and Ellis Island's familyhistory.org get some publicity, they are swamped by unanticipated hordes. If the bottleneck is at your end of the Internet connection, however, you have several options to speed up your surfing life.

Faster isn't the only reason for bumping up your connection. Many of us use "always on" connections through our cable TV companies or via digital telephone lines. The advantage of these connections is tremendous. Once you have one, you'll wonder how you did without it.

As I mentioned in the preface, before I got my own cable Internet connection at home, my family wasn't too keen on using the Internet. Things changed rapidly once the cable Internet connection was installed. Suddenly, we had all sorts of uses for the Internet. Instead of looking up the times for local movie theaters in the newspaper (or calling the theaters on their always-busy phone lines), we set up a My Yahoo portal page that lists an easy-to-use movie clock. Instead of keeping our family schedule and contacts lists on a single computer, we now had access to it from all over the world, also by means of My Yahoo pages. My daughter began using online dictionaries (such as http://m-w.com) to complete her homework. My wife enjoyed getting continuous e-mail deliveries without having to do anything other than amble over to the computer, and so forth. We are still discovering new uses. Having the continuous Internet "channel" means your PC becomes an information appliance, not just a glorified typewriter.

Using an always-on Internet connection saves time, to be sure: not only do the pages load faster when you surf the Web, but you also avoid waiting while your modem dials up your Internet service provider and makes its connection. You also avoid busy signals that you may encounter when trying to connect at peak evening times.

NOTE

An always-on Internet connection saves money. The cost of extra phone lines to handle modem calls can approach the cost of these connections, assuming that you get rid of the extra phone lines once you get your higher-speed connection up and running.

Problems

Higher-speed Internet connections aren't without their problems. Let's summarize them and go into the details.

+ **Problem 1** Picking the right technology for connecting to the Internet
+ **Problem 2** Making sure your home is wired correctly
+ **Problem 3** Buying the right access device
+ **Problem 4** Setting up your IP network correctly
+ **Problem 5** Buying a router and configuring all your PCs properly

Problem 1: Picking the Right Connection Technology

You have your choice of three major technologies: Integrated Services Digital Network (ISDN), cable Internet, and Digital Subscriber Line (DSL). Make that four choices: You still can use good, old-fashioned dial-up access, shared among your home network. Which one you pick will depend on what is available in your area.

That's the first problem: availability of all of these technologies (except for shared dial-up) is very spotty. In some neighborhoods, your friends down the street might have service, but you won't. If you are thinking of moving to a new home, consider which of these technologies is supplied there. I am not kidding: I have heard of people figuring in Internet access as part of their new home searches. After all, isn't the touchstone of real estate location, location, and location? You just didn't realize that people were talking about the location of their Internet access provider.

These aren't the only high-speed technologies you can use for Internet access. However, I don't recommend the others. Here's why. Hughes offers DirecPC (http://www.direpc.com) satellite service. It is available pretty much anywhere in North America that has a clear view to the southern sky and comes in several different confusing configurations. It is a companion to their digital satellite TV service called DirecTV, but uses a different dish to receive the "Internet channel." Some of the configurations require a phone line for uploading (while others make use of the satellite for two-way service), and the home service is geared toward single-PC connections. The company offers a network package, but the monthly price is so high and the configuration so convoluted that I don't recommend it.

Starband (http://www.starband.com) offers two-way satellite service, but for single PCs only. While some do-it-yourselfers have reportedly gotten it to work with home networks, I'd also steer clear of choosing this technology. (See the various instructions on networking at http://www.starbandusers.com.) At least wait until the company is fully supporting home networks, unless you feel that you can handle the modifications on your own and want to experiment with their equipment.

Both of these (and any other) satellite services have another problem, which is all the latency that they introduce into your Internet connection. *Latency* is the time delay it takes a packet of data to go from you to wherever it is intended out in the Internet, plus the time delay to get it back to your humble home PC. The longer the latency, the slower things will appear on your screen, and the more time it will take you to download some big, juicy piece of software from a server.

Latency varies by the time of day (the Internet has its rush hour), the location of the actual server (servers overseas usually have longer latencies than domestic ones), and who else is sharing your connection to the Internet.

Those signals that are bouncing up and back to the satellites take valuable milliseconds of time to travel, and if your home has big users of Internet-based multiuser games, then you are going to have some unhappy campers because of these latencies. Better to just forget the dish and move on to DSL if you can afford it.

Wireless broadband is coming into vogue, but the technology is too new to recommend to the average consumer. This involves a company setting up a transmitter in a big city, typically, and then installing dishes on your roof that can send and receive signals. The catch is you have to have a good line of sight to wherever the transmitter is. If you live in a hilly area, that could be a problem if a neighboring hill blocks your view of the master transmitter.

Speaking of the dish, all satellite services require that you (or someone else) climb up to your roof and install it there. You may not want to have a dish sticking out of the roof of your home, or your neighbors might not be too keen on the idea. Once the dish is screwed into the side or roof of your house, you need to run the cables down to your den or wherever your PC will be located.

Another idea is to use a combination of wireless broadband and a specialized hybrid fiber/coax/Ethernet cable network. A company in Utah called Airswitch has tried this and managed to wire up several thousand homes as an experiment, but so far this hasn't caught on.

You can also consider leased digital lines from the phone company, including T-1's, Frame-Relay circuits, and others. These quickly get expensive and aren't for the average person without a lot of networking experience. These leased lines come in a wide variety of speeds and feeds and are generally what businesses use for their Internet connections. Finally, you might have heard of Metricom's wireless Internet service, which is available in a few cities but again is only intended for single computers. Table 4-1 summarizes the connection varieties.

SURVIVAL TIP Which of my four preferred technologies (shared dial-up, ISDN, DSL, or cable) is right for you? If you want a quick answer without having to read any further, you'll probably end up with a cable modem if you are the typical consumer. You'll see why in a moment.

Type	Typical Monthly Cost	Throughput	Comments
Modem	$20	33KB	Uses phone line and not very good for sharing over networks
DSL	$40–$350	256KB up to 1.5MB	Always-on connection installed by phone company
ISDN	$40–$100	64KB to 128KB	Dial-up digital connection installed by phone company
Cable modem	$30–$50	up to 1.5MB	Always-on connection installed by cable company. Slows down because line is shared among your neighbors
Satellite	$70–$150	300 to 600KB	May require dial-up connection and complex installation
T-1, Frame Relay, etc.	$1000	Up to 1.5MB	Business-quality performance at business prices

Table 4-1. Connection Technology Comparison

Sharing your dial-up connection is only to be considered if you can't use any of the other three higher-speed technologies. For example, if your home is located in a rural area that isn't served by ISDN, cable, or DSL, then you will want to think about using shared dial-up.

ISDN looks like a regular telephone line coming into your house. ISDN uses standard two-wire cables and a beige RJ11 phone jack that most of us in the telecommunications industry can recognize at 30 paces. The only difference is that it is a completely digital circuit, and if your power goes out, so does your ISDN line. If you tried to hook your regular telephone set into an ISDN jack, you wouldn't hear any dial tone or other indication that the line is actually working. You need an ISDN router that has both an ISDN line connection as well as a standard Ethernet connection for your network.

Your only source for ISDN is your local phone company, and while ISDN has somewhat fallen out of fashion with the techno-savvy elite, it still is a good choice for many consumers who can't obtain either of the other two services. It is also the most widely available service and the slowest. Technically, it isn't an always-on connection to the Internet, although many consumers use it that way by leaving their service always connected. Some residential phone rates don't charge by the minute for ISDN connections, making this a very affordable solution, typically around $40 per month.

CAUTION

ISDN pricing varies tremendously by phone company, so please investigate your options before proceeding. In some areas of the country, you can only pay per-minute rates for ISDN rather than having flat rates like you do with standard residential voice telephone lines. This can make using ISDN for Internet access prohibitively expensive for the heavy user.

However, ISDN offers at most 128-Kbps connections, which these days are considered pokey. Talking to the right person at your phone company to order ISDN service can be a bit of a challenge. Remember, most of the phone company is set up to deliver voice services. "Data" is still a four-letter word for some of the Bells. Things are getting better, but you still have to deal with your phone company and pay them for your Internet needs. Most of us aren't too thrilled about that. ISDN routers have the most complex setup of all the technologies, which can be a challenge for networking newcomers, too.

I had ISDN service installed in my office from late 1995 until mid-1998 and generally was a happy camper. Because it was installed in my office and not my home, I couldn't take advantage of always-on phone rates and paid for each call when I wanted to connect to the Internet. Still, I can remember only a few times when my service wasn't available. For the most part, my ISDN gear was solid as a rock and didn't require any babysitting or effort on my part, once I got it set up and working. Granted, this was several years ago and the products are better now, but still the only thing that motivated me to switch to my DSL line was the ability to have a continuous Internet connection and to pay someone other than the phone company (which in my case went from Nynex to Bell Atlantic to Verizon).

Some phone companies have gotten their act together and offer a single-stop shopping experience for their ISDN line; any charges for ISDN appear on your monthly voice phone bill. You'll also pay your ISP for Internet access charges. You'll have to find an ISP that will handle ISDN connections and that has a point of presence near enough to your home so that you won't have to pay long-distance rates for each of your phone calls. In this respect, ISDN is very much like dial-up Internet service from AOL or anyone else.

Along came the cable companies, trying to grab some of that Internet data action. While cable TV networks were designed initially to be one-way broadcasts, over the past several years the cable companies have spent millions of dollars upgrading their networks to handle digital services such as pay-per-view and two-way data services. Of course, not all cable companies offer Internet service, and if they do, they haven't upgraded their entire networks. Cable Internet service is probably the most affordable, the easiest to set up, and the best price/performance technology of the three access technologies. Then, however, you have to deal with your local cable company and give them more money for your Internet needs. Some of us aren't happy with that situation, either.

Finally, we have DSL. Like ISDN, it is delivered to the home via a pair of phone wires and an RJ11 jack and is strictly a digital circuit. Unlike ISDN, it can handle much higher speeds, indeed speeds over a megabit per second, approaching the fastest digital leased-line service that normally cost more than a $1000 per month. DSL prior to1999 was everyone's darling. It was fast, it was cheap (relatively), and it was sexy.

Unlike ISDN, a DSL provider would have to install special equipment in every local phone company office to handle the Internet connection, which is one reason why DSL is still only available in major metropolitan areas and by no means universally. You also are limited in how far you can be located from your telephone central office in terms of obtaining DSL service. The farther your home is, the slower the available bandwidth, and some people in rural areas won't ever be able to obtain DSL service.

All this meant that DSL was extremely difficult to obtain, and its successful installation required the cooperation of companies who were (and in many cases, still are) mortal corporate enemies. DSL since 2001 is now in disfavor, particularly as major companies have gone bankrupt, leaving their customers in the lurch. (Putting all that gear into thousands of telephone company offices is expensive, and the precipitous decline in DSL stock prices didn't help matters.) Adding to the confusion, DSL comes in numerous shapes and sizes, depending on the upload and download speed and the type of specific DSL technology implemented by the provider.

Things continue to get more complex for DSL users. One of the most odious developments on the DSL scene is called Point-to-Point Protocol over Ethernet (PPPoE). The idea—and work with me here for a moment—is to simulate a dial-up connection, even though you are always connected. If this sounds like a ridiculous idea, invented by a phone company to try to conserve IP addresses and treat their customers to one more confusing thing to set up and configure, you are right. Unfortunately, PPPoE is catching on with a number of ISPs, including Earthlink, and it means you'll need a DSL router that can deal with this nonsensical protocol. (Most of them support this, but still it doesn't hurt to check if you need it.)

This is the long way of telling you that buying your Internet service isn't going to be as simple as going down to the local supermarket and getting a quart of milk. In fact, you can't really buy everything you need in one place, and you will probably need to talk to several people in different stores before you have everything you need to get online. Sorry about that. Perhaps the future will see changes here, but I wouldn't bet on it.

With cable Internet, you could have as close to a single-stop shopping experience as you can get. In my area, you can go to a retail store (owned by the cable company), buy your cable modem, initiate service, and obtain a "starter kit" that has cables, instructions (some almost understandable by ordinary mortals), and a network adapter should you be inclined to install one yourself. If you have cable TV service in your home, and if you have your cable TV jack near where your computers are located, you can do it yourself.

You go home, set up the gear, and then spend the next few days calling their technical support line when something goes wrong. I didn't say it was going to be easy. You do, however, get a single bill for your Internet service, which is usually less than $50 per month. In effect, the cable company acts as both the vendor of the physical connection from your home to the Internet and as your ISP. It's a major reason I almost always recommend cable connections for home network users.

What can go wrong with your cable installation? Lots of things. Your cable TV jacks may not be in working order or may be in the wrong places. You'll need to wire them correctly, find someone who can do this, or pay your friendly cable company to do it for you. Generally, a good way to debug your cable setup in your home is to carry around a small portable TV set. If you can get a clear TV signal on that jack, that usually means that the cable Internet service is working. One time I was setting up service for friends, and just as I started working on their computer, the cable company disconnected their Internet service to work on something in their office. You never know these things until you call the company and find out what is happening. Sometimes the cable modem is defective or just stops working altogether.

Cable companies are not phone companies and still don't think that their service is critical to your home. Sometimes your cable television service will go out, and sometimes so will your cable Internet access. Unfortunately, cable companies don't yet have the culture that phone companies do about being available 24 hours a day, 365 days a year with enough redundancy in their networks. You've been warned. My own cable service has been nowhere as reliable as my DSL service at the office, but it is far cheaper on a monthly basis. You get what you pay for!

DSL service can be a single-stop experience (oh, how these companies dream it could be!), but usually isn't. There are two alternatives for obtaining DSL service: from your local phone company, and from someone else, typically an Internet service provider (ISP). If you choose your local phone company, then you might be able to get all your gear from them and have a single bill for your service if your company also acts as an ISP.

Typically, there are at least three different players involved in any DSL deal: your local phone company (who has to install the line to your house, whether you obtain DSL service from them or not), the DSL provider (who maintains the actual data circuits and is responsible for running the actual network connection to the Internet), and your ISP, who collects your money every month, handles technical support questions and is usually unaware of the activities of the first two companies. If you are keeping score, you should add a fourth company, the vendor who supplies your DSL router to the ISP. Typically, DSL service starts at $40 per month and can quickly climb to ten times that, depending on the speed of the connection you purchase.

I have a final comment about how to pick your access technology. You might have heard that if you choose DSL, ISDN, or cable access, you can also piggyback a voice telephone line on these technologies. That is technically true, but I wouldn't necessarily recommend it. Remember, your telephone service is "household critical," meaning you don't want to mess around with this while you are getting your network together. Certainly, if you need another phone line for chatty teens, for an incoming fax line, or for some other reason that isn't the primary incoming voice line to your home, this might be a good time to consider using one of these technologies. Use one line for your sole phone connection to the outside world? I don't think so. Remember, your DSL service will go out if you lose electrical power, unlike your normal analog phone line, which has power supplied by the phone company. If you have a mobile phone as an alternate for emergencies, a sole DSL line might be acceptable.

Each of these three technologies has various technical wrinkles that can disrupt your voice service and cause all sorts of headaches for you. It is one thing if your Internet access goes down for a few minutes, or even an hour or two. (It will, believe me. While I was writing this chapter, my ISP was out for most of the business day. I wish I could tell you why, but I couldn't get through on their technical support line because everyone else was trying to call them and find out when service was going to be restored. Such is life in the fast lane.) It is another thing entirely for you to lose your phone service. Don't let that enter into your evaluation yet, although once your Internet access is working fine, it is something to think about.

Problem 2: (More) Home Wiring Issues

Picking a technology is the first step. What next? Your home may not be wired properly. I refer to the wire that connects your home to the outside world, as opposed to the wiring that you may or may not have in your home to connect each of your computers that we discussed in Chapter 1. Remember the cable from your satellite dish to your den that I mentioned earlier? Just because you have installed category 5 wiring in every room of your home, doesn't mean that you can connect to the Internet. Some of you may have thought you were done with wiring when you finished reading Chapter 1. One more challenge awaits.

How you make this connection depends on the access technology you choose and what wiring you already have installed, as well as where the Internet service will enter your home. If you don't currently have cable TV service in your home, your cable company will need to come out to hook up your home. They'll drill holes here and there to get the cable to the right place in your den or home office or wherever you are going to locate the cable modem. If you are getting DSL or ISDN service, the local phone company will have to string a new phone line to your home, and then they will have do some drilling to get the wires to come to the right place. In general, the phone or cable company will do this for you and usually charge you an outrageous fee for the service. There isn't much you can do about it, besides grumbling to your friends and neighbors.

You may have decided from my discussion in Chapter 1 that the best situation for you would be to use wireless networks to connect the various computers around your household together. That's great, but you'll still need to run some wire from the wireless access point to the cable or DSL or ISDN modem, and that cable will most always be standard Ethernet.

An issue here, especially for wireless users, is where this service enters your home. It is probably the worst possible place for locating a wireless access point: in your basement, buried underground, and near lots of concrete walls. The ideal place would be in your attic, but usually cable and phone connections don't enter your home there. However, if you already have a wireless network up and running and you are happy with its operations, then you'll just have to deal with this situation and run a wire from the access point to your cable modem.

SURVIVAL TIP

This section's discussion is also true for PhoneLine networks. You will need to buy a bridge device between your PhoneLine and ordinary Ethernet networks so that you can hook up your cable or DSL modem.

Problem 3: Picking the Right Access Device

The next problem is figuring out the right access device to buy, if you have a choice. If you are using cable Internet service, the cable company usually supplies the cable modem of one or more varieties to you, at a very attractive price. In my area, the company will give you a break on the price of a cable modem if you sign up for two years of service, which is a good deal. If you are using DSL or ISDN, your ISP will do something similar, selling you the DSL or ISDN "modem" as part of your service offering, and usually at a discounted price. (It really isn't a modem because it doesn't modulate or demodulate anything; you have a digital signal from beginning to end.)

If you are going with shared dial-up as your technology, there are a limited number of products to choose from. More on that in a moment.

SURVIVAL TIP

Most of the cable modems that I have seen are external devices. The DSL and ISDN modems come in either external or internal varieties, and if you can pick the one you want to have on your home network, pick the external box always. Why? Because it will be easier for you to build your network around an external box. If you have an internal DSL or ISDN modem, then go directly to the "Troubleshooting" section now and try to deal with its peculiarities.

Most external cable modems and DSL modems have at least two ports, apart from a place to plug in the power supply. One port is a standard RJ45 Ethernet jack, which you connect to your network hub. The other is the port for the cable coax, or an RJ11 jack that goes to your telephone outlet where your special DSL or ISDN line has been brought in by the phone company. Some of the cable modems I've seen also include USB networking ports, but you don't want to use them because you intend to hook up the device to your network, not just a single PC.

Setting up your access device can be dirt simple in the case of most cable modems. (Just hook them up—there aren't any switches or buttons or other obvious controls.) Setup can be complex in the case of ISDN routers. (You must configure a lot of ISDN gobbledygook commands, and many of the parameters have mind-numbing names that were invented by the phone company to confuse outsiders.) DSL is somewhere in between, depending on the vendor and type of service you obtain.

An added complication is what you need to do if you have installed wireless or PhoneLine network equipment in your home: you will obviously need an access device that supports these networking types. The vast majority of access devices are made for just ordinary Ethernet, so you'll have to consider how to bridge between Ethernet and wireless (or Ethernet and PhoneLine) networks to connect everyone.

Problem 4: Setting Up Your IP Network

Let's move on to your next task. To set up your network properly for Internet access, you must have your IP house in order. Why? Because IP is the language of the Internet, and if something isn't properly set up on your home network, you won't be able to get anywhere on the Web, download your e-mail, or do anything of use. You need to decide which device is going to dole out IP addresses to your home computers; where that device sits on your network is critical.

There are several choices here, and I'll go over them under the "Solutions" section in a moment. It is possible to have a working network that can share files but can't get connected to the Internet. That indicates something is wrong with the IP addressing and configuration of your network. (See the "Troubleshooting" section for how to resolve this.) If you have skipped Chapter 2, which talks about setting up IP, now is a good time to go back to that chapter and read what you need to know.

Problem 5: Buying a Router and Configuring All Your PCs

Finally, you'll need one other piece of gear to get everything hooked up, and this is a *firewall/router/hub* for your network. These devices go by a wide number of names, and in the interests of simplicity, I'll float one by you that I'll use in the rest of this book, called a *frhub*. The word is a combination of "firewall," "router," and "hub," because many of these products combine these functions. It doesn't quite trip off the tongue, but I hope you don't mind if I use it instead of the unwieldy collection of words it represents.

Are you getting confused about which device is which? Let's just review for a moment, starting with the bare wire that comes into your home from either the cable or phone company. That wire goes into the access device, either a cable, DSL, or ISDN modem. Coming out that box is an Ethernet wire, and that goes into a frhub in the case of cable or DSL customers. (ISDN modems can have frhubs built into them.) Coming of out the frhub are the Ethernet lines that go to your individual computers around your home.

You need a frhub, and I wouldn't recommend connecting your network to the Internet without it. The Internet of the new millennium is a nasty place, and plenty of people with lots of time on their hands like nothing better than trying to rattle the virtual doorknobs of your PCs and breaking in to do some damage. Worse yet, they'll install some software on your machine and use it to launch attacks at someone else's computer, someone else who could have some well-paid lawyers at their disposal and make your life miserable.

SURVIVAL TIP

You never want to have your home PCs connected to the Internet without some kind of protection. Please reread that sentence before proceeding. If you learn nothing else from this book but this one thing, then I will be happy. So will you. I want to impress upon you that you should get one of these devices today and start protecting your home network. If you lock your doors to your home, you need to do the equivalent of protecting your data resources.

As a sobering example and a simple justification of why you need a frhub, consider the following. Some friends of mine got a cable modem and connected their Windows PC directly to it. That's all well and good, until their machine suddenly started acting funny because someone reached out over the Internet and placed some nasty programs on it one day. These files took the better part of a day to remove. So be safe, or at least safer, and follow my advice. The money you spend now on these frhubs will save you plenty of hours if you have to rebuild your PC or clean off some virus or some other nasty thing because you don't have such protection.

A frhub separates your "inside" home network from the big bad "outside" world of the general Internet. In fact, they become two separate networks. This makes a lot of sense intellectually, and while it adds a layer of complexity for you to manage your network, once you get it set up and working to your satisfaction, you won't ever have to worry about it again. That is, until you decide to make some changes in your hardware, or if your kids decide to go in and mess up your frhub's configuration.

What you choose in terms of setting up your home IP network and which frhub will be based on the kinds of applications that you intend to run at home. If any household members are heavily into Internet-based games, you will have one set of problems because these games are very particular about your network conditions and the kind of frhub that is used. If you do lots of file downloads, you'll want to consider some other choices. What about needing special support for running Web and other kinds of servers from your home? That's another wrinkle here. You'll also need some special support if you want to have a secure network between your home and your office network, and if you run a mixed network of Mac and Windows PCs.

I'll have plenty to say about network security in Chapter 6, but for now consider that many of these frhubs also come with four-port Ethernet hubs. So if you are considering buying a hub and using regular Ethernet cabling, then jump over to Chapter 6 and acquaint yourself with some of these issues before proceeding any further with anything else to purchase.

Another reason for needing these frhubs is that ISPs selling broadband and ISDN connections are usually giving you only a single IP address for your network. That is great if you are planning on just hooking up a single PC to the Internet, but if you have an entire network that you want to connect, that is going to be a big problem. The way around this is to use a router that makes it look to your ISP as though a single PC were connected, when in reality you have plenty of other computers scattered around your home that have happy users who are independently and concurrently surfing away.

CAUTION

Several functional alternatives to the frhubs are available. However, I don't recommend any of them to beginners. These are all advanced solutions, appropriate for readers with lots of time on their hands, or for those for whom money is more important than time. A detailed explanation of these alternatives can be found at the PracticallyNetworking.com site. (Go to http://www. practicallynetworked.com/sharing/sharemethod.htm, then under the Sharing tab, pick "Choosing Your Sharing Method.")

If you have an internal DSL modem, you will need to spend some time studying these alternatives, because you won't be able to use a frhub in your home network. For this situation, as well as some of the other alternatives mentioned on the site earlier to share your Internet connection, you need to install a network adapter card (or network-capable USB adapter) in your PC with the DSL modem card installed. You'll use that PC as the router/firewall to go between your broadband DSL connection and the rest of your home network.

If you don't have an internal DSL or ISDN modem, I wouldn't recommend using two network adapters, for several reasons. First, you are asking for trouble trying to manage two network adapters in your machine. Your life will be complicated enough with one network adapter per customer. Each network adapter has to have its own IP address, for example, and if you have two of them inside your PC, the address ranges have to be different, which can get confusing. Second, you also pay a small performance penalty for this setup, similar to the performance penalty that using your PC as a print server entails. Third, this configuration still leaves a small portion of your computer exposed to the cold, cruel outside world, instead of having a frhub that is preventing the bad guys from coming into your home.

Finally, you still have to install and configure some additional software that can protect your network from intruders and other nasty situations, and this software isn't for the beginner. Microsoft has included the software called Internet Connection Sharing in more recent versions of Windows. While that sounds like something that you might need, I suggest you steer far away from this stuff because it's nothing but trouble.[1] Take my advice: Spend less than $200 and get a frhub.

Once you get all your gear set up and working, you'll have to learn how to set up your network for Internet access for various applications, such as Napster, AOL Instant Messaging, and the like (more on these in later chapters). Keep in mind as you go through the various configurations and decisions, that doing this heavy lifting now will enable your household to get their work (and play) done over the Internet. In addition, no one else will be party to your network from outside your home.

Another issue arises once you have a working network: should you just connect PCs together, or should you use one or more of the latest kinds of "Internet appliances" that aren't fully functional PCs but do allow e-mail and Web browsing? I'll leave that issue for Chapter 8, since we have more than enough on our plate just getting connected. (In case you can't wait, the answer is the former: Use true PCs.)

Solutions

You might be depressed that you have so many problems to deal with in setting up the Internet connection for your network. You *can* manage all of them and with luck still be smiling at the end of it all with a working system. It may seem insurmountable, but if you just take each problem as it comes, you can get through it.

The good news about Internet sharing is that you have a lot of different products to choose from, even limiting your choices to just the frhub class of products. The bad news is that you have so many choices it can easily get overwhelming to figure out which is the best unit to meet your needs.

Let me try to make it easier for you by asking you a series of questions so you can zero in on the features you need the most and figure out what to get.

You have two basic decisions: first, which connection technology to use (ISDN/DSL/Cable/shared dial-up)? Second, which frhub to buy?

The choice of access technology basically comes down to how much you want to pay on a monthly basis and what you can obtain in your location. If you can get a cable Internet connection, I would recommend you pick that for almost all home networks. The only exception would be if you need something more reliable because you intend to be working out of your home during the business hours, and you absolutely require continuous Internet access during the day for your business. In that case, I would choose DSL over cable. If price is the most important factor, cable could be less expensive than all the others, even a shared dial-up line when you consider the costs of two separate phone lines to deliver the kind of bandwidth that multiple home users will require.

---

1   Microsoft's ICS can be used for dial-up shared access, but I wouldn't recommend it for this purpose. Buy the Netopia R2020 and get protected.

How do you find out what is available in your neck of the cyberwoods? The best resource is the Web site DSLreports.com. Follow links to "Find Service" and enter your ZIP code. You'll see screens such as the one in the illustration that lists which ISPs offer DSL service and if there are any cable Internet suppliers in your area. You can also view comments left by various consumers about their providers, which I would advise you to take with several ounces of salt. (People are more motivated to leave complaints than kudos in these types of situations.) Still, the site is a tremendous resource and one that you should spend some time reviewing.

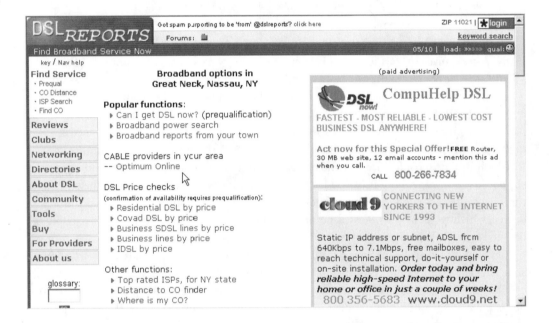

If you order cable, you typically don't have many choices in terms of the technology available and the type of service—you pretty much get whatever the cable company has decided for you, and that is that. On the other extreme with DSL service, you have numerous choices, and it can get confusing. Your biggest decision is the speed of your connection: most DSL providers offer a wide range of speeds, from 128 Kbps on up to over 1000 Kbps, and varying speeds for your upload and download links as well. What to do?

My advice depends on how many home users you will have connecting to the Internet and how often they will connect. At the least expensive end is iDSL at 144 Kbps, which is adequate for one or two users. I'd look at 192 Kbps for three users, and 384 Kbps for more than four users. If you can afford to pay for faster service, then by all means go for it. You'll find that these speeds are for the most part adequate, unless you have five or six teenagers all downloading large music files at the same time. You want to be fairly sure about the DSL circuit speed, because this decision affects what access device you end up getting. If you want to upgrade from a slower to a faster service later on, you may have to switch devices, which can be painful.

CAUTION

Another wrinkle in DSL service is that the distance you are from your phone company central office will determine the speed that you can obtain for your connection. The farther you are from the office, the slower your possible connections. How do you know how far away you are? You don't really. The phone company supposedly keeps track of this information, and you can find it on the DSLreports site by going to http://www.dslreports.com/distance.

If neither DSL nor cable is available in your neighborhood, then you should check out ISDN. A good place to start for ISDN is Dan Kegel's ISDN page: http://alumni.caltech.edu/~dank/isdn/, although Dan hasn't been doing much with the page since he got his DSL line a few years ago. Still, it is the best place to track down products and vendors and other questions about the technology.

ISDN requires you to purchase a special type of frhub that can deal with the special digital circuits that are supplied by the phone company. I recommend the Farallon/Netopia R3100. It has the most features for the price, a good user interface to set it up, and a great support department behind it. If you have decided on ISDN, then you can skip the rest of this chapter because you don't have much else to decide. You'll still need to set up this device, which won't be easy. At this point, I would recommend you getting another book devoted to ISDN that can go into more detail here.

If ISDN isn't available in your neighborhood, you are left with the shared dial-up access solution. The unit I would recommend is the Netopia R2020. It comes with ports for two ordinary modems, and you'll need to devote two analog telephone lines to these modems, to be shared among your home network. This isn't the only dial-up device available: Netgear also makes one that has one modem called the RM356.

Another choice for dial-up access is to use Apple's AirPort frhub. While it only contains one modem, it also supports wireless network users. I have heard lots of good things from users of AirPorts, but I wasn't able to obtain one to try out before writing this book. You'll also need one Macintosh to configure it, although both Windows and Mac users can use it to connect to the Internet once they are networked together.

For cable and DSL connections, you have your choice of dozens of different frhubs. The good news is that these devices are probably the easiest things to set up of anything that I recommend in this book. To make you a more educated consumer, I probably will give you more detail than you need. For most of these frhubs, the differences aren't as important as what they have in common, and that is to protect your network from outsiders who are trying to break in and damage your computers.

You probably don't need any more justification, but I want to pound this point home. Every hour, every minute, every second, hundreds if not thousands of people develop malicious software that can automatically scan thousands of computers in a few seconds and find out which ones are vulnerable to attack. Cyberspace can be a nasty place, I am sorry to report. The firewall in my office gives me daily reports of such scans. A group of programmers who are security specialists reports that within minutes of placing a new server on the Internet, it is getting scanned and poked and prodded and examined. This stuff is going on invisibly to you, the average law-abiding person who is innocent and pure as the driven snow. Please, don't skip over this piece of equipment.

Let's look at what these frhubs have in common first and then examine what distinguishes them and how you pick the right one.

All of the firewall routers that I cover in this chapter have the following features:

✦ **Support for Network Address Translation (NAT)** NAT is a way to give machines on your home network both protection and Internet access. You can consider NAT to be a primitive firewall of sorts. Basically, NAT maps each PC's IP address to a single "outside" address, which is the address of your router that is visible to the outside world. Though your router is visible with this IP address, each PC isn't reachable. All that anyone out on the Internet is aware of is this outside address, and they can't easily get into your individual PCs. Since machines on your home network aren't directly accessible to the Internet, some manufacturers are promoting it as a firewall feature. Some products also support the ability to assign a particular inbound route to one of your PCs, so that you can run a Web server on your internal network.

✦ **Support for Dynamic Host Configuration Protocol (DHCP)** DHCP is the answer to your IP address headaches. Two aspects apply here: first is the ability for your router to hand out IP addresses to the PCs on your home network. This is critical because you don't want to have to deal with making sure that every IP address is unique, in the same address range, and so on. Have a machine do it for you, so you can worry about something else that needs attention on your network. Second is the ability of your router to grab a DHCP address from the cable/DSL connection upstream, so you don't have to set this up either. All of the boxes have both capabilities. What this means is that you can drop a box into your existing network, and if your computers have been set up to grab IP addresses from a DHCP server, little additional work is involved to set things up.

✦ **Support for Point-to-Point Protocol over Ethernet (PPPoE)** PPPoE is the bizarre (at least to me) dial-up protocol used by some DSL providers like Earthlink. You may not need this if you run a cable modem or if your ISP doesn't use this connection method, but it is handy to have as part of your product's feature set. I'll show you how to set this up in a moment.

✦ **Changeable router's media access control (MAC) address**   Your cable or DSL provider can detect that you have installed some additional equipment in your home because every Ethernet device has its own unique MAC address. This could be an issue, and the frhub vendors have very cleverly added a feature to clone an existing PC's MAC address so that this equipment won't be detected by your provider. This is one of those obscure networking issues that you find out about only when something doesn't work. Thankfully, most of the products I've tested now come with this feature. If you need to set this up, see the "Troubleshooting" section.

✦ **At least two Ethernet ports**   They have one for your cable/DSL connection and one for your local network. Some products include more ports, and we'll get to that in a moment. Again, having two Ethernet ports is what makes these products a router, by definition, and allows them to protect your network from the bad guys.

✦ **Web-based user interface**   This is used to configure their features. Web-based user interface is now the de facto way all of these products operate. Some of their Web interfaces are better than others, and I'll get into that shortly so you can see what you are about to buy for your $200. (The ISDN routers don't usually come with Web interfaces because they're from a previous generation where the Web was still growing up. If you already decided on ISDN, though, why are you reading this stuff? Go set up your network and ISDN router; you'll have enough to do with that.)

✦ **A way to update the frhub firmware**   Once you buy any of these devices, the first thing to do after hooking it up to your network and making sure you can actually get Internet access from all of your computers is to check to make sure that the vendor has a new version of the firmware that runs inside the box. This is because the Internet is ever changing, and the better vendors stay on top of what is going on with their products and try to keep improving them and adding new protective features. This is done by a special piece of software that lives in the memory of the unit and can be updated with the right kind of tool from your PC, called *firmware*. Some of the boxes have very easy methods to update their firmware, while some have more obscure methods. It really depends on the version running on the box you buy and the vendor.

What distinguishes each of these products, and how do you choose? In the course of doing research for this book, I looked at over a dozen different products, to the point where I became a lending library of frhubs to my friends and family to test various ones. If you want the summary table of what to buy first, see Table 4-2. You'll notice I have also included information on their default IP addresses, costs, and other defaults. If you want to know why, read on.

Product	Ethernet Ports	Price/ notable feature	Default IP Address	Default username/ Password	PPPoE support?	MAC spoof support?
2Wire Home Portal 100W	1	$400 (Wireless/Phone Line/games)	172.16.0.1	(null)/(null)	Yes	No
Linksys BEFSR41	4	$130 (low cost)	192.168.1.1	(null)/ admin	Yes	Yes
Netgear RP114	4	$180 (content filter/logs)	192.168.0.1	admin/ 1234	Yes	Yes
Netopia R3100	8	$550 (ISDN)	192.168.1.1	(null)/(null)	N/A	N/A
Netopia R2020	8	$570 (dial-up)	192.168.1.1	(null)/(null)	N/A	N/A
Farallon NetLine Wireless Broadband Gateway	2	$260 (wireless)	192.168.0.1	(null)/(null)	Yes	Yes
SMC 7008BR	7	$100 (print server)	192.168. 123.254	(null)/ admin	Yes	Yes
SonicWALL Tele2	1	$500 (security/VPN)	192.168. 168.168	admin/ password	Yes	Yes
MaxGate 3200P	8	$270 (dynamic DNS)	192.168.0.1	(null)/(null)	Yes	Yes

Table 4-2. Recommended Frhub Features Summary

Here are the things that you need to ask yourself before picking the right frhub:

✦ **Does the frhub offer any additional ports?** The most popular addition to these products is a four-, seven-, or eight-port hub that is built in to the device, so you don't have to buy an additional hub. Some of the products also offer switched network ports, and some also offer 100-megabit ports and full-duplex ports in addition to the ordinary 10-megabit half-duplex ports. Some even offer ports that connect to other hubs, in case your network grows beyond the number of ports that they offer.

What does all this mean to you as a consumer? Generally, more trouble than benefit. Any network that is running faster than the standard 10 megabits isn't going to make much difference to you, mainly because the speed that you connect outside of your humble home is going to be much slower than 10 megabits. (There are two notable exceptions: If you play lots of network-oriented games that don't involve an Internet connection, or if you are moving files from one of your home PCs to another, then you'll appreciate the faster network connections that these products offer.)

Most of us that are using our home networks for downloading Web pages, doing e-mail and sending Instant Messages aren't going to notice the difference between 10 and 100 megabit Ethernet. If you can get by with four ports and want to spend as little as possible, then I would recommend the Linksys product: It is bare-bones protection at a very attractive $130 price. It offers an attractive user interface, as you can see in the illustration.

SETUP

require help during configuration, please see the user guide.

Host Name:		(Required by some ISPs)
Domain Name:		(Required by some ISPs)
Firmware Version:	1.37, Jan 03 2001	
LAN IP Address:	(MAC Address: 00-20-78-C7-66-E4)	

`192` . `168` . `1` . `1` (Device IP Address)

`255.255.255.0` ▾ (Subnet Mask)

WAN IP Address: (MAC Address: 00-20-78-C7-66-E5)

⦿ **Obtain an IP Address Automatically**

○ Specify an IP Address `0` . `0` . `0` . `0`

Subnet Mask: `255` . `255` . `255` . `0`

Default Gateway Address: `0` . `0` . `0` . `0`

DNS(Required) 1: `0` . `0` . `0` . `0`

2: `0` . `0` . `0` . `0`

3: `0` . `0` . `0` . `0`

Login: ○ PPPoE ○ RAS ⦿ **Disable**

NOTE: PPPoE is for ADSL user only.
RAS is for SingTel ADSL user only.

User Name:

So why do the vendors trick up their products with this stuff? Mainly for marketing appeal. If you haven't yet purchased a network hub, by all means pick a product with some extra ports, and pick one that has some room to grow if you plan on adding computers or networked printers. Remember that every print server device on your network uses up an extra port.

❖ **Does the frhub support wireless or PhoneLine connections?** If you decided in Chapter 1 to use wireless or PhoneLine networking, then you'll need to consider a frhub that supports one (or both) of these technologies. This is because, as I mentioned earlier, almost all of the Internet connections you'll install require a regular Ethernet RJ45 jack, and your frhub will connect this Ethernet line to the rest of your home network.

If you need both wireless and PhoneLine technologies, then pick the 2Wire Home Portal 100W, which offers both, but at a price of $400. (Wireless, as I have said before, doesn't come cheap.) If you only need PhoneLine connections, a good alternative is to buy the Netgear RP334 which has three RJ45 Ethernet ports along with a port that bridges Ethernet and PhoneLine networks. You hook up cables to each network, and presto, you have just enabled your PhoneLine users to access the rest of your Ethernet network. (If you need more RJ45 Ethernet ports, take a look at the description of other Netgear products later in this chapter.)

The following illustration shows the 2Wire's interface. The 2Wire product also has some nice tools, including the ability to check the speed of your broadband connection and a visual display of the servers on your home network. If you just need wireless support, a good choice is the Farallon Netline Wireless Broadband Gateway product.

✦ **Does this router offer support for gamers?** Network-based games stress the abilities of these products to function properly. Many issues are involved here, but you'll want a product that is geared toward gamers and can be set up to enable games to work across the firewall.

Some vendors call these "special applications" and place certain limitations on them in their products. For example, the Maxgate firewall/router products only allow a single PC to use the same application at a time. This is a problem if you have more than one kid who wants to play the same online game together. My recommendation is the 2Wire product for your gamer users, mainly because its interface is easier to set up these applications. Note that I didn't extensively test this product with many games, but hopefully it should do better than products that don't support any games whatsoever.

✦ **Do you need support for dynamic DNS?** Dynamic DNS services enable you to have your NAT and DHCP network, but still get some benefit from having a domain name directing traffic to a particular PC on your home network, say, a Web or mail server that you want to run from home. Both the Netgear and MaxGate products support this, and the others will probably get around to it eventually. MaxGate offers as part of its purchase price a one-year free subscription to a provider that handles the dynamic updates, although your domain address is going to be *something*.ugate.net as seen in the illustration.

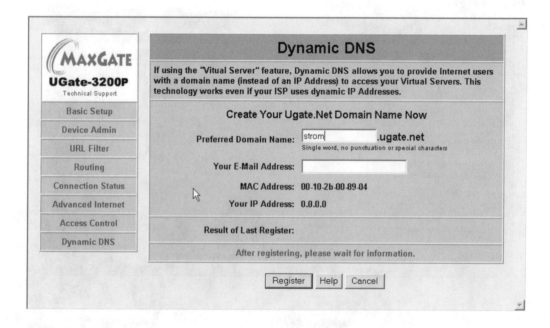

✦ **Are you willing to spend more for extra security?** Then buy the product that I use in my office, the SonicWALL Tele2 for about $500. It doesn't have any extra hub ports (meaning you'll then need to spend some money for an additional hub), but it offers the best firewall features that you can find in these products. If you are the type of person who spends the extra dough on Medeco locks for your doors, then you should get the SonicWALL. The following illustration shows their interface, and if you'd like to experiment and see more, given how much cash you'll have to part with to buy one of these, then I urge you to go the company's Web site (http://www.sonicwall.com/products/demo) and try it. It supports a maximum of five networked devices (whether they be PCs or print servers), but other than that limitation it is a fine piece of gear.

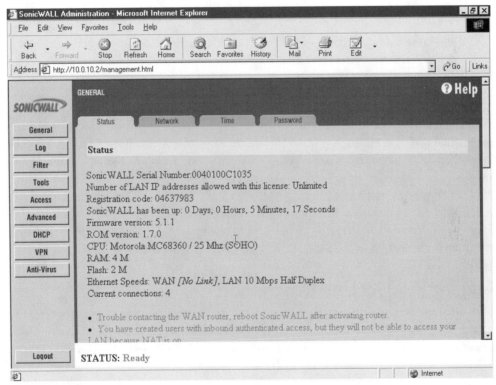

One of the additional features you pay for with the SonicWALL is the ability to connect your home network with your office computers over a secure connection called a virtual private network (VPN). This encrypts traffic between the two networks so completely that no one will be able to tap into your conversations. See Chapter 6 for more information on

VPNs and what is involved in setting them up. Some of the other products offer some support in this area, including the Netgear FR314, but none of them can match the SonicWALL for the sheer number of encryption options and features.

✦ **Do you need a print server as well?** Some of these products come with a built-in print server in addition to the firewall and routing features. The product I'd choose here is the SMC Barricade 7008BR for $100, which comes with an eight-port hub and the print server on top of it. (The print server only works for Windows and not for Macintoshes, however. If you want a frhub that has a print server that supports both platforms, check out the Asante FR3000 series.) If you choose to use a separate print server, you'll need to make sure it supports grabbing a DHCP address. If not, you'll have to set it up manually to match the IP addresses that are doled out by your DHCP server.

✦ **Do you want to keep track of your household's surfing habits**, and perhaps block certain Web sites from them? The Netgear RP114 for $180 is the best product here, although the SonicWALL can accomplish this for far more money.

That is a lot to digest. Before you get frustrated, remember that all we are talking about here is a machine with at least two network connections, one to the outside world and one to your internal network. The trick is in understanding how information flows from one network to the other, and which direction it is going. Obviously, you want all of your requests from your home network to go out to the Internet, but not the reverse. The trick with any industrial-class firewall is being able to understand its list of rules to determine how to block things (such as packets, applications, or kinds of connections) you don't want and how to allow things you do. You aren't setting up an industrial-class firewall, however; you are just trying to get Internet access. I'll say more about firewall rules in Chapter 6.

Netgear Product Line Description

At this writing, Netgear sells many different router products that you can use to access the Internet and protect your home network. Seven are used for cable and DSL connections, three are used for ISDN, and one is used to connect your home network via an ordinary dial-up line (the RM356, mentioned earlier). Let's look at the various distinguishing features of Netgear's cable/DSL products, so you can get a better idea of what to buy and what the various extra features will cost you.

At the most basic level is the *RT311*, selling for about $120. This doesn't have any hub ports, just the two Ethernet ports for your local and wide-area connections. If you want a built-in four-port hub, then you will want the *RT314*, which sells for about $150. Given that a hub these days costs about $30–$50, it is a good investment to at least get the RT314 if you haven't already bought a hub for your home network. The RT314 is roughly equivalent to the Linksys BEFSR41 in terms of features and price, and is the other basic router that I recommend. If you want eight ports, then there is the RO318 which sells for $240.

Back with the four-port hubs, spending a bit more money will bring you to the *RP114* at $180. This gives you the ability to block access to various Web sites by anyone in your home, based on certain keywords. (See the following illustration.) We'll go into details about this in Chapter 6, but the RP114 also includes the ability to keep track of which sites your household visits in a special access log. If you have a very large household, or one that is very active surfing around the Internet, it could be tedious to examine these logs and determine if any of your children are viewing inappropriate sites.

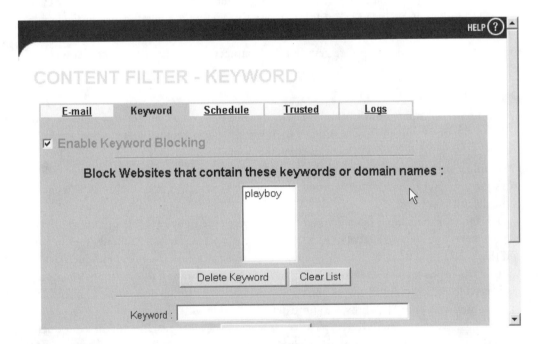

At the top of the Netgear Ethernet-only router line is the *FR314*, which sells for $350. This adds additional firewall features well worth the extra money if you will be using any of your home computers for running a business or if you are more concerned about security issues. Its cost is very competitive with the SonicWALL line of products.

Netgear has two other products as well: the MR314, which marries a four-port hub with a wireless access point for $299 and the RP334, which marries a PhoneLine port to a three-port hub for $399. If you have a PhoneLine network and know you are only going to need three additional standard Ethernet RJ45 ports, then the RP334 is a good choice. Otherwise, you should buy the PE102 for $100 along with some other frhub to get more RJ45 ports.

Keeping Track of Netopia and Farallon Products

Another company who sells many different kinds of frhubs worth considering is Proxim, which now owns both the Farallon and Netopia brands. I recommend several devices that I have used over the years for various connection options:

The *Netopia R2020* is the best dial-up frhub that I could find. If you are still stuck in the dial-up era, this is the device for you. It has the ability to use two dial-up modems and two phone lines working together, and it comes with firewall features and DHCP services and many of the other features mentioned for the broadband routers.

Farallon NetLine Wireless Broadband Gateway is a combination wireless/wired frhub, similar to the 2Wire but without the PhoneLine connector. It comes with only two hub ports, however. The access unit comes with a PC Card slot, where you insert your wireless network adapter.

The *Netopia R3100* is one of several ISDN routers sold by the company and is the one that I recommend to those who are getting ISDN connections for their Internet access.

Setting Up Your Frhub

Setting up these frhubs is fairly simple. Typically you use a Web browser and connect to it with the default IP address that was listed in Table 4.2. Some require a user name; some require a password as well. The good news is that you should be able to drop one of these boxes into your existing network and reset the IP addresses of your PCs, and they should work just fine. With most of these products, about the only thing you might want to change is the default password.

For the most part, their defaults out of the box were the right choices in terms of offering enough protection without a lot of hassles. Most of them will take about 15 minutes to configure, and that is counting the time it takes to read the slim manual that usually comes included. Many of the products have their own Windows-based configuration software, but you don't really need to even install this if you aren't going to change the initial defaults and can connect to the router with your Web browser at the default IP address.

Having a Web user interface also means that Macintoshes can easily set up these products, too, and you don't have to worry about having a particular piece of software to run your router. Well, almost. You'll find that some of the router products require a special piece of software to upload their firmware, and naturally this software is only available for Windows. (Asante and Farallon products are the exception here, as you would expect.)

The simplest way to set up a frhub is to know both that the *DHCP server is turned on,* so that your network will be able to obtain IP addresses from it, and that it can also *act as a DHCP client* and grab an IP address from your cable or DSL provider. Typically, these are the default settings of most frhubs, so you have nothing to do. If your provider has given you a static IP address, then you'll have to enter it into the frhub yourself.

If you need to set up special games or your own Web server at home, you'll need to enter this information. If you need to set up PPPoE, then you'll need to enter this information, typically the user name and password that your ISP has assigned to your "login" for your DSL line. The illustration shows how it looks on the Netgear frhubs.

WIZARD SETUP

ISP Parameters for Internet Access

Encapsulation	PPP over Ethernet ▼
Service Name	Earthlink
User Name	davidstrom
Password	**********
Idle Timeout	300 Seconds.

Back | Next

Setting Up Frhubs on Cable Systems

I should give you one additional caveat. Most cable systems, and some DSL systems, detect the media access address of the frhub when the cable modem (or DSL modem) is turned on. This means that if you first test your cable modem by plugging it directly into the PC's Ethernet card, then unplug the Ethernet cable and plug in the frhub between the cable modem and the PC, things won't work.

Here is the correct order to get everything set up properly with a cable modem:

1. Plug in all the RJ45 cables: the cable from one of your PCs to the frhub and the cable from the frhub to your cable modem.

2. Plug in the cable coax to the cable modem.

3. Turn on the cable modem. Wait until all the lights have finished flashing, and wait until the light that indicates an Internet connection is solidly on.

4. Turn on the frhub. Wait until all the lights have finished flashing, and wait until the light that indicates a connection to the cable modem is solidly on.

5. Turn on your PC. The light on the frhub port that it is connected to should turn on. It should also acquire an IP address.

6. Make any configuration changes to all of your PCs as needed to connect to the Internet.

Finishing Up the Job

No matter if you chose a cable, DSL, shared dial-up, or an ISDN connection, you will have one final step to finish setting everything up and making sure that your network is functional. When you bring home your new Mac or Windows PC, it comes with an Internet Connection wizard (in Windows) or an Internet Setup Assistant (for Mac) icon. Either of these will help you establish the various configuration parameters you need to get online. Once either of these tools finishes its task, your computer should be working and be able to see the Internet.

That's all well and good, but you have one or more PCs that you didn't bring home new and have been using for the longest time with dial-up modems or nothing connecting them to the outside world. That is where this final step is important because you need to change your PC from the slow lane to the fast lane.

NOTE   If you followed the instructions in Chapter 2 in terms of setting up your IP network, you have done the hard part. You have to make some changes to your IP configuration to grab those DHCP addresses from your frhub instead of using fixed IP addresses as detailed in that chapter. See the "Troubleshooting" section on using WINIPCFG (for Windows 95/98), IPCONFIG (for all other versions of Windows), or the Mac's TCP/IP control panel.

If you haven't done anything about your network installation yet, then continue reading and follow these instructions to switch your computers from dial-up to local area networking.

If you like the wizard/assistant approach, you can rerun them and adjust your machine accordingly. The desktop icon is probably long gone, so you'll need to track them down. For Windows 98/ME/2000, go to Programs | Accessories | Communications, and you'll find the wizard there. For Macs, go to the Internet folder, and you'll find the Setup Assistant there. In either case, you want to tell your PC that you now have a continuous network connection for your Internet needs, and you don't have to mess around anymore with that annoyingly slow dial-up connection. (That is the last of the three options in the Windows wizard. For the Mac, on the second step, you'll choose to connect via the "network" setting rather than your modem.) You can follow along the screens in either wizard and change the settings to look for your Internet over your network rather than your modem.

Windows XP has a bit more complicated situation, because in the interests of making your computer more home friendly, Microsoft has thrown in a bunch of new wizards to confuse you.

First, as you can see in the following illustration, you can choose among five options rather than the three in previous versions of Windows. Picking the right one will depend on whether you have a network and if you are going to connect to the Internet through it. Most readers should choose the third option.

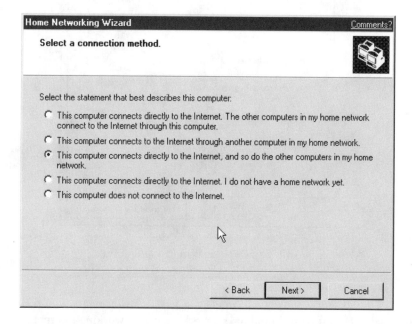

XP has some other additional wrinkles, including the ability to set up a firewall on that computer. We'll return to that discussion in Chapter 6.

If you are feeling confident, don't want to run the wizards, and are running Windows Internet Explorer, go to Tools | Internet Options | Connections. You'll see the screen depicted in Figure 4-1.

At this point, select the Never Dial A Connection option, and make sure that your LAN settings are correct. That should enable you to go online without having to deal with your modem from now on. Remember to repeat this procedure with all of your PCs.

For Macintoshes, you should be able to switch things over to your network connection by running the Internet Connection Assistant, as I mentioned earlier. You also may need to switch the IP settings from a fixed IP address to grabbing a DHCP address from your frhub, and you do that in the TCP/IP control panel.

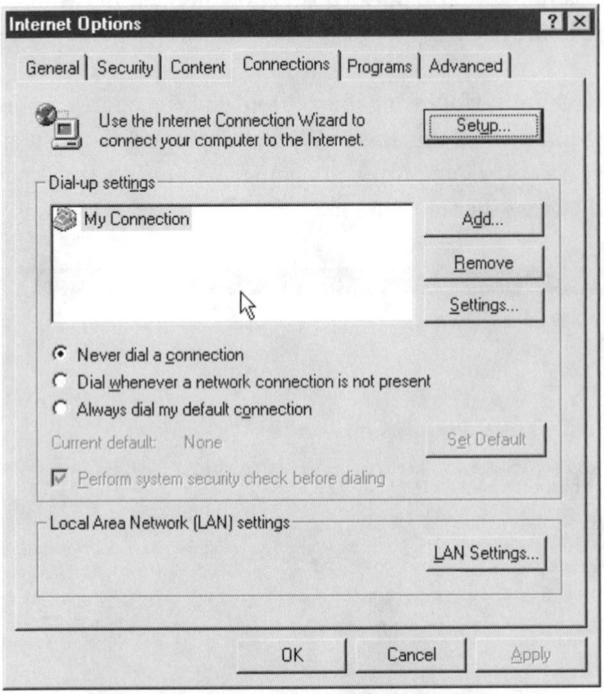

Figure 4-1. Internet connection options for Windows 98/2000

Whew! That's about it. You should have a working frhub, working Internet access, and the ability for each of your computers to browse the Web and get e-mail. Wait a minute, I haven't yet told you how to deal with e-mail; that's for our next chapter. If something isn't quite right, see the "Troubleshooting" section that follows and with luck find some information on how you can get whatever isn't working fixed.

Troubleshooting

Let's cover several situations that may not have worked out according to plan.

Suddenly, the Internet Seems Slow

Once you have everything working properly, you'll get used to the high-speed Internet connection so quickly that you won't be able to deal with dial-up modems anymore. You can never have enough speed to make everyone happy. Trust me, it will take your household about a day before they start complaining about how slow the Internet is. Before you panic and think something is wrong, realize that you have now moved the bottleneck for your connection from just outside your computer to someplace down the road or halfway around the world.

Before you become concerned, let's do a few rudimentary tests to see how fast things are going. A good place to start is this Web page, which contains links to various "speed tests" you can run to determine how fast your connection really is:

http://www.wwc.com/techsupport/Installation.htm

Try doing one of the speed tests at various times of the day over the course of a week and see what the variations are. That should give you a good idea that your actual throughput is going to vary tremendously. Without seeing the results, it is hard for me to make any specific statements, but I can almost guarantee you that there will be considerable difference between doing the tests at 3 A.M. and 3 P.M., say.

These speed tests measure the speed of sending packets from a particular test site (such as c|net's servers or Microsoft's servers) to your network and back again. Depending on where you are located and the path between you and the test servers, you can get better or worse results. The issue is that these communication lines are shared. No matter where you are trying to get to on the Internet, chances are someone else is also trying, and they may have monopolized critical resources, delaying your connection. Think of it as everyone leaving the big city for their vacation homes on a Friday. If you leave at noon, it won't take as long as leaving at 7 P.M.

SURVIVAL TIP

The problem is figuring out where the new bottleneck is located and if you can do anything about it. Chances are you can't do either and have to live with the temporary slowdown.

Everything Seems To Be Working, but You Can't Access the Internet

This is the same situation if you want to swap the IP address configuration from using a fixed address (as mentioned in Chapter 2) to using the dynamic addresses given out by your frhub's DHCP server.

The first thing to try is to renew your DHCP addresses. If you are running Windows 95/98/ME, go to Start | Run and type **WINIPCFG** and press ENTER. You should see a list of the various network and modem connections. Scroll down until you find the one that lists

your network adapter, and then click Release, wait a moment for the box to blank out the various entries, and then click Renew. In a moment, it should find your DHCP server, and you should be ready to roll across cyberspace. (See Figure 4-2.)

If you are running Windows 2000/XP, you need to open up a command window, and then type **IPCONFIG \RENEW**. Note the space between the two words, and press ENTER after each command. If you are using a Mac, go to Control Panel | TCPIP | Configure, choose Using DHCP Server, and then close the control panel to try renewing your address.

You may also need the Domain Name Services (DNS) server information from your cable modem or DSL provider, and you may need to enter this information in one of your frhub's Web configuration screens. How do you know if you need this? Try bringing up a Web browser and typing in some random Web site address, say www.microsoft.com. If nothing comes up, your name server information is required, or you might not have set up your DNS properly.

DNS is the way that all computers on the Internet translate the numerical IP addresses into ordinary names that you and I can remember, like www.microsoft.com instead of

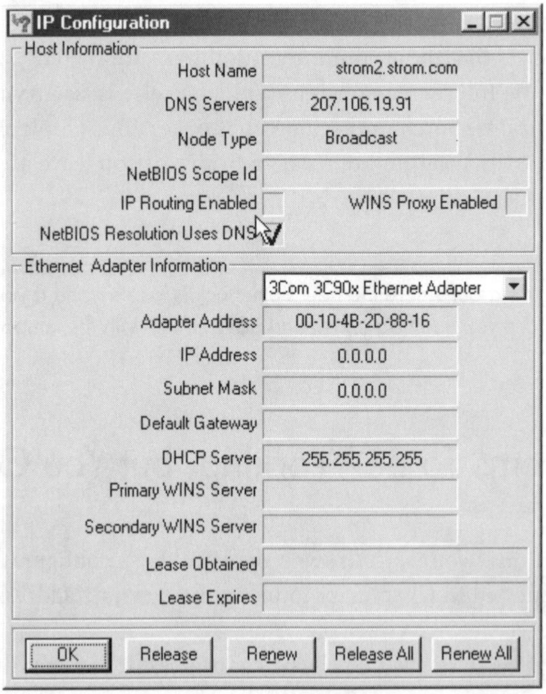

Figure 4-2.　WINIPCFG dialog box for renewing DHCP addresses

207.46.131.199, or whatever they have set this up to be these days. Every network comes with a series of name servers, and sometimes you can get away without having to worry about finding the exact IP addresses for these servers. Usually, when you obtain an IP address from a DHCP server, it obtains the DNS server information at no additional charge or aggravation. Sometimes, however, you won't be able to obtain these servers for one reason or another.

To set up DNS servers manually, you'll need to find the place in your frhub or ISDN modem setup screens to enter this information and also need to know from your provider what the DNS servers are. Probably your provider did supply this information to you when you signed up for an account, but you have either misplaced this information or didn't realize the importance of what they were telling you. You can try going to the support Web pages of your provider's Web site and seeing if they have documented this information here.

You Get the Message "Server Not Found"

Speaking of DNS servers, this could be the cause of this problem. If you mistyped the DNS information, or if something is wrong with your Internet service provider's DNS servers, then you won't be able to get anywhere in cyberspace. Bring up a command prompt window if running Windows (or use WhatRoute if running a Macintosh, which you can download from http://homepages.ihug.co.nz/~bryanc), type **ping yahoo.com**, and see if you can get a response back from Yahoo's servers. If not, then something is wrong either with your Internet connection or your frhub, or the provider's own network is having problems.

To see if it's something under your control, try to ping your frhub's IP address to at least establish that you have a working local network in your home. Next, try to ping the DNS server at your provider's network. If that seems to work, maybe you're just unlucky, and the server that you are trying to get to is out of commission.

The best tool to see what is going on between you and any particular server on the Internet is called TraceRoute. It displays the route between your computer and a particular server out on the Internet, and gives you an idea if there are any problems on the path between you. Mac users can use WhatRoute. To use this tool, bring up a command-line window, type **tracert yahoo.com** (or some other destination), and watch as it describes the route between you and Yahoo's server. The larger the numbers displayed, the longer the latencies between one router and the next. If one of the lines says "destination host unreachable" or something similar, you know that the path between you and Yahoo (or whomever else you are trying to reach) is having a problem and is out of your control.

Interpreting the Lights on the Frhub

The blinking lights on the front or the back of your frhub are sometimes the only clue you have to ensure that things are or are not working on your network. In general, there are two kinds of lights: One indicates whether a PC's Ethernet cable is plugged in and operating on that port, and the other indicates whether a 10- or 100-megabit connection has been established with that particular PC.

Sometimes the lights are labeled "Link/Act" and "100." Sometimes they are just placed very close to the top of the RJ45 connector that is part of the frhub: one on the left side of the connector and one on the right side of the connector, and you have to figure out what they mean on your own. Sometimes the Link light blinks on and off when data is passing through the hub to and from that particular port, indicating network traffic and not just that it has a connection with your hub port.

If your PC is on and your Ethernet adapter is working, you should see at least one of the lights go on when you plug in a cable that connects the frhub to the PC. If not, chances are your cable is bad, you have the wrong kind of cable, or your PC's networking adapter isn't configured properly. You might try swapping with a known working cable or moving the cable to another port to see if the situation changes. Your hub or frhub might also have a small switch that changes the polarity of the port from a straight-through to a crossover cable, so you don't have to swap cables. Again, look at the lights on each port, and see what happens when you press the switch in and out a few times. If the light comes on, you have the right combination of cables, and you should have communications working between hub and PC.

Wireless adapters also have one or more lights, and these also indicate that the adapter has found a wireless access point and is communicating with it.

One additional note: 10Base-T Ethernet specifications are 325 feet for the longest distance from hub to one of your PC's. PhoneLine specifications are 1000 feet for the total amount of wiring among your networked PCs. If you suspect that you have run more than this amount of wire around your home, try bringing your computer to the room where your hub is, and hook them up together with a short piece of cabling.

How to Set Up a MAC Spoofing Address

Some cable and DSL providers don't want you to have networks. They try their best to keep you from setting up a network by requiring that you specify the media access control address of your PC's Ethernet card as a way of ensuring that you won't swap out PCs or add additional ones to your home Internet connection. Vendors have thwarted these feeble attempts by adding special features to their frhubs so you can specify whatever media access control (MAC, not be confused with Mac[intoshes]) address you need to get past your provider's security checks.

Every Ethernet adapter sold in the world has a unique address that is burned into its chips when it is manufactured. I find this whole subject somewhat tiresome, but all the products that I checked had support for "cloning" the MAC address. There are various ways to do this, and I'll show you how both Netgear and Linksys handle this.

With the Netgear frhubs, you run the wizard setup, and one of the screens will look like this:

WAN IP Address Assignment

- Get automatically from ISP (Default)
- Use fixed IP address
  - IP Address   `0.0.0.0`
  - IP Subnet Mask   `0.0.0.0`
  - Gateway IP Address   `0.0.0.0`

DNS Server Address Assignment

- Get automatically from ISP (Default)
- Use fixed IP address --- DNS Server IP Address `0.0.0.0`

WAN MAC address

- Factory default
- Spoof this PC's MAC address --- IP Address `192.168.0.2`

| Back | Finish |

Select the option labeled "Spoof this PC's MAC address," and enter the IP address of the PC that you registered with your provider. Of course, you now need to know this PC's IP address. Trundle over to that particular PC, bring up WINIPCFG or IPCONFIG (if Windows 2000) (or if you originally registered a Macintosh, bring up the TCP/IP control panel), and check the IP address that this PC is using.

This works even if your PC has had its IP address changed because it is now getting it from the frhub, rather than your provider's DHCP server. This is a neat trick.

For Linksys, the process is more involved. When you bring up your Web browser interface, first click on the DHCP tab and then the button that says "DHCP Clients table." Make note of the PC with the appropriate IP address that you want to copy, and then write down the MAC address listed for that PC. Be careful to copy this address correctly. Now click on the Advanced tab and then on "Mac Addr. Clone." You'll see the following screen.

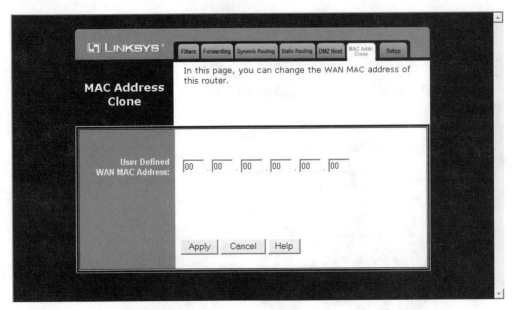

Now enter in the MAC address that you copied down.

Using an Internal ISDN or DSL Modem

You have some hard times ahead, I'm afraid, if you want to run a network in your home and connect all of your machines to the Internet. You will have to set up a router inside the PC that has the ISDN or DSL modem card, and also install an Ethernet (or PhoneLine or Wireless network) adapter in the same machine. Both the ISDN/DSL modem and the Ethernet card will have separate subnet addresses, meaning one might be on the 10.0.0.x subnet and one might be on the 170.1.0.x subnet. You will probably have to use fixed IP addresses on the rest of your network, too. See the practicallynetworked.com site for specific instructions on how to set this up.

You Can't Access the Internet After Resetting or Powering Off/On Your Cable Modem

Try powering off/on your frhub first, and renew DHCP leases using the procedure mentioned earlier in the section on "Can't get access to the Internet." Also, make sure that you followed the procedure in the section under "Solutions" for setting up your frhub with cable systems, and carefully follow the order of how each device is powered-on.

You Have Trouble Connecting Your Router to Your Cable Modem

As mentioned in Chapter 1, there are two types of Ethernet cables: straight-through and crossover. The former is usually used between two PCs or two hubs; you might need one of these, depending on your frhub and cable or DSL modem. Some products automatically sense which type of cable you are using and adjust themselves accordingly, while others have a small switch that needs to be set so you don't have to go rooting around to find the right kind of cable.

In general, you know you have the wrong kind when you plug in the cable between your PC and hub port, and the little port light doesn't immediately come on. Look through the box of your cable/DSL modem and frhub, and see if you can find another cable. Otherwise, go to your local computer store, buy the straight-through cable, and see if that works. You could also have a bad cable, as wires can get bent, cracked, or cut apart: with my friends at Family Z, the local rabbit or dog had chewed through their cable enough that it worked sometimes, but not consistently. When they replaced their cable, all was well.

You Can't Update Your Router's Firmware

There are a number of issues here, but first check to see that you changed the default IP address or administrator's user name/password. With some products, such as the SMC Barricade, you have to first reset these values back to their defaults, the ones that came with the router out of the box. Then you can upgrade the firmware. The Linksys devices have a more cumbersome firmware upgrade process than either the Umax or Netgear units. The latter two have menu items inside the Web interface to make updating the features and protective measures easier.

Don't Update Your DSL or Cable Modem's Firmware

Unless you are having problems with the cable/DSL modem, don't mess around with any firmware updates. While I recommend that you keep fairly current with your frhub's firmware, when it comes to the DSL or cable modem, I suggest leaving well enough alone. While I was writing this chapter, I noticed that my Flowpoint DSL modem was running an older firmware version, and I thought I'd be a good camper and update it while I had the chance. A bad move: all of a sudden, I had terrible problems.

When I went back to the Flowpoint support page, I read the instructions that told me *not* to update firmware unless I was experiencing particular problems. Let this be a lesson learned the hard way—keep the DSL or cable modem as is, unless you have reason to suspect it is no longer working. While you are at it, if you can make a backup copy of your DSL modem's firmware, do so. The moral of this story is if it works, *don't fix it!*

Don't Use PhoneLine and DSL on the Same Phone Line

If you only have a single phone line in your house, and it is running DSL services, then you can't reliably make use of PhoneLine network products. The trouble is that the digital codes used by the DSL service will interfere with the digital codes used by the PhoneLine networking products. Either install a separate phone line for your network, or else make use of one of the other products. Sorry about that.

Futures

Sharing your Internet connection is probably one of the most active product development areas in the home-networking arena. With the combination of wireless access points, new low-cost firewalls, and cheaper chipsets to deliver fully switched 10/100 Ethernet ports, expect to continue to see prices drop and features bundled in at a very high rate.

A number of companies have begun to sell their products that offer more in the way of security and better features to track household usage, two active areas for product development. This is one situation where reading a book isn't much use, since anything that I write is going to be out of date by the time you read this book. Nevertheless, I'd check out the Web site practicallynetworked.com because they tend to post reviews of these products on a timely basis.

Let's move on to discuss how you can use the application that you and your household will be spending most of their computing time with, sending and receiving e-mail and instant messages.

Chapter 5

Using E-Mail on Your Home Network

E-mail has become our family lifeline. We use it to communicate with each other to set up family gatherings and to inform each other about important events, setbacks, and accomplishments. A few years ago, a single e-mail contact per household was acceptable and, to some extent, usual. In some cases a parent brought his or her e-mail account home from the office and accessed it from the home PC. Those days are behind us now, and everyone has his or her own e-mail address—often more than one. Soon e-mail addresses will proliferate like phone numbers: You'll have an e-mail address for work, for home, for sending e-mail to your two-way pager, for your Web-enabled cell phone, for mailing lists, and for tons of other reasons.

Ordinary e-mail has grown beyond one-to-one messages with the rise of Instant Messaging (IM) from various vendors. For those of you still living under a rock or far removed from teenagers, IM has almost become more important than ordinary e-mail itself. The ability to converse with someone, or several someones, halfway across the planet is a powerful tool for everyone from chatty kids to ad hoc workgroups. Indeed, the words "to IM me" are now part of our normal vocabulary.

Probably no company more than AOL has been responsible for the popularity of both e-mail and IM. With tens of millions of e-mail addresses, AOL is the gigantic water cooler in cyberspace. For teenagers, it is the de facto communications medium. I've seen kids give out their "screen names" when asked for their e-mail address—without using the "@aol.com" that is the usual Internet format. While AOL defends its IM perimeter from competitors, millions of non-AOL members have IM accounts and continue to use its system to chat.

AOL is what I usually recommend to people new to e-mail and IM. They have made it relatively easy for newcomers to pick up the necessary skills to communicate and compose messages, and to manage their correspondents' addresses and contacts. If you buy a new PC, AOL is usually included. If not, chances are the company will mail you a CD with its software and an offer for a free first month of use.[1]

AOL didn't accomplish the e-mail explosion on its own. Having the Internet as the backbone and major glue to bind together disparate e-mail systems helped move things along enormously. As recently as a decade ago, "e-mail" still meant using multiple systems that didn't communicate with each other very well. You had to maintain separate addresses because there was no way that someone on MCIMail could communicate with someone on BITnet or an IBM DISOSS system. (Don't worry about what these acronyms mean. These systems are still around in some form, although most of us would only care how they could connect to the Internet.)

One of the first things that most of us do when we sit down at our computers is bring up whatever e-mail program we are using and check to see if we've got mail. We probably

---

1   These "700 hours free" offers really bug me. If you read the fine print of the offer, it only applies to that portion of the calendar month when you sign up. If you decide to start your service late in the month, there aren't enough hours to use all of them. Nevertheless, AOL's marketing prowess is remarkable, and those CDs find their way to my mailbox with some regularity.

spend more time at our computers reading and sending e-mail and IMs than any other task, regardless of what else we do with the machine. Certainly, e-mail traffic still accounts for the majority of data that is transmitted on the Internet, despite the growing popularity of the Web.

Problems

The popularity of e-mail brings several problems with it, some general and some that are unique to domestic situations.

Having a continuous Internet connection into your home does wonders for e-mail, because you are getting nearly continuous delivery of messages to your desktop. That could become a problem, especially if you have family members who are more in tune with checking their mailbox than checking in person with what the rest of the household is doing. While I am not prepared to give you family counseling sessions on how to avoid these problems, you should certainly monitor your family members' use of e-mail and set some realistic guidelines about when it is appropriate to check messages. (Presumably, you do the same thing for TV usage.) Certainly, steering clear of the computers just before dinnertime is a good idea. (How many times have I heard, "I'll be there in a minute. Just let me finish reading one more e-mail…"?)

Various problems can arise in terms of managing the ebb and flow of messages to your inbox, given that e-mail is now nearly universal.

Make that "inboxes" (plural), please. Until recently, it was difficult to run any e-mail software that could handle multiple personalities and accounts on a single PC. This is one reason why AOL is so firmly entrenched as a household legacy application, because handling multiple mailboxes for household members is something it has done well almost since the beginning.

It isn't just having accounts for each household member that presents the problem. You probably have multiple e-mail identities yourself, even if just to segregate work and home e-mail traffic, and how you handle these separate inboxes can be a challenge. For example, you might check your e-mail on your home machine as part of your morning ritual on the way to work. However, once you collect your messages on your home machine, how do you make copies of them that will be available on your work machine? Not easily. Consider this the technological equivalent of leaving your wallet in your other suit, for those of you who wear suits.

Managing multiple e-mail identities has become more of a necessity than a luxury these days, especially as the number of Internet-accessible devices continues to increase and as the number of free e-mail service providers mushrooms. Some service providers require an e-mail account as part of a package of other offerings, such as My Yahoo's portal of various contact-management and personal services, JungleMate's Web-accessible address book, and Visto's synchronization service. I've lost track of how many e-mail accounts I have set up for myself over the years—it has passed several dozen by now and could be approaching 100. While it is great to have choices, things can quickly get out of hand for many of us who have taken advantage of these services.

Having multiple e-mail identities doesn't always have to mean that you have to check multiple e-mail inboxes for your messages. As more people purchase their own Internet domain names, they can readily forward the e-mails to their existing inboxes, but that means they have to manage these new domain addresses and make sure that the proper forwarding rules are put in place. Depending on who hosts your domain, this could be easy or impossibly difficult.

Multiple accounts are just the tip of the iceberg. My wife has a two-way pager and forwards her e-mails from her regular desktop account so she can be connected when she is away from her desk or out of town. (She didn't set this up herself—that is where having in-house technical support can come in handy.) A year ago I would have thought such a situation was for the ultra-geeks among us and a distant hope for the average citizen.

Now I take it in stride. As more people use two-way pagers with Internet connections, more people will want to use them in this fashion. My cell phone has an e-mail address so I can receive messages from the Internet. Other digital assistants like the Palm and the Blackberry come with their own e-mail identities. Some desktop software products even will forward your e-mail from your existing desktop account to these devices.

That's just the beginning of managing your e-mail mess. You have to deal with spam,[2] one of e-mail's biggest frustrations.

Spam is a fact of modern Internet life. What makes it hard to fight is that a spammer doesn't have to have a physical office: he or she could be doing business the next minute under a new identity. There is nothing you can do about it.

Microsoft Outlook and other e-mail programs have ways to block junk mail, but the problem is that the minute you block out all e-mails from makemoneyfast.com, a spammer will set up a makemoneyfast2.com domain and start hammering you from there. I'll have more to say on how you can try to cope with spam later in the "Solutions" section, but I warn you that none of my suggestions will do much, and you will still have spam messages filling up your inbox.

You *can* do something about e-mail viruses and other infections you receive from the Internet. This is such an important situation that I have devoted a good portion of Chapter 6 to this discussion.

Surely porn spams, solicitations from shady merchants, and other junk e-mails can quickly overflow your mailbox and bury you in messages that you'd rather not read. Another issue arises, however. If your children have accounts outside of AOL, you may worry that some of these inappropriate messages will hit home, so you'd like to block them. No system is

---

2   The term spam originated from a Monty Python routine, and the proper noun is really a trademark of the Hormel Corporation for its food product. There are probably better terms that are more descriptive, such as unsolicited commercial e-mail, or what my friend Brad Templeton calls SPUME for "system polluting unsolicited mass e-mail." Whatever you call it, you will be guaranteed at some point in your e-mail life to receive a message that you have no interest in getting, didn't ask to get, and don't want to be on subsequent mailings from this company or correspondent.

perfect, and these obnoxious come-ons will continue, no matter what technology you put in place.

If you currently are using AOL and want to move away from that system, then you'll have some work to do to migrate all of your household members, some of whom might not want to move. You'll also have to make changes in the way that your AOL household uses AOL Instant Messaging, and retrain them on the new e-mail and IM software that can handle their existing AOL applications. That may be more than you bargained for when you set up your home network. I'll show you how to do this in a moment when we get to the "Solutions" section.

AOL has another shortcoming that home networkers quickly figure out: Concurrent logins are not allowed. In other words, only one household member can use the "master" household account at a time. I'll mention ways around this in the next section, but this is another reason I recommend families move away from AOL.

If you do want to use something else, choosing an e-mail software product can be a challenge. This is especially true given the numerous warnings about security breaches with Microsoft Outlook and Outlook Express products. (I'll get into some of the specifics of these problems in the next chapter, when we address security and virus protection issues.) In addition to Microsoft and AOL, there are e-mail programs from Netscape (now part of AOL), CompuServe (now part of AOL), Eudora (as of this writing, *not* part of AOL), Opera, and numerous other vendors. Each program handles the basics well, but you may need more than the basics and thus some advice on which one to use. The good news about Internet e-mail protocols is that you can use any of these programs (with the exception of AOL) interchangeably. That means if you get tired of one, you can switch without too many consequences. The bad news is that you have to pick one to use and set it up properly.

E-mail is useful for other tasks, especially when it comes to notifications and reminders about upcoming events. Things have gone to a new level lately, as everything from your car to your coffeepot can send you e-mail reminders about when it needs servicing (or just an oil change or a new supply of grounds). I am not making this up.

Coffee machines aren't the only things sending reminders these days. My e-mail box is filled to overflowing with various automated reminders. I have reminders from My.Subaru.com about when it is time to service my car. My.Yahoo.com reminds me of family birthdays and other significant events. Webpartner.com tells me when my Web site is unreachable to the world. Amazon.com sends me e-mail when my favorite authors have new books, or when they think I might be interested in buying a new CD or video, based on my previous purchase history. Fedex, UPS and most of the package shipping companies can send you reminders when your package is shipped or when it is supposed to arrive, including the tracking number in the e-mail message for easy reference. Tracerlock (at http://www. tracerlock.com) sends me e-mails whenever my name (or whatever other keywords I specify) is mentioned somewhere out on the Web, which still amazes me!

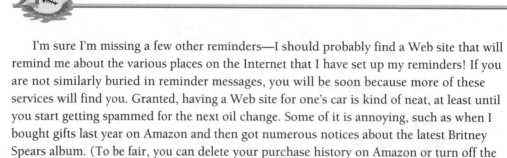

I'm sure I'm missing a few other reminders—I should probably find a Web site that will remind me about the various places on the Internet that I have set up my reminders! If you are not similarly buried in reminder messages, you will be soon because more of these services will find you. Granted, having a Web site for one's car is kind of neat, at least until you start getting spammed for the next oil change. Some of it is annoying, such as when I bought gifts last year on Amazon and then got numerous notices about the latest Britney Spears album. (To be fair, you can delete your purchase history on Amazon or turn off the reminders, but who has the time?)

In the past few years we have also seen the growth of e-mail list service providers. As more people use e-mail, a greater need arises to manage groups of these addresses. Everyone from the local church choir to the soccer team to the extended family planning their next reunion has a mailing list these days.

Becoming your own mailing-list publisher sounds easier than it is. Apart from figuring out which service provider to use, you have to learn a whole new language and etiquette in terms of what and how you send messages to your list. You also have to learn how you maintain your lists as your members switch to new e-mail identities often and without notice.

Speaking of mailing lists, keeping track of your own subscriptions to lists that you are interested in is another challenge. What happens when it is time to change addresses, or if you want to unsubscribe from a list that you long ago signed up for and for which you have since lost the unsubscribe instructions?

Finally, consider the issue of e-mail privacy. There are two dimensions to the privacy issue: the first is protecting and controlling who has access to your e-mail address. You may not want everyone in the world to know your e-mail address, but it is hard to find the equivalent of an unlisted phone number in the world of e-mail. As the Internet e-mail directories get better at discovering your address, you won't be able to hide for much longer. The second dimension is ensuring that your communications remain private and are sent to the intended correspondents, either through authentication services or encrypted e-mails or both. You'll see what you can do about these in the next section.

Solutions

Here is our plan of attack for getting through various e-mail pitfalls and problems. While this seems like a long list, you don't need to work on every point right now. Come back to this section when you have a specific problem.

1. Select the right e-mail product and set it up properly.

2. Run multiple accounts on a single PC.

3. Handle AOL issues, including multiple concurrent logins, migration off AOL, and setting up AOL IM.

4. Manage mailing lists, both from a participant and from a list-publisher perspective.

5. Deal with spam and filter your messages.

6. Encrypt and protect your conversations.

Selecting the Right E-Mail Product

You can use and be perfectly content with numerous e-mail programs for little to no additional money. Most of them are either already installed on your computer or are only a quick download away (especially now that you have a working high-speed Internet connection for your network). Which is the best one for your needs?

The main choices are programs from Microsoft, Eudora, Netscape, and others. They are equally capable, in either their Windows or Macintosh versions. If you don't like using Microsoft products, aren't happy with the AOLization of Netscape, and don't like Eudora, then consider some of the freebie e-mail clients. I prefer Microsoft, Eudora, and Netscape.

Microsoft has two e-mail programs: one is included with Internet Explorer (and hence in every copy of Windows) and is called Outlook Express, and one, called Outlook, is included with many versions of Office. The former is designed just for Internet-based e-mail, while the latter can work with both Internet e-mail and Microsoft Exchange servers. I use both and like them for different reasons.

Outlook comes with its own address book that is the source of potential virus infections, but it is a solid piece of programming. It has its own calendar program, so you can remind yourself of meetings and such. If you have thousands of contacts to manage, then it makes sense to use Outlook for your e-mail needs. Outlook also has a better system to block junk e-mails, but isn't good when it comes to managing multiple inboxes and mail identities. If you have a laptop that you take between home and work and that is for your exclusive use, I would recommend Outlook. If you have to share a computer among several household members, all of who have their own e-mail identity, then read on.

Outlook Express does shine when it comes to managing multiple identities. It is the program that Microsoft recommends for reading newsgroups,[3] and while the address book isn't as capable as Outlook, it can do an okay job for a few hundred or so contacts. It doesn't do as good a job as Outlook at blocking junk e-mails. If you plan to use Outlook Express, make sure that the version included with your computer is the latest version that is available from Microsoft's Web site. Chances are it is not, and you might have to either uninstall it

---

3   Newsgroups are usually unmoderated discussions that have been popular in the past among many in the technical community. There are close to 100,000 different subjects, ranging from sports to computing to fans of just about every major actor and celebrity. They are somewhat raucous and raw but never dull. If you haven't seen them before, it is worth taking a look. You'll need to find out from your Internet provider how to connect to their news server, however.

completely, or update it with one or more patches to fix some security problems. See http://www.microsoft.com/windows/oe/ for the Windows version and http://www.microsoft.com/mac/products/oe/ for the Mac version.

If you don't want to run either Outlook because of virus issues, I suggest you look at Eudora, which is also available in Windows and Mac versions. Eudora used to be my favorite e-mail software before I went over to the Microsoft side. It has the best power tools for doing all sorts of message management and an active community of supporters. You can use one of three versions:

- ✦ **Sponsored mode** Eudora displays banner ads. After a trial period, Eudora will ask you to profile yourself to continue to use the full free Eudora.

- ✦ **Paid mode** Eudora does not display ads, and you get the full power of Eudora, but you do have to pay for the software.

- ✦ **Light mode** Eudora has many fewer features, but is free of charge and without ads.

Most of us will probably be content with running Eudora in light mode, because we won't miss the extra features and the price is right. However, if you plan on supporting multiple users from one machine, you'll either have to pony up the cash for the paid mode, or else deal with the banner ads in sponsored mode, because the light version doesn't support more than a single user account per machine. Still, it is worth checking out Eudora.com's Web site and getting more details before you decide which version to use. You'll need to download the same file no matter which version you end up using. When you install it, Eudora asks you which mode to operate in and will set itself up accordingly. Mac users will need OS 8.1 or better to run it.

If this is too confusing, or if you already use Netscape's Web browser because of an anti-Microsoft bias or because you just like it better, try Netscape's Communicator software for your e-mail needs. It is also available for both Windows and Macintosh platforms. Note that this differs from Netscape's Navigator product: Communicator includes the browser software along with the bits and pieces you'll need to run your e-mail life. If you have already downloaded Navigator, you will need to uninstall it and then download Communicator if you want the e-mail software. Mac users will need at least OS 8.6. Netscape Communicator comes with the AOL IM client software as well, which is probably something you will want to use no matter which e-mail software you end up with. This is because just about everyone that your kids communicate with will be using AOL and AOL IM.

No matter which product you end up using, you will need to do the following basic tasks. First, you want to be able to set up your mail accounts for both sending and receiving e-mail. Second, you want to understand how to save and find your attachments.

Much more can be said about using e-mail than I can cover here. Indeed, you might think that you should go out and get another book on the subject. I have just the book for you:

Internet Messaging: From the Desktop to the Enterprise, which I co-authored with Marshall T. Rose (Prentice Hall, 1998). Marshall is one of the inventors of the Internet e-mail protocols. Our book is filled with the kind of practical information that you'll need to become an e-mail expert, written in the same witty and breezy style and full of authoritative and useful advice such as you have come to expect from reading this one. You can also check out a sample chapter or two on my Web site at http://strom.com/email, if you need more convincing.

Set Up Your E-Mail Accounts

Every e-mail client requires four basic pieces of information. Of course, how you specify each piece of information varies depending on the version of software you are using and whether you are running on a Windows or Mac, so I will try to be as generic as possible. All of the current versions do a moderately good job of walking through the account setup process. Once you collect this information, you should be able to type it in and start sending and receiving messages within a few minutes of installing the software.

The items are

✦ Your actual name that you intend to have displayed on all of your messages.

✦ The e-mail address, like "david@strom.com," that will be used for people to reply to your messages and that is the address given to you by your Internet provider.

✦ The password that was supplied by your provider for this address.

✦ The name of the two mail servers that you will use to send (sometimes called SMTP server) and receive (sometimes called POP or IMAP server) messages. With some providers, this is the same name. With others, it differs. See the "Troubleshooting" section for more details about the names of the sending server and special situations about sending e-mail.

That's it. If you have these four things, you should be able to set up your account. Note that you will need these four things for each account, such as different accounts for yourself and members of the household. Some providers, like my cable company, allow you up to five e-mail accounts on the same master account. You must set them up yourself, using an obscure series of Web screens. One of the nice things about most cable Internet providers is that if you get stuck at this point, you can always call their 24-hour help line, and someone will help you through the process.

Dealing with Attachments

Perhaps the biggest problem for e-mail users, once they get everything working properly, is figuring out how to handle attachments. One of the more useful things you can do with e-mail messages is to send files worldwide. The trouble is, once the file actually enters your computer, it becomes very difficult to track down and bring up on your screen with the right application to open the file. The easiest way to do this is to look for the little paper clip icon that indicates an attachment is attached to your message. Most of the e-mail products use this icon. (AOL indicates attachments with an envelope icon.) Generally you can either open the message, right-click on the icon itself, or use the File | Save Attachments command and put that darn file someplace where you'll be able to find it again.

Outlook Express has the annoying habit of burying the file deep within a series of nested folders, all with hard-to-remember names. I recommend clicking on the My Documents icon. (Alternatively, you can browse your file system until you find the folder name, as shown in the illustration below.) Store the attachment in that folder, so you can find it again. The illustration shows where the My Documents folder happens to live in one of my Windows 2000 systems, to give you an idea that it isn't always easy to find.

With Eudora and Netscape Communicator, you open the message, right-click on the attached file icon, and then save it to an appropriate folder on your hard disk.

Running Multiple Accounts on a Single PC

If you absolutely require multiple mailboxes per PC in your home—meaning that you have more people than computers—then my strong recommendation for you will save you the trouble of reading the remainder of this section. Install Microsoft Outlook Express; you'll be happier for it. Outlook Express has the best support of multiple mailboxes of any of the major software programs I discuss here. You can password protect each profile and include multiple e-mail addresses in each profile, so you can pretty much make it do what you want and keep each household member's e-mail safe from prying hands and eyes. It works the same way on Windows and Macs. You go to File | Identities | Manage Identities and create a new identity for each household member, with your screen looking like that in Figure 5-1.

Notice that you are presented with a list of the various identities and also a default identity to bring up whenever you start the Outlook Express program. After you name your identity, you are next asked whether to specify a password each time you use this. I'd recommend that all adults use a password, to prevent household conflicts and mistakes

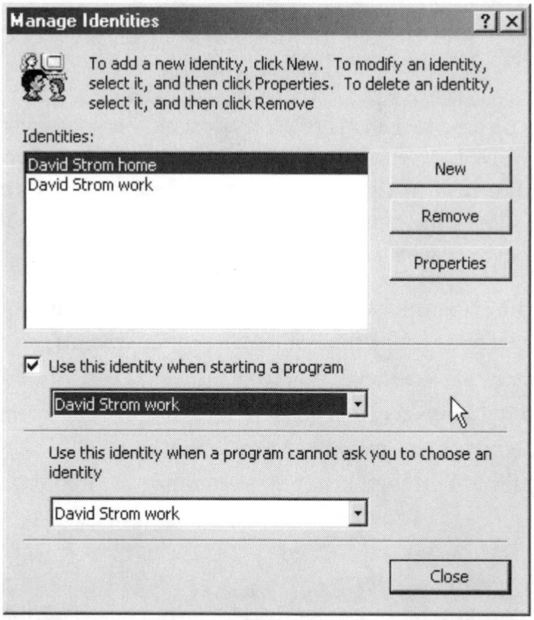

Manage Identities

To add a new identity, click New. To modify an identity, select it, and then click Properties. To delete an identity, select it, and then click Remove

Identities:

David Strom home
David Strom work

New

Remove

Properties

☑ Use this identity when starting a program

David Strom work

Use this identity when a program cannot ask you to choose an identity

David Strom work

Close

Figure 5-1.   Managing identities in Outlook Express

down the road. Note that this password can be distinct from your e-mail server password or any other password: it is unique to Microsoft's Identity Manager. Once you set up the identity, you then add one or more of your e-mail accounts to it.

If you do choose to use passwords to protect your e-mail account, remember to leave Outlook Express by going to the Manage Identities menu option and clicking the Log Off Identity button. If you just exit the program without doing this and don't power-off your PC or log off Windows, anyone can bring up Outlook Express and gain access to your e-mail.

Outlook doesn't offer this feature; only Outlook Express does, and only more recent versions of Outlook Express for that matter. How do you know if your PC has the more recent version? Easy: if you bring up the File menu, and you don't see the Identity menus, then you know you have too old a version. Sorry, but you'll have to go to Microsoft's Web site and download the latest and greatest. Since you have to download something, you might as well download the latest and greatest version of Internet Explorer, which usually includes Outlook Express as part of the package. Now are you beginning to see how Microsoft works its way into our lives?

I am not recommending Outlook Express because it is from Microsoft. Indeed, Microsoft also sells (or gives away) another program called MSN Explorer, and it is a dog of a program.

CAUTION

MSN Explorer can be used to manage multiple accounts. I don't recommend using it, unless you are wedded to using MSN as your main Web portal and Hotmail as your main e-mail system. It is big and bloated and will mess up some things on your computer that are already working. Given a few more years of development, Microsoft might have a workable piece of software here, but from what I have seen so far, I would steer clear of it.

If managing multiple accounts isn't important to you, or if you are opposed to running any Microsoft software in your home for political or other reasons, an alternative is Netscape Communicator. Netscape calls its identities "user profiles," and you use a separate piece of software, called the Profile Manager, to switch among them. Note that for this software to work, you first have to exit all Netscape browser, e-mail, Instant Messenger, and any other windows you have running. You then bring up the manager, and your screen should look like this:

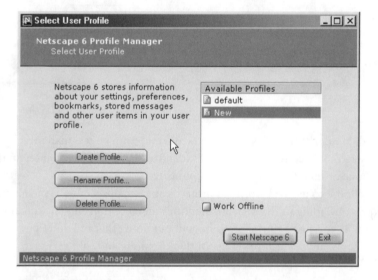

You next click on the Create Profile button and walk through the screens to set up a new profile. Then you save the information, come back to the manager to switch to the right profile, bring up Netscape's browser, click on the little envelope icon at the bottom-left portion of the screen, and add one or more e-mail accounts to your profile. Does this sound like a lot more work than with Outlook Express? Now you know the reason behind my preference.

I used to like Netscape's Communicator program back when the company was a scrappy little Silicon Valley startup that had yet to be tainted by fantastic stock options and huge corporate buyouts from AOL. Um, anyway, Netscape 6 is big, bloated, and difficult to deal with, and I think you'll find that managing multiple personalities—or profiles—isn't as easy as with Outlook Express. Plus, you can't password protect these profiles, so that may be an issue for you. This means that your household members can gain access to your e-mail accounts or at least view the messages you have in your Inbox and saved folders. While it is nice to be able to trust our children, I don't trust them that much that I would give them carte blanche access to my e-mail account.

Another choice is using Eudora, in either sponsored or paid mode. As I mentioned earlier, the light version of Eudora doesn't support multiple e-mail accounts on the same machine, so you'll either have to pay for the software, or deal with the pop-up ads in sponsored mode. To set this up, go to Tools | Personalities, right-click anywhere inside the Personalities window on the left pane, and choose New to create what Eudora calls a "personality," which is the configuration of one e-mail account.

SURVIVAL TIP

You can have only a single e-mail address per personality, and you can't protect each personality with a password. This is the least capable of the three products when it comes to multiple accounts. However, if you want to use Eudora, follow the wizard and provide the e-mail server names and your name in the appropriate places. When you want to switch personalities, you can go to Tool | Personalities and switch to the appropriate account by clicking on that entry.

If you are not happy with these programs, I can suggest elsewhere for you to look for e-mail programs that are specifically designed to handle multiple personalities, or identities, or profiles, or whatever you want to call them. The first place to look is if you are already a customer of Earthlink's service. Earthlink sells a version of software (starting with version 5.0) that comes with a very capable personality management feature. It is designed to be used by families and to share PCs, and its profiles can be password protected, too. However, it is only available to Earthlink subscribers.

If you want to replace your Web browser from Microsoft or Netscape with Opera, you can use its support for multiple e-mail accounts. It doesn't protect them with passwords, however, so that may be an issue for you. While I wouldn't replace your browser just for this feature, if you'd like to try an alternative to the Microsoft/Netscape/AOL hegemony, it is a worthy alternate. You can download the software from http://www.opera.com.

Finally, a $25 program from Pocomail.com that also handles multiple Internet e-mail accounts is available; it is a good alternative to the Microsoft/Netscape/Eudora trio.

AOL Issues

If you are an AOL household, meaning that more than one person in your home has an AOL screen name, then you will quickly find out one of the biggest limitations when you get a home network connected to the Internet is that it is first come, only served. Whoever logs onto AOL first is the only person that can use the service. Everyone else who is party to the same master account can't get connected.

When you were back in the dinosaur dial-up era, this usually wasn't a problem, because you probably didn't have more than one phone line in your home that had a modem, anyway. However, once you have all of your computers connected together, and connected to the Internet, this becomes a big issue.

One of the useful things that AOL implemented with its service is the "bring your own connection" feature. Rather than having to deal with busy signals trying to connect to its dial-up network of modems around the country, you have an alternative. If you have a continuous Internet connection care of your cable or phone company, you can set up the AOL software to use that connection to connect to its services. It is cheaper[4] and faster, and you don't have to listen to all those beeps and grunts as your modems do their dance.

If you are running version 6 or later of the AOL software, "bringing your own connection" is relatively easy: you bring up Setup, specify TCP/IP connection, and you are done. If you are running older versions of the software, you might have to go through a few screens to change your connection profile. You might want to remove the dial-up profile if you are confident that your cable or DSL connection will be stable and if you don't want your kids to be using the modem and tying up your phone line. Or you might want to keep the old profile if you want the security of having a backup in case your high-speed Internet connection goes south.

What can you do about the concurrent user limitation? You have several choices. First, you can migrate some or all of your household members off of AOL software and use the e-mail addresses that are supplied by your cable company or Internet provider or even a free e-mail service like Yahoo or Hotmail.

I found migrating my family took about nine months of intermittent nagging. What finally brought my wife around to my point of view was the ability to get continuous (or nearly so) e-mail delivery, without any intervention on her part. She went from being a die-hard AOL user to having four different e-mail accounts for various purposes in a matter of a few weeks. (As I mentioned earlier in this chapter, she now gets her e-mails on her pager as well.) This is an important but subtle distinction: with an AOL dial-up account, you have to check it

---

4   Provided you don't require the dial-up access to AOL's network, such as when you are traveling or
     not at home. Then you are charged for access by the hour, which can add up.

periodically to see if "You've Got Mail." Once you have a broadband connection, you can check for new messages every minute, if you are that eager for your messages.[5]

Leaving AOL e-mail behind also gives you much better control over your mailbox and message management, and I'll get to that in a moment. The one downside is that your children are now exposed to the world's spammers. AOL does offer a useful feature to protect children from receiving attachments or from getting e-mail from strangers. These features are not really available in any of the alternative e-mail products, and if you have younger children, you may feel more comfortable sticking with AOL until your kids get to the point where they know everything.

Second, you can replace the AOL software with the AOL IM software. If your kids will be doing a lot of IMing anyway, they might be just as happy, and there is little difference between the current version of the IM client and the overall AOL client program anyway. You can download either Windows or Mac IM versions at http://www.aol.com/aim.

Third, you can use the AOL Web client to read and respond to your messages. Go to www.aol.com and log in with your screen name and password, and you will see your mailbox. It isn't as pretty as the Windows or Mac clients, but it works and gets around the one-person limitation. Finally, if you are feeling like you need to give AOL more of your money, you could set up a second or third or whatever master account. I wouldn't recommend this, but for some of you that may be the only possibility.

SURVIVAL TIP

If you run the AOL IM client, it does not limit the number of people using IM over your network. I have seen multi-PC families where everyone is IMing each other late into the evening. Hey, you've got to take your family conversation wherever you can find it, and it beats everyone staring at the TV, right?

If you do plan on migrating your household from the full AOL software to AOL IM, make sure first that you are running version 6 or later of the software. This is because with version 6, AOL has done something helpful. All of your "buddies"—the screen names of the people you and your kids communicate with—are automatically saved to that big AOL server in the sky (actually, I think it is in Virginia) when you run version 6. That means that you don't have anything else to do when you install the AOL IM software. Your kids will thank you, especially because it took them a long time to type in all 300 or so buddies on their lists.

---

5   Technically, AOL can check continuously over a broadband connection, so it actually has a slight advantage over pure Internet email solutions. When using its dial-up network, AOL will automatically disconnect you if you have been inactive for a period of time.

If you are running an older version of the AOL software, you'll need to either upgrade to version 6, or save the buddy list as a file on your hard disk and then import this file into your AOL IM software. (To upgrade, either download the software from their Web site, or wait a few days until the AOL CD you request comes in the mail.) If you do the upgrade, AOL has the annoying habit of not cleaning up after itself, so you might want to delete the "America Online 4.0" or whatever the older directory folder is called. Not to worry: The version 6 upgrade copied your saved messages and settings to its new directory structure.

Managing Mailing-List Subscriptions

Mailing lists have become popular for all sorts of reasons: You might want to subscribe to the airlines list that tells you about upcoming special fares. You may want to subscribe to the mailing list about new Broadway musicals or the schedule of sports events of your local team or a hundred other things. Once you get your Internet connection and start looking around, you'll find lots of mailing lists that you can join.

A mailing list is nothing more than a group of e-mail addresses. E-mail sent to the mailing list name gets "exploded," or copied to every member on the list. Several kinds of mailing lists are used. One type is the kind that any of you use as part of your desktop e-mail software. Typically, these lists are found in an address book. The address book contains information on your correspondents, such as their actual name and e-mail address, and perhaps other information including postal addresses and phone numbers. Most e-mail software has similar techniques for creating lists: You go into their address books, create a new list name, and add members to the list. When you want to send mail to a group, you first create the group, and then click on the group name in your address book or type it into the mail program. That's not too difficult, is it?

This is just the tip of the mailing-list iceberg. There are plenty of other mailing lists besides the ones that you maintain in your e-mail program. Some mailing-list programs operate on special e-mail servers: These run without any human intervention. You send e-mail to a special address, called the *listserv* address (named after a popular piece of software that is used for this purpose), which subscribes you to (or removes you from) the mailing list. Of course, this includes the exact instructions for these commands and where they are placed in your e-mail message, depending on the listserv software being used.[6] If your e-mail isn't formatted correctly, the listserv can't process your instructions, and it sends back an e-mail with a sometimes-cryptic error report.

---

6   For example, some listservs require the subscribe command to appear by itself in the Subject:. Others
     require that the word subscribe be followed by the actual e-mail address and separated by spaces.
     Others require the word "subscribe" to appear on the first line of the message body. Some use another
     command word, such as join instead of subscribe. And these commands are supposed to be sent to
     the listserv processor address, rather than to a separate address that is used as the actual broadcast
     address for the group. This makes for annoying situations when users trying to join the list mistakenly
     send their e-mail containing the sign-up commands as broadcast messages to the entire list.

As I said, computers maintain listservs. This makes it easy for you to forget about them when you change your e-mail address. The trouble begins when the listserv attempts to deliver mail to your old address. Eventually a carbon-based life-form must manually intervene and remove your old and no longer functioning e-mail address from the listserv.

There are mailing-list service providers, some of whom offer their services for free or nearly so, as long as you don't mind that they will append a small advertisement or other promotion to every e-mail that you send through their services. I can write an entire book on mailing-list procedures and suggestions (and part of my first *Internet Messaging* book is devoted to this subject), but let me give you a few pointers if you are interested in joining a few lists or in running your own lists.

First, set up a special folder on your computer where you can store the subscription messages for those lists that you subscribe to. You'll find that they contain all sorts of information that isn't important to you now, but it will become extremely important once you want to remove yourself from the list. This folder can serve as an easy reference to which lists you have subscribed and how to get off a list when you tire of deleting unread e-mails, day after day.

Second, make sure you understand what your subscription will entail. Some lists are very chatty, sending tens or hundreds of messages a day. Others are more parsimonious, and you'll be lucky to get one message a week. If you don't like having your inbox filled to overflowing with the list chatter, then look into subscribing in what is called "digest" form. This typically bunches 10, 20, or more messages and sends the accumulated wisdom out in one single, long message. Sometimes you don't necessarily know what is involved, although with some lists you can check their archives and quickly see what the expected message traffic will be.

Also, if you are planning on going on vacation or being away from your e-mail for a long time, you might want to consider unsubscribing or putting your subscription on vacation hold. Depending on the listserv you are using, this may be easy or hard to do.

Finally, make sure you understand what you are trying to accomplish. You want to make sure that you are using the listserv address and not the administrative address. The same goes when you want to send a removal or digest command—make sure you don't send this to the entire list when you are just trying to deal with your own subscription. (Believe me, this happens every day, and it used to be a big badge of shame to carry. You'll get over it quickly, and so will the members of your list.)

Publishing Your Own Mailing Lists

You may want to start your own mailing lists, whether to send a group greeting to family for the holidays or for organizing your local Boy Scout troop or other community happenings. Suddenly, you are now your own publisher.

The trouble comes when you aren't aware that a member's address has changed. I've found that about one or two percent of my mailing list changes every week. That doesn't sound like much, but it takes time to track down new addresses and make the changes. If you are considering starting your own list, you have plenty of choices when it comes to finding a provider who is willing to host your mailing list. Depending on the size of the list, whether you want to support one-way or two-way communication among your members, and numerous other features, you probably have several dozen vendors who range from completely free to charging you several hundred dollars a month for their services.

It's great having all these choices, but with choice comes confusion. Let me try to clarify the options. To give you an idea of where I am coming from, I have used a number of mailing-list technologies. As I mentioned in the Preface, I began my own series of self-published essays back in the fall of 1995 and still send them out under the rubric of Web Informant.

◆ The first 43 or so issues were sent out with custom perl scripts using UNIX sendmail, sending out HTML-encoded messages. (Boy, was I ahead of my time.)

◆ I used Intermind's Communicator push client software to send the next 20 or so issues, in parallel with those who wanted to continue to receive plain e-mail.

◆ I experimented with PointCast's software in fall 1996 and tried that for a few years, still in parallel with my perl/sendmail system.

◆ In June 1997, I replaced sendmail with a series of Allaire's Cold Fusion scripts combined with a list maintained in a Lotus Approach database. It sounds odd, but it was a good system, given the technologies at the time.

◆ Around the publication of issue #90 in the fall of 1997, I switched over to Revnet's Groupmaster service, which was one of the first mailing service providers.

◆ Most recently, I began using the eGroups service in May 1999 with issue #156. When Yahoo purchased eGroups, I became unhappy with their service and switched to a mailing-list server running EZMLM under UNIX. I have come full circle, so to speak.

You probably don't want to be switching from one provider or technology to another, so carefully consider the choices. There are two Web sites that I recommend you take a look at: http://list-business.com/list-service-providers/ and http://www.gweep.bc.ca/~edmonds/usenet/ml-providers.html. Both sources give lots of information about the various providers, including pricing and the underlying technologies used.

Two of the more popular mailing-list programs that are used by providers are Lyris and L-Soft's Listserv. Both have been around long enough to be well tested and well developed.

Both come from the command-line UNIX world, but have Web interfaces to help you configure them. To get a feel for the Web interface of Lyris, you can go to this page at Dundee.net (http://www.dundee.net/isp/p-list.htm), one of the providers using this software. There you can see the various parameters you'll need to specify to set up your list.

NOTE What do I recommend for mailing lists? I continue to use Yahoo Groups (http://groups.yahoo.com) for noncommercial purposes, such as to support nonprofit organizations or social clubs.

Within minutes of setting up your account on Yahoo Groups, you can have your mailing-list set up and working, sending messages to several dozen of your closest friends and family. Of their competitors in the free mailing-list hosting arena, Yahoo offers the best interface, tools, and controls for your groups. You have all sorts of other features besides mailing lists: you can store common files, share a common group calendar, and poll your list for opinions as well.

Yahoo has an option to pay to remove much of the advertising, but they still tack on their own bit in each message footer. You'll need to establish a Yahoo identity and a Yahoo e-mail address to administer any mailing list on their service.

If you want the best e-mail list processing service and can afford to pay for it, I would choose Listserv and the Ease hosting option at L-Soft (http://www.lsoft.com/products/default.asp?item=ease). If you are cost-conscious and don't mind wading through some Web pages to set things up, the folks at Dundee have a reasonable offering.

I also recommend taking a look at Margaret Levine Young and John Levine's book called *Poor Richard's Building Online Communities* (Top Floor Publishing, 2000). The book is especially useful if you are new to mailing lists and want to know how to set them up, including explanations of some of the more arcane command syntax for Listserv-, Majordomo-, and Listproc-based lists. The book goes into detail about other community-building tools, including newsgroups, IRC, and the legal issues over running your own mailing lists.

Dealing with Spam

Spam is a fact of life for all of us who use e-mail. I wish it weren't so, but that's for another universe and in another dimension. If you use your e-mail address on the Internet, you will attract spammers. If you use your real e-mail address as the owner of an Internet domain, you'll get spam. If your name is on a publicly accessible mailing list, you will get spam. If you have a Hotmail or Yahoo account, you will get spam. I have even gotten spam on new e-mail accounts that I set up and then never used to send any e-mail, just to see how long it would take before I got spam: a matter of a few weeks! How do these guys find you? You've got me.

**SURVIVAL
TIP**

I recommend that you never place your e-mail address on any Web page. Several programs can search through your Web site and collect e-mail addresses. Of course, this may not be very practical for you to implement, particularly if you want people to contact you for business reasons.

One anti-spam tactic is to set up a filter to delete any messages that come from typical spam addresses, such as hotmail.com. This could also delete messages from legitimate correspondents on these domains, however. If you are using Microsoft Outlook, you can right-click on any message and identify it as a Junk E-mail; then all messages from that address will go straight to your trashcan. You can do something similar with Eudora and Netscape, but it isn't as straightforward. You would have to create a filter, matching the address of the sender, and choose to send the message directly to the Trash. You set this up in Communicator by choosing Edit | Message Filters | New, as shown in the illustration.

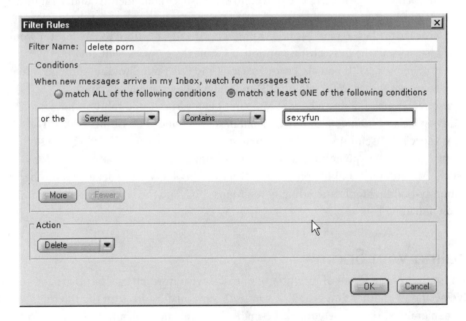

Several Web sites will put you on lists to avoid spam. I have tried these lists, but not every spammer will check first to see if you have opted out of mass mailings. You can find a list of these sites at Yahoo, under "Junk E-mail Registration Services." Some of these sites carry rather interesting domain names, such as nothankyou.com and junkmail.com. I'm not sure that listing your e-mail address there will do anything, but if you have some spare time, it might be worth trying.[7]

Spam *is* aggravating. None of us likes to have our mailboxes polluted with these messages, and frustration can certainly mount. However, you need to keep cool and not go nuts trying to fight spam. Scott Hazen Mueller has several good suggestions on what *not* to do when fighting spam:

> *Don't threaten violence or vandalism; don't mailbomb the site; don't mailbomb the alleged spammer, who may be an innocent third party such as myself (due to spoofing one's e-mail address); don't ping-storm or SYN-flood the site; don't hack into the site; don't try in any way to bring the site down illegally. And, above all else, don't use spam to fight spam. This also applies in Usenet— don't follow up to spam postings, lest your posting also become spam.* (From spam.abuse.net/spam/dontdo.html)

Finally, if you are really concerned about fighting spam, then I suggest you take a look at the paper prepared by Dave Crocker and Paul Hoffman(http://www.imc.org/ube-sol.html), two e-mail professionals. I know there are no perfect solutions. I recommend judicious use of your DEL key and plenty of patience.

Encrypting and Protecting Your Conversations

My last series of suggestions has to do with protecting your e-mail conversations by using various electronic mechanisms. Truly, all of us should do this, even if we are simply sending birthday greetings to Aunt Sadie on the other side of the country. Encrypting your messages means that no one, other than you and your recipient, can read the message, particularly as it travels around the Internet from server to server. What, you didn't know that your messages were open to such inspection? They are. Think of all your e-mails as sending postcards and giving them to your nosiest neighbor to take down to the post office to mail for you. That is about the level of security that your correspondence has these days.

E-mail is wide open because of the protocols that were used to create the overall Internet messaging system. In other words, it is a feature, not a bug. If someone were to target your e-mail server, they could quite easily read all of your correspondence.

---

7   For more helpful hints about how to deal with spam mail, see Paul Hoffman and Dave Crocker's paper called "Unsolicited Bulk Email: Mechanisms for Control" at www.imc.org/ube-sol.html. This suggestion for removing your e-mail address from your Web pages is just to avoid any personal spam: You still want to have some e-mail address on your Web pages for your customers to contact you.

There are two methods to secure your messaging life. First, attach a special digital signature that proves you are you, and not someone else who is pretending to be you. One of the problems with Internet messages is that anyone can pretend to be you: all they have to do is change that one parameter in their e-mail program from their address to yours. That's all it takes.

You may not think that anyone would want to do it, but I can tell you one horror story from my own experience. Shortly after I set up my Yahoo Groups mailing list of Web Informant, my list got sent a bogus e-mail from someone pretending to be me. I hadn't set all of the security parameters properly and left a door open such that anyone using "david@strom.com" as their e-mail address could send messages to my mailing list. Someone did. And it took them about a minute to reconfigure their e-mail client.

Authentication isn't enough, however. You also will want to scramble your messages, so that no one else can unscramble them without the right key. This is called *encryption*.

Doing both authentication and encryption is not fun. The tools are terrible, they don't always work as intended, and they require a great deal of skill to set up.

I recommend that you begin by using a product called PC-Encrypt (available at http://www.pc-encrypt.com) to scramble your files. It's a simple product that pairs of correspondents can use without a lot of trouble and with minimal cost. If you are looking for something more capable, or something that is used more in the corporate world, then I would next consider the free version of Pretty Good Privacy (PGP), which can be found at http://www.pgp.com and http://www.pgpi.org for the international versions.

If you want some motivational reading to convince you that this is a serious issue and you should attempt to start doing this, look at some of the essays written by my friend Fred Avolio (http://www.avolio.com/columns) on his Web site.

Troubleshooting

As I have said several times throughout this chapter, there are numerous troubleshooting situations. Here are tips for solving some basic problems.

Can't Connect to Your Mail Server

Before you try to do anything, make sure that the four pieces of information you have specified for your e-mail account are correct. Maybe you copied down the password incorrectly or have made some other typo in your e-mail server names. It can happen. Check to see if you are the only one with a problem or if all household members are having trouble connecting to the same e-mail server. The former situation means something is wrong with your computer's configuration, while the latter means a more systemic problem. You should bring up your Web browser and check to make sure that you can access any random Web site. Your Internet service could be down, or your network could be having problems.

To see if your mail server is still working, bring up a command window and type **ping** *servername*.**com** on the command line, substituting the real name of your mail server for *servername* and leaving a space after the ping command. (Mac users, you'll have to find some software such as WhatRoute that lets you ping a server.) If you get a response showing the number of milliseconds that it takes to communicate with your server, that means two things: First, your Internet connection between your home and your e-mail server is working. Second, your mail server is probably working, so the problem is something at your end.

If you get no response from the pings, then either your mail server is down, or your Internet connection is down, or both. Try pinging another Internet site, say, Yahoo.com, and see if you get a response. If you do, then something is wrong with your mail server, and you can't do anything about it. You can try to connect in a few minutes, or call your provider and see what is going on with them.

To make sure your own network is operating properly, bring up a Web browser and see if you can connect to your frhub's configuration screens, using the IP address that you specified for the frhub in the last chapter. If you forget this address, bring up a command window, and type **IPCONFIG** to see the Gateway address listed, which is the address of your frhub. You should see on the frhub's status screen a listed IP address for the Wide Area Network (WAN) connection: that indicates that the frhub was able to communicate with your cable or DSL modem and obtain a proper address. You could also ping that IP address to make sure that you have a working network between you and the frhub.

True, you might find that a cable is chewed or that someone messed up your basic network setup. What if these aren't the problems? Let's dig deeper.

Can Receive but Can't Send Messages

One of the more curious situations is when you have messages queued up to be sent to your correspondents and the messages are stuck in that queue, not going beyond your hard disk. You can still receive messages from your server just fine, but these awaiting messages are going nowhere fast. Why does this happen?

There are two reasons. The first is that something in your configuration was changed, if your messages were being sent just fine previous to this situation. Chances are you did the changing, so check your configuration of your account, and see if other household accounts are having this problem. However, perhaps your provider either has blocked you from sending messages or made configuration changes on their end and hasn't yet told you about them. (Shame on them, but it does happen.)

Some Internet providers put blocks on their networks to deter spammers from using their mail servers to send out spam. While the details of this are beyond the scope of this book, basically you can't use any other mail server to send your messages with these providers. Earthlink is one example: If you use Earthlink's network to connect to the Internet, then you must use only Earthlink's mail servers to send your mail. Any other SMTP server will be blocked from sending messages on their network.

Coping with Error Messages

The biggest challenge you'll have troubleshooting is when you get an e-mail "bounce" or error message and try to figure out what you did wrong and how to fix it. You don't always know why something is wrong with the message you sent. You need to be able to match the error message and the recipient name with the suspected e-mail that contains the incorrect information. Then you need to find that name and either delete the now-defunct recipient or figure out why his or her address is no longer valid. Did you make a typo? Did this person change jobs or job locations? Did this person decide to switch Internet providers and e-mail identities? It sounds messy, and it is. There really isn't any other way to fix the problem.

Figuring out what error message was generated by which piece of e-mail you sent isn't always easy. There could be days between when you tried to send your message and when you received the error report, or you could get multiple error reports for a single piece of e-mail. I don't have any good advice, other than to tell you to sort your outgoing messages by recipient and to try to match that recipient's domain name with the one from your error report. You could spend more time tracking down the error than you spent composing the original message!

Let's look at some sample error messages I have received and try to decode them. First is a report that is probably one of the more helpful ones I've seen:

```
Subject: Returned mail: Service unavailable
From: Mail Delivery Subsystem <MAILER-DAEMON@pgh.nauticom.net>
The original message was received at Wed, 7 Jan 1998 17:53:14 -0500 (EST)
from [208.215.131.25]
Your e-mail message could not be delivered. Common causes
are listed below:
User Unknown:           The username you entered is not valid on
                        the system you addressed the e-mail to.
                        (ie USER@somehost.com - USER does not exist.)
Host Unknown:           The hostname you entered is not valid or there
                        is a problem with the user's service provider.
                        (ie user@SOMEHOST.COM - SOMEHOST.COM does not
                        exist.)
Disk Quota Exceeded:    The user you entered has used up his/her
                        available disk space for their account on
                        their Internet Service Provider.
Below you will find the error that caused your message not to
be delivered:
    ----- The following addresses had permanent fatal errors -----
<ryhome@viper.nauticom.net>
    ----- Transcript of session follows -----
fclose: Disc quota exceeded
binmail: cannot append to /usr/spool/mail/ryhome
Mail saved in dead.letter
554 <ryhome@viper.nauticom.net>... Service unavailable
Reporting-MTA: dns; pgh.nauticom.net
Received-From-MTA: DNS; [208.215.131.25]
Arrival-Date: Wed, 7 Jan 1998 17:53:14 -0500 (EST)
Final-Recipient: RFC822; ryhome@pgh.nauticom.net
Action: failed
Status: 5.5.0
```

My diagnosis of this situation is a full disk quota. Resend this message in a few hours and see if it gets through.

How about this message:

```
From: Mail Delivery Subsystem <MAILER-DAEMON@ix.netcom.com>
Subject: Returned mail: Mailbox full, Please try later.
Auto-Submitted: auto-generated (failure)
The original message was received at Thu, 22 Jan 1998 06:14:53 -0800 (PST)
from caldera.com [207.179.18.1]
    ----- The following addresses had permanent fatal errors -----
<sparksb@ix.netcom.com>
    ----- Transcript of session follows -----
554 <sparksb@ix.netcom.com>... Mailbox full, Please try later.
```

This seems clearer. Once again, my diagnosis is a full disk quota. This time I don't have to have a medical degree to find it. The error message even tells us to try again later.

Here is another example of a full mailbox, this time from CompuServe:

```
From: CompuServe Postmaster <postmaster@compuserve.com>
Subject: Undeliverable Message: ? EMDNRM - Mail Delivery Failure. No
room in mailbox. 72631,73—Web Informant #96, 18 December 1997 (Truth in
advertising?)
Sender: auto.reply@compuserve.com
```

Again, a very clear statement of the problem, and contained in the Subject line as well, so we don't have to go searching through the message text itself.

Take a look at this message:

```
From: Mail Administrator<Postmaster@magnum.sohonet.com>
Subject: Mail System Error - Returned Mail
This Message was undeliverable due to the following reason:
Each of the following recipients was rejected by a remote mail server.
The reasons given by the server are included to help you determine why
each recipient was rejected.
    Recipient: <Mstrange@fonorola.net>
    Reason:    User unknown
```

This is a relatively easy call. The user name no longer exists at the particular domain name. We need to find out what happened to this user and change his or her address. Diagnosis: Someone has changed his or her address and is no longer home.

Here's another error message:

```
From: Mail Administrator<Postmaster@magnum.sohonet.com>
Subject: Mail System Error - Returned Mail
This Message was undeliverable due to the following reason:
Your message was not delivered because the Domain Name System
(DNS) for the destination computer is not configured correctly.
The following is a list of reasons why this error message could
have been generated. If you do not understand the explanations
listed here, please contact your system administrator for help.
     - The host does not have any mail exchanger (MX) or
       address (A) records in the DNS.
     - The host has valid MX records, but none of the mail
       exchangers listed have valid A records.
     - There was a transient error with the DNS that caused
       one of the above to appear to be true.
You may want to try sending your message again to see if the
problem was only temporary.
     DNS for host sv.tbgi.com is mis-configured
The following recipients did not receive this message:
     <SRBENJ@sv.tbgi.com>
```

This looks like a problem, but it is relatively minor. The most likely cause of the error is the third reason in the list, a "transient error" with the particular domain name server that supports this host. Diagnosis: a random Internet error. Try to resend the message tomorrow.

These are just a few examples of the kinds of errors you might see in your own correspondence. I wish there were better tools to help you figure this stuff out.

Blocking AOL IM Access from Your Network

Before we leave troubleshooting e-mail issues entirely, I'll discuss one other issue. There comes a time in every parent's life when we need more control over our children's computing activities, and nothing is more addicting, more time-consuming, and more troublesome than your kid logged into IM and logged off of his or her homework or dinner or getting chores done. So for those situations where you need to take back control, I offer the following as a way to shut off IM on your home network and to show your kid who is in control, at least for a little while.

You could take the brute-force approach and shut down the computer that she or he is on, or disconnect your home from the Internet entirely. That's a little heavy-handed. A better and more technologically elegant way, and one that will show your children that you know a bit more than they do about computers, is to disable just IM access on your home network and leave everything else running.

I speak from personal experience. My daughter knows that I am far more savvy about computers than she is; still, every once in a while it is good to flex your parental mental muscles. There were and will be times when her use of IM is too much, and she needs to be doing something else. So I threaten to turn it off, and since I have done it in the past, she knows I can do it, listens to me, and logs off. At least for now.

So what do you do? Go to your frhub, find the screen that allows you to control individual ports, and disable any communications from port 5190. As it turns out, that is the port number that AOL IM uses for all its communications. By disconnecting traffic from this port, you don't mess up anything else on your network, and you can easily restore access once the household crisis has passed.

On the Netgear frhubs, you are out of luck and can't do this easily. On the Linksys frhubs, go to Advanced | Filters and under Filtered Private Port Range, choose Both, 5190, and 5190 in the entries, as shown in the following illustration.

Filters enable you to prevent certain PCs on your network from accessing your Internet connection.

FILTERS

Filtered Private IP Range: (0 to 254)

1:	192.168.1.|0	~ |0
2:	192.168.1.|0	~ |0
3:	192.168.1.|0	~ |0
4:	192.168.1.|0	~ |0
5:	192.168.1.|0	~ |0

Filtered Private Port Range: (0 to 65535)

1:	Both	5190	~ 5190
2:	Both	0	~ 0
3:	Both	0	~ 0
4:	Both	0	~ 0
5:	Both	0	~ 0

Make sure you save this configuration (by clicking the Apply button at the bottom of the screen) to disable the IM port. When it is time to turn it back on, delete this entry and save the change again. On the Umax frhubs, go to Access Control and select the Block All Internet Access By Port Number option. Then enter the magic port number of 5190. You can find a similar configuration page in your own frhub device to do this, by looking for "Port Blocking" or "Port Filtering." Your kids will look at you with new respect, believe me.

Futures

E-mail is becoming a critical part of our lives, and we'll see more devices that use Internet e-mail as a key component in their operation. I was only being somewhat tongue-in-cheek when I said that you should expect to receive e-mails from your coffeepot and car. The day isn't so far off when both devices, along with many others, will have some integrated e-mail system in place.

While the future looks bright for e-mail hardware and embedded devices with e-mail capabilities, the future looks dim on the software side. The current versions of Eudora and Netscape Communicator both bear the signs of feature bloat, and Outlook Express is getting somewhat trickier to deal with as newer versions arrive from Microsoft. These three have all but pushed the remaining players off the e-mail landscape, and if they continue to produce more and more bloated software, all of us will suffer.

If you have older versions of Eudora or Communicator available to you, try them before you download the latest and greatest from these vendors' Web sites. I think you'll like them better.

While mailing-list service providers have proliferated, it is still hard to find a service provider that really meets your needs without doing a lot of technology evaluation and careful research. Hopefully, these providers will improve their user interfaces and make their systems more transparent to novice mailing-list publishers over time.

I had high hopes for Yahoo when they purchased eGroups. Since the merger, however, things have gone downhill for Yahoo Groups. The service still is one of the best ones available, but it could be better with a few small improvements and some additional technical support.

The future for encrypted e-mail also looks pretty grim. While a number of smaller vendors have put together some impressive products, few advances in secure e-mail technologies have been made, and the interoperability among various secure e-mail products remains painful and problematic. PGP is still the champion in terms of corporate use, but there really isn't a product that will work simply and for the home user without a great deal of babysitting and care. Hopefully, the next few years will change this.

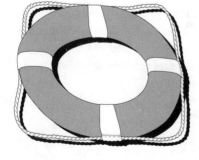

Chapter 6

Securing
Your Network

So far, our discussions have focused on building your network step by step, from the basic wiring and operating systems support for networking to rudimentary applications. If you have been following along and implementing my suggestions, you have a working network, are doing all sorts of fun things on it, and are enjoying the high-speed connection to the Internet. It is time to get a little more serious and start to tighten things up.

If you have ever had a break-in or been robbed, you know how important it is to protect our homes and families. The sense of personal violation is strong, you feel stupid for it having happened, and you vow to strengthen your protective measures and to improve locking down your doors and other entry points.

While it is relatively easy to protect our homes from physical entry, the same isn't true when it comes to protecting our home networks from potential break-ins. It is harder for us to understand the nature of a break-in, to detect such intrusions, and to prevent further attacks. It isn't as if we were to come home one evening and find the computer missing from the den—computer break-ins are far more subtle and involve more complicated situations than the mere removal of our physical property.

Problems

At the heart of the problem of securing your data is a simple fact: Your computer is now connected to the Internet whenever you turn it on, thanks to all of the hard work you did by following my directions thus far. Your always-on connection gives thieves and mischief-makers an opportunity to commit mayhem with your files. Why? A connected computer is a lot harder to protect.

NOTE

The best way to secure your PC is to keep it off any network, and to not hook it up to the Internet or any other communications network.[1] Once your computers are part of the Internet, they can come into contact with other computers run by people who can try to compromise your programs and data.

Some people spend their lives on the Internet trying to damage others' computers. They develop computer programs that poke and prod until they find someone who has left his or her PC defenseless or weak. They develop new programs that can enter your computer via seemingly innocent e-mail attachments. They use other computers, typically at universities and government research labs that have little or no security measures, to try to attack your computers, making their efforts harder to track down and prevent. Even if you do everything in your power to try to

---

1   If you want to take things to extremes, the only truly secure computer is one that is powered off.

stop these people and programs from entering into your system, the people you know and work with every day can still harm you. These people can unknowingly attack your system on behalf of the bad guys by forwarding harmful e-mails and other programs.

This is happening every hour of every day, 365 days a year. It is happening while you sleep and while you get up from your machine to get a cup of coffee.

You may think I exaggerate these threats, but consider that scarcely a week goes by without reports of a new virus being discovered by some hapless user, who inadvertently has spread it to hundreds of his or her closest friends. Reports of various Web site break-ins or of graffiti writing over legitimate pages on the site are almost as frequent. Those are the incidents that we hear about—numerous others happen without any fanfare.

Threats from E-Mail Attachments

There are basically three types of threats that you should be aware of. The first and probably biggest threat is receiving a virus or worm or some other program via an e-mail attachment. Since e-mail has become such a universal communications tool, the threat of virus infection is quite real. I don't know anyone who has escaped being infected by a virus. It has happened to me, and I am very careful about the messages that I open and how I go about my day-to-day business.

For our purposes, we don't have to differentiate among these programs—all of them can harm your system and need to be stopped before they enter your network. All of them destroy parts of your system, some more important and harder to recover than others. The differences are in how they enter our network and how they go about their dirty business.[2]

Sometimes these infected e-mail messages arrive with pretty innocent-sounding subject lines, such as "in reference to your e-mail" or "please check out this homepage." Sometimes they have spiced up the subject lines with promises of lurid porn or making money fast or other come-ons that rarely, if ever, deliver. (Indeed, as I was finishing this chapter I got one of those messages, talking about Snow White. Jeez!)

Sometimes the e-mail messages are from your usual correspondents: they have been infected, and the virus rips through their address books, sending out e-mails to everyone in them. If you aren't a suspicious person, or if you are new to e-mail, then I have to warn you that this sort of thing happens every day. It happened to me, and I sent a virus to a neighbor. This virus clogged up their entire corporate e-mail system so badly that the company had to shut it down before they could clean it out. All because of one message that I sent with the virus attached.

---

2   For a complete discussion about various threats and how to tell their differences, see the Practically Networked page (http://www.practicallynetworked.com/sharing/securitythreats.htm).

The biggest opportunity for virus authors is Microsoft products, which are the products most of us use. The Windows versions of Microsoft Outlook and Outlook Express in particular are extremely easy to use as virus culture media. Think of them as the virtual equivalent of a piece of ripe fruit, attracting all sorts of insect life. These two pieces of software are often the focus of virus authors and can quickly send a copy of some nasty program to friends in your address book. They are also extremely difficult to lock down to prevent virus infections.

Why did I recommend Outlook and Outlook Express in the last chapter? The additional features are worth the risks, but you still need to protect yourself.

Here's why these programs are so risky. Microsoft has designed Outlook/Outlook Express to work effortlessly with a series of programs, in the hopes of making it easier to integrate e-mail with a wide variety of applications. While they have succeeded in this design, they also have succeeded in making it easier for virus authors to integrate their mischief into a wide variety of applications, such as a program automatically e-mailing everyone in my Outlook address book a copy of a virus.

The problems aren't limited to Outlook. Even if you use a Mac or some other e-mail program, you are still at risk. E-mail programs are set up to make it easier for you to use them, and one of the worst things as far as security is concerned is to automatically run programs associated with particular kinds of files.[3]

In the old days, before Windows 95, say, it was harder to use your e-mail system because you had to know the type of program that created a particular file that you received as an e-mail attachment. Now you can click on an attachment, and the operating system will bring up the software it thinks you need to view your file. That is exactly the kind of feature that virus writers play into, and why receiving e-mail attachments is generally not a good idea.

There's no good way to eliminate attachments from our lives. For a few weeks, I set up my copy of Outlook to automatically reject any e-mail messages that contained attachments. That wasn't realistic and vexed some of my correspondents when they received the rejection message. You can set up more complex screening techniques and filters, but many viruses come from people you know and want to communicate with, so these filters don't really help. You can convert all your e-mail over to a host-based system such as Yahoo Mail, which includes virus screening as part of its service, but that isn't practical if you already have another e-mail address that people know you by. Your choice is limited to using an antivirus program that can check your e-mail somewhere in the process and eliminate any problems before they creep into your computer.

---

3   You can break the connection between the type of file and the associated program that will automatically open it, to give you a running start in fighting these types of viruses. However, doing this properly will take lots of work. See Appendix B for more information.

Threats from Microsoft Office Users

E-mail attachments aren't the only security problems. Microsoft Office contains a wide array of small executable programs that go by various names, including macros, templates, and scripts. All of these have been exploited by the bad guys to wreak havoc on unsuspecting users' systems. Also, all of these can easily and sometimes inadvertently be transmitted via e-mail or other Internet communications, including instant messages and Web site visits.

Suppose you are collaborating with someone on a series of presentations, documents, or spreadsheets and are sending them back and forth via e-mail. (Such is the process by which this book was created, for example.) If one of your correspondents has lax security, they could infect your machine with one of these virus files quite easily. Or they could mess up your default settings for your documents to the point where you could spend several hours trying to restore the original settings.

Some nasty people out there create these awful programs. Sometimes people create viruses inadvertently, as a result of a programming project gone wrong that destroys large amounts of data. Either way, you can do nothing about it. We will continue to see their work proliferate on the Internet. As the various means to protect your PCs increase, these people will figure out new ways to circumvent them and new ways to design viruses and worms. That doesn't mean you have to give up hope. You need to get the right set of tools and be better prepared.

The first thing you need to do is obtain an antivirus screening program. Make sure that it is installed and kept up to date on every computer on your home network. I mean each one. You need to do it now. To delay by even a day is to put your household's computers at risk of infection. Some virus screeners are free, while most just cost a few dollars. I'll get into this in the "Solutions" section and give you tips on how to maintain these products, because that is even a bigger commitment than just buying and installing the software.

CAUTION   Virus authors have gotten cleverer as time goes on. In May 2001, I heard about a virus that looks like a message from Symantec. The message tells you about a new virus their research team has discovered. It comes via an e-mail message with the subject line "FW: Symantec Anti-Virus Warning" and claims to contain a description of a nonexistent worm in an attached file named www.symantec.com.vbs. The message, of course, is not from Symantec, and it does contain a virus! As if you didn't have enough to worry about. A list of other hoaxes can be found at Network Associates' Web site: (http://vil.nai.com/VIL/hoaxes.asp).

E-mail-borne viruses are just one means of infection. A second "disease vector" (as epidemiologists would call it) for viruses is via floppy and Zip disks that are moved from computer to computer. If you bring work home from your office on a disk, and then place the disk into your home computer and copy these files, you are at risk on both machines of transferring a virus between your home and work networks.

I have numerous computers in my office, including many that I use only for testing and run infrequently. Over the years I got lazy and didn't install any virus screening programs on some of the test machines. This was mainly because I didn't use them for extended periods or because I just didn't feel like going through all the motions to get the antivirus stuff set up. This was a mistake. One day I found all my boot floppies that I use to create new operating systems were infected with a virus. The virus wasn't particularly destructive (otherwise I would have found it sooner), but it was annoying to have to go through all my floppy disks and clean them. I also had to install the current version of the antivirus software on all of my machines and make sure that all the virus files were deleted from every machine. Just one floppy, one instance where you drop your guard, can be enough to infect your entire home network and potentially your work network.

This is one reason that many businesses have given up on floppy or Zip or other removable disks, although if you have a CD burner at home, it is also possible to inadvertently place a virus on it and then infect other computers. (Microsoft and several other software vendors have had this happen to some of their beta copies of their production software, much to their collective chagrin.)

Have I convinced you yet to install an antivirus scanner? I hope so. Of course, you still need to set it up properly and make sure floppies and Zip disks are scanned upon insertion, otherwise the best scanner in the world won't help you.

Threats from Visiting Web Sites

The antivirus programs can do only so much, because a third means of infection exists. Being connected to the Internet with your computer is enough to get you into trouble. Even if you turn your computer on and do nothing else—receive no e-mails, go to no Web sites, do absolutely nothing other than supply power to the box and have it running with some kind of Internet connection—your computer is at risk. This is perhaps the scariest part because the dirty business happens completely independently of what you are doing and is hidden to you as an everyday user of your computer.[4]

---

4   This risk is the same for people who use dial-up connections. I have seen reports that users who
     spend large blocks of time on dial-up lines can become victims of attacks.

NOTE

You are also at risk whenever you visit a Web site. We can thank Microsoft for this last security wrinkle. As a feature to their Internet Explorer browser, they developed the security cesspools called Active Content and ActiveX. This is content that can add all sorts of excitement to ordinary Web pages, including animation, updates from databases, and other visual tricks. However, it can contain malicious programs that can be automatically run on your computer, without any intervention or action on your part other than visiting the particular Web page where the content is stored. This means that your computer is at risk merely because you view a particular Web page—and you don't have any prior warning when you are going around the Web innocently surfing.

If you took my advice in Chapter 2 and enabled file sharing on one or more of your Windows or Macintosh computers, you might be at risk because this opens up your machine so that others can view your shared files, even others that are out on the Internet and halfway around the world from your humble home. I'll have more to say on how to set this up properly. Chances are good if you are using a frhub that these file sharing network broadcasts are being blocked by your frhub and that no one else outside of your home can see them. Chances are also good that if you aren't using a frhub, you are in deep trouble and need to fix that situation, pronto.

Even if you haven't turned on file sharing on any of your computers, you are still at some level of risk. Security consultants report that their machines are constantly being scanned by potentially malicious programs doing the computer equivalent of rattling their door locks to see if these programs can gain access to the machine's resources. These consultants have tuned their PCs to report on these intrusions and are experts at detecting and repelling these invasions. You are probably not an expert at either and may wonder, why you? What does your modest and unknown home network have to offer these people?

Being scanned is a democratic process. It happens to everyone, whether you are a small two-PC home network or a large corporation with hundreds of Web servers and networked computers. The scanners don't necessarily target their dirty work at anyone in particular. Some people develop programs to exploit particular operating system vulnerabilities. Some are looking for Web servers that have unprotected back doors or other easy entry points. Some just set up their programs to run through a particular range of IP addresses that happen to be located nearby or across the world.

Understanding IP Network Traces

What are these scanning programs actually doing? Recall that in my discussions about IP networks, I mentioned that every computer that is connected to the Internet must have a unique IP address. Each IP address is usually part of a range of addresses that are owned by your ISP or that bear some relation to your employer's network or some other identifying information. (Or, if you are using a frhub, they are a private range of IP addresses from your DHCP server.) Think of it as a listed phone number, only the way the phone numbers are given out, bears some special meaning. Just as there are reverse phone directories, where you can locate someone's postal address if they have a listed phone number, you can do the same with an IP address and find out what network a person is connected to and who is their ISP.

Let's try it now. If you are running Windows, bring up a command window and type the following command: **tracert yahoo.com**. (Note the space and press ENTER after you type in the command.) If you are running a Mac, you should have downloaded WhatRoute from our discussions in Chapter 2.

You are asking your computer to tell you how data gets transmitted from your computer to Yahoo's main servers, and all the places along the way these packets are routed. You'll notice a series of lines that look something like this:

```
Tracing route to yahoo.com [216.115.108.243] over a maximum of 30 hops:
1    80 ms    80 ms    70 ms  pos1-0.core2.mcl.cais.net [63.216.0.14]
2    30 ms    40 ms    30 ms  208.49.231.5
3   100 ms    91 ms   100 ms  pos7-0-2488M.cr2.SNV.gblx.net [208.50.169.86]
4    90 ms   100 ms   101 ms  206.132.254.41
5   101 ms    90 ms    90 ms  bas1r-ge3-0-hr8.snv.yahoo.com [208.178.103.62]
6   100 ms   100 ms    91 ms  img3.yahoo.com [216.115.108.243]
```

Each of these lines shows you the time (in milliseconds) it takes for the packets to get to this point, the name of the router, and its IP address. You can see on line 3 that Yahoo's data at this moment goes through gblx.net. You can also see that the Internet thinks Yahoo.com is located at the IP address of 216.115.108.243.

Once you know the IP address, you are practically inside their computer. Now you need to know what programs they are running and whether they have any open doors that you can enter. Your computer also runs a bunch of programs as part of its operating system. No matter whether you run Windows, MacOS, Linux, or OS/2, your computer uses a series of port numbers to handle its day-to-day business. These port numbers are the way your computer distinguishes various applications and keeps them from getting in each other's way.

Remember how I showed you in Chapter 5 how to turn off AOL's Instant Messaging software by blocking port 5190? A lot more port numbers are out there.

These port numbers are also markers for what is available on your system that can be exploited by hackers. They include numbers for well-known applications, such as Web servers (port 80), e-mail servers (ports 25 and 110), our friendly AOL IM (5190), and other tasks. They are also for more obscure things, such as the port to run particular network-based games. Napster's port number is 6699. Any malicious programmers know these ports and know how to examine your computer to see whether they can get inside.

CAUTION

If someone can figure out your IP address and which ports are open on your machine, they know where you live and what you do and how your computer is vulnerable. They will know what kinds of applications you have running and whether they can access any of them and do some damage.

You don't have to be a server to be vulnerable. For example, if you load Windows Peer Web Services in Windows 98/Me, you may be exposed to attacks coming in over port 80. Even though it goes by some fancy name, this is still a Web server as far as some anonymous hacker is concerned.

Anyone can easily obtain a list of these port numbers. In fact, they are part of the Internet standards process. When someone wants to reserve a port number for their particular application, they have to file a registration document with the appropriate Internet standards-keepers. You can view a complete list of the known ports at the IANA Web site (http://www.iana.org/assignments/port-numbers).

Scan Your Ports

Am I getting through to you yet? Do you think that these are scare tactics, that it can't happen to you? Let's do some analysis of your particular situation with a few simple test tools. I hope to convince you. My aim is to motivate you into acting to protect your network to the strongest extent possible. Part of being security-conscious is understanding the level of the threat against you, and then being able to harden your defenses with the appropriate tools and techniques.

Let's start with a simple port scan of your computer, care of Steve Gibson's Shields UP! service. This simple tool addresses the issue of what parts of your computers are vulnerable to attack. Go now to his Web site, http://grc.com, and click on the graphic for that program. You will see lots of information about what it does and how to proceed through its tests. There are two buttons to click on; choose Probe My Ports, and in a few minutes you will have the results of its analysis.

You'll notice that the first thing Shields UP! tells you is the IP address that your computer is using to connect to the Internet. If you have already installed a frhub as I instructed you to do in Chapter 4, then this IP will actually be the address of the frhub and not your individual machine. More on this in a moment.

Shields UP! examines each of the popular application ports and tries to connect to them, the way a bad guy's program would try to do so over the Internet. When the program tests each port, several possible outcomes can result:

+ **Open**   This means that the port is wide open and can be exploited by hackers. The trouble is, the more stuff you run on your computer, the more likely you have opened ports available for hackers to exploit.

+ **Stealth**   This means that Shields UP! didn't detect anything going on with this port. This is the best circumstance you can hope for. You want to hide as much as possible about your computer from outsiders, and the best way to do this is as if the port doesn't exist on your computer.

+ **Closed**   This means that the port and the application that uses this port have been detected by Shields UP!, but that the program couldn't obtain access to it. This is almost as good as Stealth, and better than having any of your ports wide open.

Ideally, you should run Shields UP! on every computer in your home that is connected to the Internet. More than just telling you if someone has left a back door to your system unlocked, Shields UP! also tells you what to do about it—how you can secure your system and keep your assets protected. Gibson has provided lots of advice on how to correct the problems Shields UP! discovers. This advice is actually more important than doing the tests themselves, because it will get you thinking about how your systems are exposed and how hackers try to force entry into your home network.

If you took my advice and bought and installed a frhub for your home network, the most likely situation to occur is that you have a report full of Stealth results, which is good. You should congratulate yourself on doing what you can to protect your domestic computing environment. You could still be in trouble, however, depending on what else is running on your computer.

Perhaps you were so excited when you got your cable modem that you ignored my advice (or hadn't yet bought this book) and hooked up one of your computers directly to the cable modem without any protection. In the time that it took you to read this paragraph, your computer already could have been compromised, and someone could have installed a piece of software on the machine without your knowledge.

No port scanner in the world is necessarily going to divulge this sort of information, unless it thoroughly scans all 65,000 ports on your computer, and you carefully review its results and understand the implications of the port numbers that it finds open. While this scenario isn't likely, it can happen. Getting rid of these rogue programs isn't easy and is outside the scope of this book. You might have to completely reinstall the operating system from scratch, erasing your entire hard disk.

If you want to learn more, I suggest getting your hands on a more in-depth book on security and following some of its suggestions. There are plenty of network security books, but unfortunately, none is really geared toward beginners. Most are written for administrators of large corporate networks, who often don't know much more than you do, but are willing to spend more time to lock things down since they have more to lose with break-ins than your small home network does. See the section "Recommended Reading" near the end of the chapter for a few books and Web sites to visit.

Solutions

There are several things that you need to do to secure your systems from potential harm. Let's review the items and then cover how you go about installing and maintaining them one by one:

1. Install and configure an antivirus software scanner.

2. Protect Windows operating systems, and remove any harmful Windows defaults and Microsoft programs.

3. Ensure that specific firewall options on your frhub have been properly set up.

4. Remember to do ongoing maintenance of your antivirus software and to periodically review your firewall logs.

Antivirus Software

There are numerous antivirus programs on the market. Most cost about $50 and include several months' worth of updates as part of their purchase price. While I have used several of these programs, the one I keep coming back to is Symantec's Norton Anti-Virus (NAV), available for various Windows and Mac operating systems. The program works well, is relatively easy to install and set up, and the company is constantly providing updates to the virus scanning libraries that are used to keep your protection up to date. You can't go wrong with this program, and I'll show you how to set it up properly. If you would rather choose some other antivirus software, go ahead—you are better off getting something rather than nothing—but NAV is the one that I'd use.

In the past several years a number of Internet-based antivirus service providers have sprung up from such well-known vendors as Mcafee/Network Associates. Instead of buying a software package and installing the software from CD, you download a small piece of software from the Internet and use a Web page from the service provider to manage your antivirus situation. The advantage of using these providers is that you minimize the downloaded software to your machines, and supposedly they are simpler to operate and do just as good a job as the software-based antivirus products. I have tried a few of these providers, but don't yet recommend them even though others have used them with good results. It is still too early to tell in terms of effectiveness, and I would wait until there is more experience with them.

Another twist to the antivirus scene is the inclusion of antivirus screening software on various firewalls and frhub devices. SonicWALL began this trend, and Linksys is also offering this feature. While it sounds like a great idea, since you minimize the amount of software that you install on each machine, I don't recommend the practice. The tools aren't as good as NAV, and getting rid of them once they are installed is painful. If you do want to try this, you'll have to pay an additional subscription fee (beyond the initial purchase price) for this service. See the "Troubleshooting" section later for further comments about this topic.

Many new computers come with preinstalled antivirus software, or you can order the software at the time you place your order for a new computer. If you have some other antivirus software, I recommend replacing it with NAV. This may mean uninstalling the other antivirus software first, and then installing a copy of NAV. This is more work than you bargained for, but trust me, you'll end up doing this later. It isn't any fun to deal with multiple versions of software that do things in slightly different ways.

Choosing your antivirus product has one additional wrinkle. You should purchase and install a separate copy of the program for every machine in your home. This is the method I recommend for most households. Remember that you must install it for every machine: if you leave one unprotected, a virus could enter your home from that machine and infect the rest of your network.

If you are running the original version of Windows 95 and want to install the latest version of NAV on it—you can't. (Note that the current version of NAV supports Windows 95B, also called 95OSR2, which is a more recent version.) At this point, you are faced with a difficult choice: either continue without any virus protection on this machine, upgrade it to a newer version of Windows, or try to find an older copy of NAV that will run on the original Win95. None of these alternatives is great. I'd choose the upgrade path to Windows 98 or 2000 if you were going to upgrade the machine anyway, and if the Win95 version has some problems running something else that you would like to fix. You might be able to find an older version of NAV on the Internet or from a friend.

You can also purchase an enterprise version of the software and set up an antivirus server. The advantage is that you only have to download the virus pattern files once, and then the server will copy these files to all your machines on your network. However, I have found that the server versions are expensive and geared toward networks of several hundred computers, not your average home network situation. I would stick with the separate copy method. You should purchase a license for each machine you intend to run it on, and the antivirus vendors offer multiple license packs.

Finally, Symantec sells NAV as part of several different packages, depending on if you want other software along with the antivirus checker: SystemWorks (which includes troubleshooting utilities and fax software), Norton Internet Security (which includes a personal software firewall and banner ad blocker), and a bundle of NAV with fax software. I recommend purchasing the basic NAV version; you don't need all these other things. Besides, the additional programs can add up to a lot of dough. The basic NAV program also works on the widest selection of operating systems (but not on NT Server and Windows 2000 Server versions if you should be using either of these versions).

Setting up NAV requires you to set up two separate programs: the actual antivirus software and an additional program called LiveUpdate, which is used to schedule and update the virus definition files. As new viruses are discovered on the Internet, the product team at Symantec makes updates to these definitions, so that their scanners can catch the newest viruses. The trick becomes downloading the updates as soon as they are available and making sure that you stay current with them. Otherwise, you run the risk of being infected.

That doesn't mean that you won't ever get infected with a new virus, because it is possible for something to arrive at your desktop before the good folks at Symantec have had time to process their own update and send it to you. That does happen, and if your company has European offices that are connected via e-mail, you could be the first person in the United States to catch a new virus. This is because Europe is a few hours ahead of us here in the States, and often viruses begin their propagation there as businesses open and as people fire up their e-mail software when they come into work. Sometimes, it pays to go into work late and not be the first one to get your e-mail in your office!

Before you install NAV, make sure that all your computers have your e-mail software installed and set up correctly. While you can do this after you get NAV on your machines, it is best if you have the e-mail software configured properly beforehand, since NAV will discover which e-mail accounts you have set up and will ask you if you want to protect them before finishing up its installation. Of course, if you are reading the chapters in sequence, you've already done that in Chapter 5. If you skipped over that chapter, now might be a good time to go back to it and get your e-mail house in order.

Enough caveats. Put this book down, get a copy (or copies if you want to be legit) of the software, and install it on all your machines. Make sure after you install NAV that you run LiveUpdate immediately and update your virus definition files. You may have to do a few reboots to get everything working, so you might want to pick a time when the rest of the household is out at the mall or sleeping, so you don't interfere with their computing needs.

Once you install the software, you should be careful about several configuration parameters. Let's take a look at some of these screens, which you get to by clicking on the NAV icon in your System Tray (if you are running Windows), or go to the Norton Anti-Virus folder (if you have a Mac). Note that the layouts of these screens have changed somewhat in the 2002 version of NAV.

For Windows, you want to pay attention to three different places on the NAV configuration: the general automatic protection features (see Figure 6-1), the floppy disk scanning features (see Figure 6-2), and the e-mail protection features (see Figure 6-3). Each is important. You need to go through this process for each of your home computers. It sounds like a lot of work, but once you get this set up, you don't have to deal with it again—at least until you get a new computer.

You basically want to set up NAV to work as seamlessly as possible, so you don't have to remember to do anything, yet your computers are still protected. Choose the options that I have selected on the various screen shots for your own computers, and you should be set. The only difference you might see would be if Symantec were to change the program options.

Macintosh users of NAV don't have as many options to set up. You should check the boxes labeled "Scan floppies" and "Treat all removable disks as floppies," and that should do it for you.

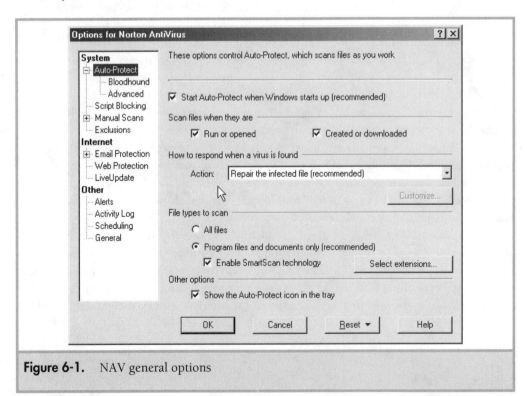

Figure 6-1. NAV general options

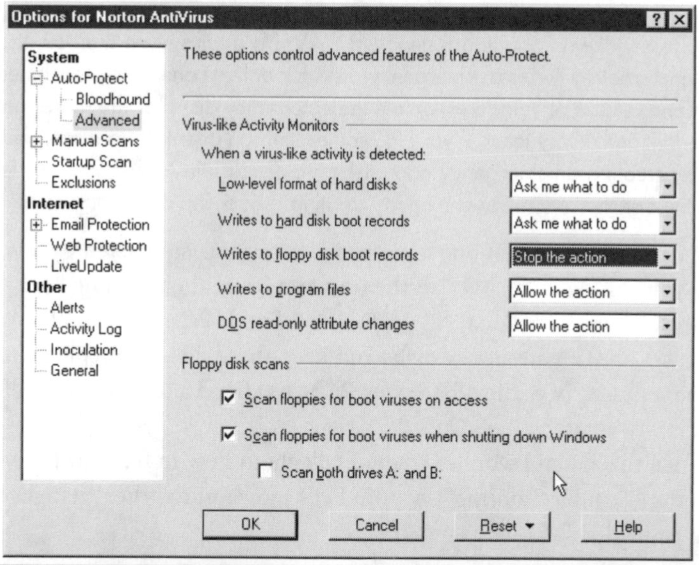

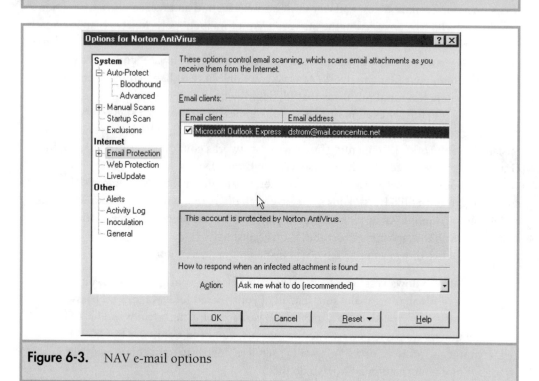

Figure 6-2. NAV floppy scan options

Figure 6-3. NAV e-mail options

**SURVIVAL
TIP**

I'd like you to do take an additional step with NAV: Do a full system scan on each of your machines and create a series of emergency disks for at least one of the machines. If you have more than one version of Windows, create the emergency disks for the more recent operating system version, at the very least. If your PC comes with an internal Zip drive, you can speed things up by creating an emergency boot disk on a Zip disk instead of on a series of floppies. You'll see the appropriate menu choice for creating a boot Zip disk in this situation.

You'll need emergency disks if one of your machines gets so toasted by a virus that this is the only way you can easily recover all the files and bring the machine back to working order. You can boot from the original NAV CD-ROM if your PC supports a bootable CD drive. It is far better to set up the emergency disks and keep these disks someplace that you'll remember in the moment of panic when your PC is rendered a useless hunk of metal and plastic by some nasty virus.

If you've gotten this far and wonder where I talk about how to fix your PC when it receives a virus, turn to the "Troubleshooting" section. Let's move on to other changes you'll need to make to secure your PCs.

Windows Changes

If you own one or more Macs, you can skip this next section and feel somewhat superior to your friends who have invested in the Microsoft Windows monopoly. MacOS is an inherently more secure operating system, mainly because Microsoft mucked up Windows with so many designed-in security problems. You should still use antivirus software, and you should still put a firewall on your home network. At least you don't have to baby-sit the numerous operating system leaks and problems that I'll describe here.

If you want to further explore various security issues on your Macs, I suggest trying out or purchasing software from these vendors: Open Door Networks (http://www.opendoor.com), Sustainable Softworks' IPNetSentry (http://www.sustworks.com), and MultiRouter Traffic Grapher http://people.ee.ethz.ch/~oetiker/Webtools/mrtg).

Maybe one day we will see a version of Windows that will equal the Mac in terms of security strengths, but it isn't likely. XP adds some new back doors that will require your attention, and if you are running XP or planning on buying a new computer that comes with XP, then you should read that section and set things up accordingly.

There are five things you need to do on just about every version of Windows:

1. **For all Windows versions, lock down your network configuration.** If you have enabled file sharing, make sure that all of your shared folders require a password as I instructed you to do in Chapter 2. If you are *not* using a frhub and have your computers connected directly to the Internet, you need to unbind the TCP/IP protocols from Windows Networking services. (See http://grc.com/su-explain.htm for more information on how to do this.)

2. **For Windows 95/98, disable Windows Scripting Host (WSH).** This is one way Bubbleboy and other scripting-style viruses get into your life. Go to Control Panel | Add/Remove Programs | Windows Setup | Accessories | Details and clear WSH. Then click Apply. Unless you are running Visual Basic scripts, you won't miss this piece of software, and you are better off without it.

3. **For all Windows versions, if you are running Internet Explorer version 5, download the "eyedog" scripting patch.** This plugs another hole in the scripting side of things. Get the patch from Microsoft (http://www.microsoft.com/TechNet/IE/tools/scrpteye.asp).

4. **For all Windows versions, you should change your browser's Internet security options** to prevent scripts and ActiveX controls from automatically running. This will take some fooling around with the options, depending on which browser version you are running and whether you are totally paranoid and want to turn off cookies and scripts entirely.

5. **For all Windows versions, remove automatic VBS execution ability.** Thanks to *PCWorld,* this is how to set this up: In Windows 95/98 Explorer, open Folder Options under the View menu (or Tools in Windows Me/2000). Select the File Types tab, and scroll to VBScript Script File. Click on the Edit button (the Advanced button in Windows Me/2000). Another window will open showing the possible file actions, with the default action indicated in boldface type. The default action is likely Open. Highlight instead the word "Edit," and click the Set Default button. "Edit" should now appear in boldface.

   In some older systems the Edit function may not appear. In such instances, click the New button and enter **Edit** in the action field and **Notepad.exe** in the application field. Once Edit appears, make it the default action, as just described. While in the file-type screen, also make sure the boxes for Always Show Extension and Enable Quick View are also selected. Click OK to close the open windows.

You can also follow the instructions in Appendix B to eliminate other more troublesome file extensions.

If you would rather download a utility program called VBS Defender that makes some of these changes for you, go to *PC World*'s Web site: http://www.pcworld.com/downloads/file_description/0,fid,8106,00.asp.

I realize that all of these suggestions are a lot of work, particularly since you have to do them on *all* of your Windows computers that you have at home. You'll thank me later, when you hear from one of your neighbors that they are infected or under attack.

Firewall Issues

One of the biggest differences between cable and DSL connections is the potential security options that are part of the device used to connect you to the outside world. The cable modem has none, while the DSL router/modem comes with some significant security features. The trick is in setting them up or knowing how to get them set up for you.

This means that if you do your homework and get your DSL router configured properly, it can serve as a firewall and block potential attacks before a single data packet makes it further into your home. With a cable modem, you don't have the possibility of this protection, which is why I strongly recommended the frhubs in the last chapter.

Let's talk about how you set up your frhub for specific security issues and then return to how you can harden your DSL router if you went that route.

With some of the frhubs, there is little you can do to increase their default security options. I'll mention a couple of things to check and then cover how to set up real firewall rules on the SonicWALL, which has a fully featured, rules-based, inspection-type of firewall that you can use to lock down just about everything on your network.

The first thing that you want to turn off is the ability for Windows networking broadcasts to leave your home. This is one way that intruders find out what you have on your PCs, and also a way for them to attach to your computer and start examining your files. All of the firewalls turn this off by default, but it is a good idea to check it nonetheless if you can. The Netgear frhubs don't have any mechanism for changing this, so you don't have anything to do.

On the Linksys frhubs, go to the Advanced | Filters page, select Enable for Block WAN Request, and select Disable for both Remote Management and Remote Upgrade. This will make your network go to Stealth mode and make sure that no one else from the outside can mess with your configuration. (See the illustration.)

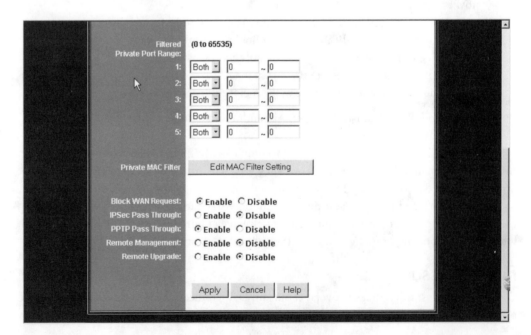

On the MaxGate frhubs, you want to go to the Device Admin. page and choose Disable for External Admin., Yes for Block WAN Probing, and Yes for Block WAN ICMP. (Why all the vendors can't use Yes and No universally is beyond me, but let's not get into that rant right now.) On the Sohoware Broadguard frhub, enter your e-mail address, as shown in the illustration, so the firewall can send you alerts when it encounters various security breaches.

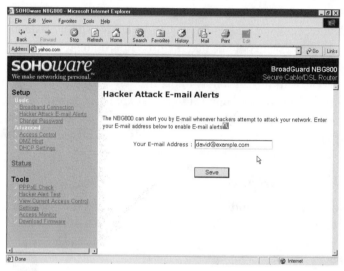

On the SonicWALL, go to Access | Services and make sure that the check box is clear for Windows Networking Broadcast Pass Through. This will keep your networking commands strictly in-house. It is also a good idea to select Enable Stealth Mode. This will ensure that the SonicWALL won't respond to any requests from the Internet, making it as invisible as possible to potential hackers. (See the illustration.)

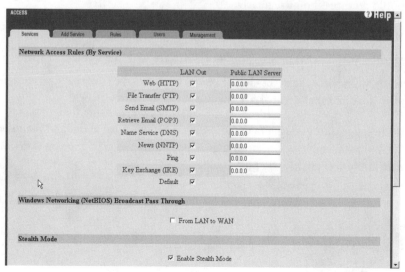

If you want to be even more thorough, you can specifically block certain ports, just as we did in the previous chapter when it came time to turn off AOL IM. I don't recommend you fool around too much here, but know that you have at your disposal a way to isolate your network, should the need arise.

Enterprise-class firewalls come with the ability to set up a series of rules to prevent all sorts of mischief from creeping into their networks. The SonicWALL is the most capable unit of the frhubs I recommend here, and it can be set up in a similar fashion. Why would you want to use these rules? It could be that the firewall is doing too good a job at blocking your applications from actually working, so you might need to relax their prohibitions (what computer geeks call "poking a hole in the firewall") so that these applications can work unimpeded. The kinds of applications that are usually in the most trouble are various network-based games. This is outside the scope of this book, but you can find some good information on how to set up the firewalls to let the games continue if you go to PractiallyNetworked site (http://www.practicallynetworked.com).

Ongoing Maintenance

Our discussion of firewalls and antivirus software is really just the beginning. Keeping your network secure doesn't have to be a full-time job, unless you work as a security consultant for a large corporation.

SURVIVAL TIP

You do have to spend some time each week routinely maintaining your computers if you want to take true protective measures. Think of it as being the security guard who makes his or her rounds and rattles the doors in a building, to ensure that they are still locked and no one has broken in.

You should do three things regularly:

1. Periodically scan each computer's hard disk for viruses and irregularities.

2. Periodically update your virus scanning software with the latest virus pattern files.

3. Periodically review the access log of your frhub to make sure that everything is hunky-dory and that there aren't any break-ins to your network.

Each of these measures doesn't take more than a few minutes to do, and with the right kinds of software, you can have certain things happen automatically (so you don't have to remember to do them explicitly). Let me explain.

If you are using NAV, the first two steps can be automated completely, provided you have set up both NAV and LiveUpdate properly. I recommend having NAV perform an automatic scan of your entire hard disk once every month and having LiveUpdate check every day for new virus patterns.

To set up these parameters, you'll first need to bring up the Configure Anti-Virus screens by right-clicking on the icon in your Windows task bar and then choosing the LiveUpdate menu, as shown in Figure 6-4. Make sure the Enable Automatic LiveUpdate check box is selected, and make sure that the button Apply Updates Without Interrupting Me is also selected. This way, your computer can grab those updates without you having to worry about them.

Next, bring up the NAV program itself, click on the Scheduling button, and then click Add Event. A wizard will walk you through the process. Add two events: one that does the daily LiveUpdate request and one that does the monthly hard disk scan. You can set up both

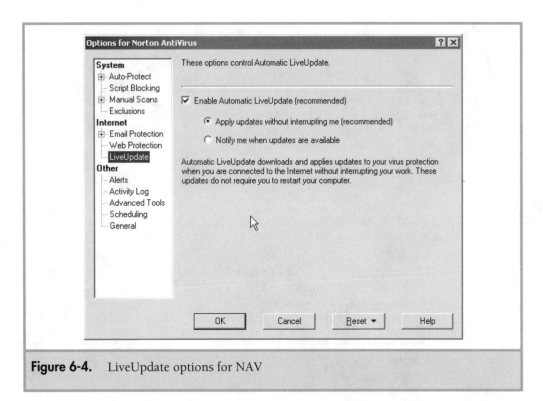

Figure 6-4. LiveUpdate options for NAV

activities to run in the middle of the night, when you aren't usually using your computers, as long as you leave them turned on all the time. If you tend to turn off your computers at night, then schedule these events for times when you won't be using them or when you can afford to have them go do their thing without interrupting some important work. When you are finished, your Scheduling screen should resemble Figure 6-5.

Mac users of NAV go through a similar sequence of steps to accomplish the same thing.

Finally, you need to examine your frhub's access logs and set its particular features. I'll show you what to do with the Netgear RP114 and the SonicWALL, both of which have this feature. (Some of the other Netgear frhubs may or may not include this feature.) Either product can send you e-mail notifications when someone tries to break into your network as well as send you periodic information when other events occur.

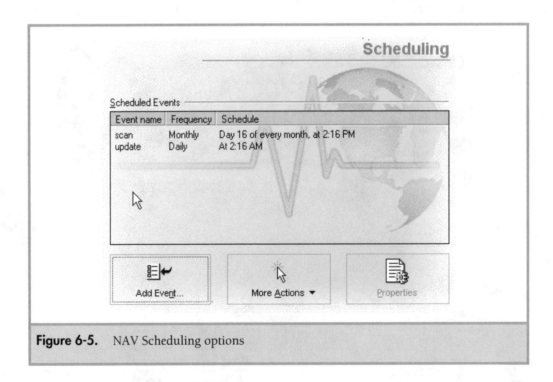

Figure 6-5. NAV Scheduling options

For the SonicWALL, bring up your browser, and enter the IP address of your SonicWALL firewall. Then log in with the correct user name and password, and go to the Log button and Log Settings tab.

You'll notice in the following illustration that I have put in my e-mail address and mail server information, along with instructions to e-mail me the log every Sunday. I have also selected the various categories of events that I want to be notified about, including system errors, attacks, and dropped packets.

Sending the Log

Mail Server	mail.example.com (Name or IP Address)
Send log to	david@example.com (E-mail Address)
Send alerts to	david@example.com (E-mail Address)
Firewall Name	Strom Tele2 Sonic (Name)
Syslog Server	(Name or IP Address)

Email Log Now   Clear Log Now

Automation

Send Log: Weekly ▼   When log overflows:
Every: Sun ▼   ⊙ Overwrite log
At: 0 :00   ○ Shutdown SonicWALL

Syslog Individual Event Rate: 60   (seconds/event)
Syslog Format: Default ▼

Categories

Log		Alerts
System Maintenance ☑	Attacks ☑	Attacks ☑
System Errors ☑	Dropped TCP ☑	System Errors ☑
Blocked Web Sites ☑	Dropped UDP ☑	Blocked Web Sites ☐
Blocked Java etc. ☑	Dropped ICMP ☑	
User Activity ☑	Network Debug ☐	
	Denied LAN IP ☐	

You might want to choose these parameters or to experiment with others once you are more comfortable with seeing the reports that are generated. To test to make sure that you have set up everything properly, you can click on the button E-mail Log Now, and the SonicWALL should send a copy of the log to your e-mail address within a few minutes.

Now you are set. You will get notifications from your SonicWALL when your network is under attack and also have your computers updated with the latest Norton software when they are available.

For the Netgear RP114, bring up your browser and type in the IP address of the frhub, and then enter your user name and password to log in. Next go to Advanced | Content Filter | E-mail. Fill out the screen as shown in the following illustration, again with your e-mail server and e-mail address, and selecting the appropriate boxes to send you the log every Sunday.

CONTENT FILTER - E-mail

| E-mail | Keyword | Schedule | Trusted | Logs |

Address Info :

Mail Server : example.com (Outgoing SMTP Server Name)

E-mail To : david@example.com (E-Mail Address)

Send Log or Alert :

☑ Send immediate alert upon attempted access to a blocked site

Log Schedule : Weekly

Day for Sending Log : Sunday

Time for Sending Log : 0 (hour) : 0 (minute)

Time Zone : (GMT-05:00) Eastern Time (US & Canada), Indiana(East)

Current Time : 00 : 01 : 42

Apply   Cancel

Changes to Windows XP

Windows XP has introduced the concept of its own built-in firewall as part of the expanded range of services for the operating system. While no software-based firewall can match the abilities of the SonicWALL and other hardware firewalls, it is probably worth a closer look to see if this can help protect at least those machines on your network that are running XP. I don't recommend that you upgrade your older Windows operating systems to XP just for the firewall feature—you probably can't since XP needs lots of memory and processing power found on newer computers. If you have to buy a new computer, and that new computer comes with XP preinstalled, then it is worth turning on the firewall feature, if only to serve as additional protection for that PC.

To get started, go to Control Panel | Network Connections | LAN Connections and right-click on Properties. Then go to Advanced | Internet Connection Firewall | Settings, and you'll see a series of screens, as shown in the upcoming figures. While some of this isn't absolutely necessary since you should be protected by your frhub, it doesn't hurt to also protect your XP machine with these measures, too.

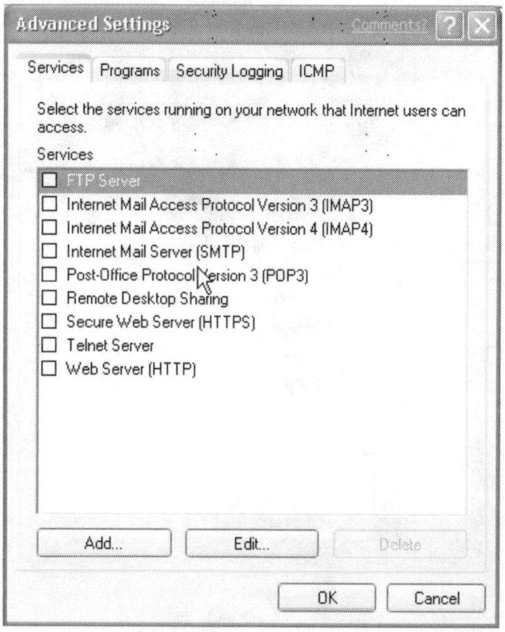

Figure 6-6. Advanced firewall settings on XP firewall

Ensure that no one can access the services you have running on your XP machine, that your machine appears in Stealth mode whenever possible, and that you log any possible break-in attempts on your machine. (See Figure 6-6.)

For the first series of settings, select any of the services you have running on your machine that you wish others to have access to. Ideally, none of these should be selected, so that no one can see your machine. However, if you want to run a Web or e-mail server on your XP machine, and you can set up your frhub to allow outsiders access to these services, then select these boxes. Of course, you also have to ensure that your Web and e-mail and whatever server is set up properly. If you now click on the Security Logging tab, make sure to select Log Unsuccessful Inbound Connection Attempts, as shown here.

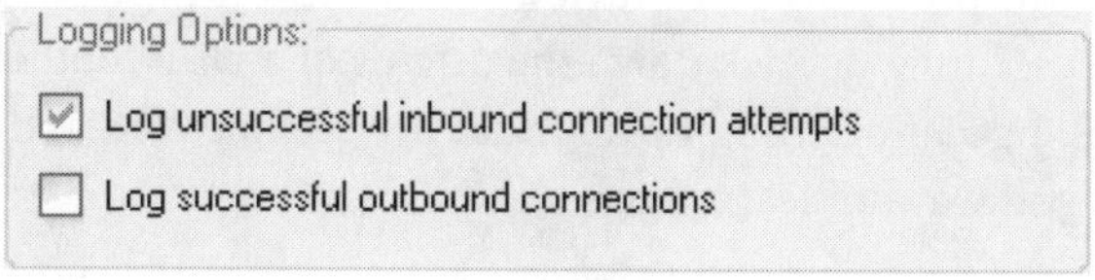

Figure 6-7 image:

> Services | Programs | Security Logging | ICMP
>
> Internet Control Message Protocol (ICMP) allows the computers on a network to share error and status information. Select the requests for information from the Internet that this computer will respond to:
>
> ☐ Allow incoming echo request
> ☐ Allow incoming timestamp request
> ☐ Allow incoming mask request
> ☐ Allow incoming router request
> ☐ Allow outgoing destination unreachable
> ☐ Allow outgoing source quench
> ☐ Allow outgoing parameter problem
> ☐ Allow outgoing time exceeded
> ☐ Allow redirect
>
> Description:
>
> Messages sent to this computer will be repeated back to the sender. This is commonly used for troubleshooting, for example, to ping a machine.

Figure 6-7.   XP ICMP requests

Finally, go to the ICMP tab. ICMP is the protocol that computers use to communicate with each other, mainly used by routers, but it can be used by hackers to penetrate your systems. Again, to be as stealthy as possible, all of these boxes should remain unchecked. You might have to check one or more of them to enable certain games or applications to run on your XP machine. (See Figure 6-7.)

Troubleshooting

Our coverage of security issues wouldn't be complete without touching on ways that you can troubleshoot various problems. Let's review some of the ways you can remove a virus once you are infected, see how to track down the origins of a virus, and examine alternatives to NAV. As promised, I go into setting up a virtual private network and give you plenty of additional reading if you want to learn more.

Is It Really a Virus?

Sometimes, the e-mail warnings that you get from your well-intentioned correspondents about viruses turn out to be wrongheaded. Let's take a look at one message that a friend of mine received:

```
It was brought to my attention yesterday that a virus is in circulation via
e-mail. I looked for it and to my surprise I found it on my computer. Please
follow the directions and remove it from yours. TODAY!!!!!!! I do not know
how long it has been on my computer, but no virus software can detect it. It
will become active on June 1, 2001. It might be too late by then. It wipes
out all files and folders on the hard drive. This virus travels thru E-mail
and migrates to the 'C:\windows\command' folder.

To find it and get rid of it off of your computer, do the following : Go to
the "START" button. Go to "FIND" or "SEARCH" Go to "FILES & FOLDERS" Make
sure the find box is searching the "C:" drive. Type in; SULFNBK.EXE. If it
finds it, highlight it. Go to 'File' and delete it. Close the find Dialog
box Open the Recycle Bin Find the file and delete it from the Recycle bin
and you should be safe.

The bad part is: You need to contact everyone you have sent ANY e-mail to in
the past few months. Many major companies have found this virus on their
computers. Please help your friends !!!!!!!! DO NOT RELY ON YOUR ANTI-VIRUS
SOFTWARE. McAFEE and NORTON CANNOT DETECT IT BECAUSE IT DOES NOT BECOME A
VIRUS UNTIL JUNE 1ST. WHATEVER YOU DO, DO NOT OPEN THE FILE!!!
```

Before you do anything like delete the file indicated in the message, you should first check and make sure that you are at risk. Let's go to Symantec's Anti-Virus Research Center Web site and track this down. Go to http://www.symantec.com/avcenter, click on the Virus Encyclopedia, enter in the search box **SULFNBK.EXE**, and see what turns up. As luck would have it, this is a hoax, not a virus, and the message is asking you to delete a legitimate Windows executable file, so you should ignore the message.

When Not to Give Someone Your Credit Card Number

While we are on the subject of e-mail hoaxes, I should mention one other situation that comes up with disturbing frequency: the scam of trying to get you to divulge your credit card number to someone who may not be whom you think they are. Let's take a look at a typical e-mail request:

```
Subj: AOL Billing Center

From: BillingRep46@aol.com

Below is the result of your feedback form.  It was submitted by

(BillingRep46@aol.com) on Sunday, May 27, 2001 at 07:43:44


-------------------------------------------------------------------


Hello from America Online,

We apologize for the inconvenience, but the credit card information for your
account has expired.

In order to enjoy your America Online experience and keep your account
active, you must enter new, *valid* credit card information within 24 hours
of receiving this e-mail. To enter new credit card information and keep your
account active, please click here.

Our Regards,

Matt Glazer

America Online Billing Department and Staff
```

What is wrong with this message? First off, AOL never asks people to send their credit card numbers in this way. Second, your AOL is active forever; those who have tried to discontinue service can attest to the zeal with which AOL will attempt to keep you subscribed. Finally, the e-mail address is suspicious: "billingrep46@aol.com" doesn't sound like a legit AOL employee, now does it?

Beware of these and other kinds of scams, particularly if someone you don't know is asking you for your personal information. If you get something like this, report it to abuse@aol.com (or whatever domain it purportedly came from).

Removing a Virus from Your PC

No antivirus program is perfect, and a time will come when your computer gets infected. The trick is to limit your exposure and get rid of the virus without mangling your PC.

If you realize that the e-mail attachment (or floppy disk file) that you just opened contains a virus, don't start cursing. Immediately, and I mean immediately, reach over behind the computer, grab the Ethernet cable, and disconnect it from your computer. You should take care not to rip the cable off from the RJ45 plastic connector if at all possible. Why the Ethernet cable? That's the fastest method of isolating your machine from the rest of your home network and the Internet at large. If you can't reach over to the cable fast enough, or don't have the presence of mind to do this, then press the power switch to turn the computer off.

Either way, you have to bring up NAV (or whatever antivirus program you're using) and try to eliminate the virus. If you turned off your PC, boot from those emergency repair disks that you created earlier in the chapter. Oops, decided to skip that step, did you? Don't despair. You might be able to boot directly from the original NAV CD-ROM, if you can find it and if your computer is set up to boot from CD drives. (If you are running Windows, you should be able to press DEL or F1 and see some setup options that you can fool around with to select the boot device order.)

If it is a virus that NAV doesn't recognize, which is likely because it should have stopped it before you opened your attachment, then you will have to figure out a way for it to clean the darn thing off your machine. If you have a working machine elsewhere at home, try going to Symantec's antivirus Web site (http://www.symantec.com/avcenter). See if you can track down some specific advice on how to remove the virus. Depending on what you have caught, you may be in for a rather long period to disinfect your PC.

You should also review your configuration settings; make sure that the automatic protection features have been set properly and that you have the latest pattern file to recognize what that you just caught.

Tracking Virus Origins

If you have isolated the virus on your computer and want to spend some time tracking down where it came from, more power to you. Once I find the darn things, the last thing I want to do is spend any more time with them, but I am not the type of person who slows down when he sees a wreck on the side of the freeway. You might be more of a gawker than I, in which case, this section is for you.

I did spend some time tracking down why I got a copy of the "Snow White" virus. It is one of the Hybris class, which are a series of viruses well-known to security experts. Like many people, the first thing I did was look at where the virus was coming from in the e-mail message header. The e-mail message I received said it was from hahaha@sexyfun.net.

Naturally, I thought it was just another porn site, but I was surprised when I did a whois lookup on this domain. (If you go to the Web site http://easywhois.com, you can enter the domain name, in this case, sexyfun.net.) I found an interesting result: it was almost as if some Good Samaritan was trying to provide antivirus information in the actual whois record, anticipating that I (and others like me) would try to track this stuff down. The record looks like this:

```
BLACKBURN, CASEY (CXB1127)

Research.the.Hybris.virus.The.e-mail.is.not.from.us@sexyfun.net

For Virus/Spam Help or Questions Go To

WWW.SEXYFUN.NET. NC 27609 US 919-875-4974

The From Field Is Faked
```

If this information was to be believed, it meant that the sexyfun.net domain wasn't actually where the virus originated. This sort of thing is very typical with many viruses, which can rewrite e-mail header information to some made-up address. What was curious was how Blackburn had manipulated the whois record for his domain. To get more information, I spoke to Gary Moe, who hosts the sexyfun.net Web site.

Both Moe and Blackburn are network system administrators with good hearts. Moe's company provides the Web hosting resources for the domain, while Blackburn did most of the work creating the content. Moe told me, "Our main goal was to help people who were running into this problem, and raise public awareness. We aren't into this for making money. Indeed, we have turned down several offers to post banner ads pushing particular products on our site."

A nice sentiment, indeed. If you go to Blackburn's Web site, you'll be impressed, too. It was filled with helpful information on how to eradicate this virus, along with lots of tips on how to set up mail filters to prevent future attacks. Blackburn and Moe also provide links to the major antivirus software vendors, so you can research the virus yourself if you don't believe them. Moe told me that they have received plenty of angry e-mails from people who think they created this virus. (The latest information is that a Brazilian group is the author.)

I did learn a few things in the process. First, I came across a helpful newsgroup called alt.comp.virus that discusses things you can do to keep your system virus-free. (Remember newsgroups from the last chapter?) While there were several thousand messages when I checked this morning, I could easily sort through them to find out more about Snow White and Hybris.

When I followed a link on Blackburn's site, I found a discussion about one "feature" of Windows Me that isn't widely known, the ability to automatically restore a system to a previous state. I remember when I first came across this feature, I thought, what a great idea. However, as you see from a bulletin from Microsoft—http://support.microsoft.com/support/kb/articles/Q263/4/55.asp—you'll find out that the restore function can keep virus scanners from completely removing infected system files. You might have to turn off the automatic restores before you can get rid of the infection completely.

I mention this not to knock Windows Me but to point out that things have gotten complicated. Even the most experienced computer user will have to keep up to date on the developments to stay ahead of the twisted people who create these viruses.

Let's praise people like Blackburn and Moe. They are a reminder of the culture that was common on the Internet ten or so years ago. Blackburn and Moe didn't have to go through all this trouble to buy the domain name and host a site and prepare all these pages. Instead, they are helping others who possess less knowledge than they do, by providing tools and helpful advice. Of course, you have to know where to look for this advice, and sometimes tracking it down isn't easy. Their site offers a great starting place. More people should emulate them.

Using Alternative Antivirus Programs

While I am partial to Norton's Anti-Virus products, if you want to use some other virus scanner besides Norton, here's what you do. Read *PC Magazine*'s review about other products on ZDnet (http://www.zdnet.com/products/stories/reviews/0,4161,397221,00.html).

They still rate Norton the highest of those tested, but you might be attracted to another product. Maybe you have some other product that you are familiar with because you use it at work or because it came preinstalled on your new computer, and you don't want to go looking for something else. It really doesn't matter: While there are subtle differences among the various products, the important thing is to install one, get it working, update its virus pattern files regularly, and scan your complete hard disk once a quarter. Just make sure that with any product, you cover the basic operations: automatically scan all floppies, screen e-mail attachments, periodically update patterns, and regularly scan your entire hard disk.

Setting Up Antivirus on the SonicWALL

Another alternative to individual virus-scanning programs on each desktop is to stop the infections where they first penetrate your home network, at the firewall. SonicWALL was the first to include this on their frhubs, and other vendors have announced similar products. For an additional yearly subscription fee, you can purchase virus scanning protection and install a small piece of software on each of your desktops, as long as they happen to be Windows machines. You can buy an annual ten-user license for about $300. Macs are not yet supported. More details can be found at the company's Web site (http://www.sonicsys.com/anti-virus).

Going this route has advantages. You have to do absolutely nothing once you get everything set up. The Sonic AV takes care of scanning, updating, configuring, blocking and tackling, and keeping your network safe and secure. You don't have to worry about e-mail attachments because they never even enter your PC: They are stopped by the SonicWALL, which isn't even running Windows, so you don't have to worry about the viruses messing it up either.

While this sounds attractive (and perhaps expensive, since you can't just buy a couple of licenses, but have to pony up for that ten-license minimum nut), I don't recommend this solution. My impression (and this is more anecdotal than based on lots of testing) is that the Sonic AV software is not as robust or as fastidious as the NAV that I know and love so well.

If you do want to set it up, you'll have to purchase the upgrade and install the software by activating it. (Bring up your browser, go to the IP address of your SonicWALL, go to the Anti-Virus page, and click on the Activation button.) Then register your SonicWALL on the company's Web site. It sounds more complex than it is. You'll then have to download software to each of your Windows desktops and probably have to reboot them before your protection kicks in. If you have Macs on your home network, you are out of luck since Sonic doesn't have software for them yet.

Setting Up a VPN on the SonicWALL

I mentioned virtual private networks (VPNs) a few times before and suggested that if you need to be extremely careful about the kind of data that you are sending and receiving over your home network, you might want to consider them. As you should know by now, just about every e-mail message that you send or receive is sent in clear text that anyone could read, should they be inclined to monitor your conversations. A VPN prevents this sort of eavesdropping by encrypting your traffic using one of a variety of encoding mechanisms.

Any VPN comes with two components: a client piece and a server piece. You locate the client on your home desktop, and the server piece is located someplace on the target network that you wish to communicate with securely. You can have a VPN client running on your remote firewall, or either inside or outside the firewall's boundaries. There are advantages and disadvantages to each method, and most likely you'll have little say in where the VPN server is running and what software it is using. You can also have VPNs running on two firewalls and two separate networks so that all network communications between the two are encrypted.

To set up a VPN—no matter what the configuration—is beyond the scope of this book. The instructions for the SonicWALL are obtuse and obscure, and will confound most of you and take some careful study plus probably a few calls to their technical support phone lines to clarify some things. It took me several hours to get my own VPN working, and that was after lots of personal coaching from the SonicWALL engineers.

If you are interested in learning more about VPNs, you should take some time to read the chapter on IPsec protocols (the underlying protocol that all VPNs are built on top of) in the Norberg book cited in the next section. Windows 2000 and XP come with support for IPsec built into the operating system in both client and server versions. This is probably as good a place as any to get started understanding the issues involved with setting up a VPN. Plenty of documentation is available on the ICSAlabs.com Web site, an organization that tests IPsec implementations and interoperability issues.

Recommended Reading

The point of this chapter was to introduce you to the bigger security issues and give you some solid foundations to start protecting your home network. Obviously, you can and should do much more to protect your computing resources. If you are interested, I recommend the following books that will guide you through the next steps.

A good book for beginners is *The Happy Hacker* by Carolyn Meinel (American Eagle Publications, 1999) which is available from her Web site at http://www.happyhacker.org. It contains plenty of illustrations of how hackers work and is written for non–computer experts.

If you want to learn more about what hackers can do to gain access to your systems, a very readable book is *Inside Internet Security—What Hackers Don't Want You to Know* by Jeff Crume (Addison Wesley, 2000). Crume gives you a detailed explanation of the methods that hackers use and practical advice on securing your network.

If you are planning on running NT or Windows 2000 servers on your home network, say a Web or e-mail server, then you need to harden those systems accordingly. The best book for this is *Securing Windows NT/2000 Servers for the Internet* by Stefan Norberg and deborah Russell (O'Reilly, 2000). It details on what you have to do for both operating systems to eliminate their security vulnerabilities.

The most technical and detailed of these books is *Hacking Exposed* by Scambray, McClure, and Kurtz (Osborne/McGraw-Hill, 2000). It covers both Windows and UNIX systems in detail and gives lots of tool recommendations and examples on how to understand the weaknesses in your systems and how to lock them down.

Another resource worth taking some time with is Project Honeynet, at http://project .honeynet.org. An informal group of Internet security consultants put together monthly challenge puzzles that use real-world situations and problems. Solutions are posted the following month. You can learn a great deal from the information posted on this site. With one puzzle, I learned that the hard part isn't understanding how your network has been compromised, it is figuring out how to fix it and return it to a state where it won't be threatened again.

The average time spent to investigate the attack used in this one puzzle by the people who turned in their answers turned out to be about 34 hours per person. That is a staggering amount of person-hours, and these are the supposed experts with years of security training. Yet the attack, which happened to a university Linux computer last fall, took all of about a minute for someone to break into the system and install some automated attack tools. I particularly liked (in the white papers section) the conversation recorded between D1ck and J4n3 (Dick and Jane), two bad guys talking about various exploits, over an IRC channel, giving plenty of insight into some of their motives.

You should also periodically go back to the Web site of your antivirus software vendor, and check to see what is going on in the ever-changing world of viruses and their prevention. Most of the major vendors maintain quite good sites, where you can search for information about specific viruses and updates to their software, along with other security-related matters.

Futures

Network security is getting more potent and easier to use, and is slowly finding its way to home networks. As more people get continuous Internet connections, the growing need for easy to use and easy to set up devices motivates the major vendors to pack more security features in a wider selection of their product lines, at increasingly attractive prices. Having purchased a frhub, you have gone a major step toward improving your chances of practicing "safe hex," as one Web site calls it. Don't congratulate yourself too long, because being secure means continuously maintaining vigil over your network and desktop computing resources, and making sure that new and nastier ways haven't been found to penetrate your virtual home in cyberspace.

All of these measures and countermeasures are aimed at people from the outside trying to break in. An entire other set of circumstances covers what happens when people from the inside try to break out. In our next chapter, I'll go into details about another potential threat to your family's peace of mind—what can happen when your children are viewing potentially harmful and inappropriate materials on the Internet, and ways you can at least keep track of their surfing habits.

Chapter 7

Keeping Track
of Your Family

N ow that you have taken steps to keep your home network safe from intruders, your next step is to protect your family from their own actions, intentional or not. As I stated earlier, the Internet can play host to people with a twisted sense of values. Since your children could come into contact with them, you should know how to monitor these situations.

Problems

The biggest opportunity for home networks creates the biggest problem: once you obtain high-speed Internet access, your computer is always connected to the Internet. Your children may be tempted to roam freely around in cyberspace, where they might view inappropriate Web sites and chat with strangers.

SURVIVAL TIP

It is important for you as a parent to establish the policy on Internet usage as early as possible. This issue is part of your job of protecting your children and should be presented to them as part of your discussions about fire safety, not talking to strangers, and so forth. As a friend of mine says, "If you're at the point where you have to rely on threats and direct monitoring, you're already in trouble."

Several problems arise for parents when it comes to keeping track of what the kids are doing on the Internet. First, there is the sheer amount of content on the Web that contains porn, hate speech, and other X-rated stuff. It is out there in such staggering quantity that anyone can use any search engine to find it in seconds. "It" can cover the waterfront. Pick whatever kind of porn and hate speech you'd like, and you will find it on the Internet. If you haven't tried to track down some of this garbage, try now. I am certain you can find something offensive to some parent that is easily available to children.

Even if you manage to keep your kids away from this garbage on the Web, they can trip over it plenty of other places around the Internet. I already spoke about e-mail spam in Chapter 5, and almost every day I receive at least one porn offer via e-mail. Your kids can download thousands of pictures and messages a day from hundreds of porn and hate newsgroups, should they know how to find them. There also are chat rooms where they might meet shady characters. In addition, they could receive threatening e-mails from their peers at school, which is something else entirely, but still disconcerting.

The notion of movie ratings is a quaint idea when it comes to the Web. An international standards body called the Internet Content Rating Association (http://www.icra.org) has tried to promote self-rated Web sites over the past several years, but has been woefully unsuccessful to date. Most Web sites don't carry any ratings whatsoever. Even if they did, there isn't an easy way for parents to set up their computers to avoid these sites.

CAUTION

Sometimes the domain name of a site can be misleading. Sites like MartinLutherKing.com and Whitehouse.com aren't what you think they are—the former was a hate site, the latter a porn site. Even the most well-intentioned parent would have a hard time distinguishing these from more benign sites that actually are places that pay tribute to the slain civil rights leader and the repository of the executive branch of the U.S. government. There are thousands more where these two came from.

By their nature, children can give rise to the second problem. Most kids are natural communicators and aren't shy about talking about themselves. That can and has gotten them into trouble when they chat with strangers over the Internet. While we admonish our kids not to talk to strangers in person, it's a more difficult proposition when it comes to cyberspace. How do you know to whom you are talking over the Internet? You don't. You can't see them, and all you have to go by is a screen name, an e-mail address, or a brief chat "handle" that could be fabricated by just about anyone.

Third, the technology to block inappropriate sites is still primitive, and the operators of these sites are much cleverer than you and I. You will always be playing catch-up when it comes to keeping the most obnoxious materials out of your home, and it doesn't help that your kids are probably smarter than you when it comes to figuring out ways around your controls and methods. You just have this book and a few meager references at your disposal; they have their friends and loads of spare time.

Fourth is the lack of privacy that anyone has when using the Internet, but this is especially serious for children who may not realize the consequences of giving out your unlisted home phone number or the name of their school. Many e-commerce Web sites that are geared toward children don't take appropriate steps to guard privacy of the data they collect, putting your children and you potentially at risk.

Finally, it doesn't help that many parents view the computer as inherently good and encourage their kids to spend time online. Even households that limit television viewing think that sitting in front of the PC for hours is acceptable. Many children have computers in their own bedrooms, or in relatively private places of the house, making monitoring difficult.

Solutions

What is a concerned parent to do? You can take several steps, but I warn you: none of my solutions is anywhere near perfect. If you have to be absolutely sure that your kids are protected, then I suggest getting rid of any means of connecting to the Internet from your home. Nothing you will do is foolproof, and most of it will leave some risk for your kids.

As a parent, I think about the risks that my kid takes when she travels out in physical space, let alone cyberspace. You can't live in a vacuum, of course. Your kids will see stuff from their friends, or see it on TV, or hear it from the parents of their friends. There isn't much you can do about it, other than educating them about these dangers and giving them some instructions on how to avoid them.

The strategy that you pursue depends on the ages of your children and their particular stage of development, and whether they have any interest in finding out about the seamier side of the world they live in or are relatively innocent creatures still. I can't really help you on these scores, but I can give you some pointers on how to proceed.

First, examine these tips from the Federal Bureau of Investigation to see if any of them apply to your child:

---

1. Your child spends large amounts of time online, especially at night.

Most children who fall victim to computer-sex offenders spend large amounts of time online, particularly in chat rooms. Parents should consider monitoring the amount of time spent online. Children online are at the greatest risk during the evening hours. While offenders are online around the clock, most work during the day and spend their evenings online trying to locate and lure children or seeking pornography.

---

2. You find pornography on your child's computer.[1]

Sex offenders often supply their potential victims with pornography as a means of opening sexual discussions and for seduction. Child pornography may be used to show the child victim that sex between children and adults is "normal." Parents should be conscious of the fact that a child may hide the pornographic files from them on floppy disks.

---

3. Your child receives phone calls from people that you don't know or is making calls, sometimes long-distance, to numbers that you don't recognize.

While talking to a child victim online is a thrill for a computer-sex offender, it can be very cumbersome. Most want to talk to the children on the telephone. They often engage in phone sex with the children and seek to set up an actual meeting for real sex. While a child may be hesitant to give out his or her home phone number, with Caller ID, the offender can readily find out the child's phone number. Some computer-sex offenders have even obtained toll-free 800 numbers, so that their potential victims can call them without their parents finding out.

---

4. Your child receives mail, gifts, or packages from someone you don't know.

As part of the seduction process, it is common for offenders to send letters, photographs, and all manner of gifts to their potential victims. Computer-sex offenders have even sent plane tickets in order for the child to travel across the country to meet them.

---

1   By following some of my instructions, you could find questionable pictures or other files that your child has deleted. Be careful not to rush to judgement when you find something.

5. Your child turns the computer monitor off or quickly changes the screen on the monitor when you come into the room.

A child looking at pornographic images or having sexually explicit conversations does not want you to see it on the screen.

6. Your child becomes withdrawn from the family.

Computer-sex offenders will work very hard at driving a wedge between children and their family or at exploiting their relationship. Children may also become withdrawn after sexual victimization.

7. Your child is using an online account belonging to someone else.

Even if you don't subscribe to an online service or Internet service, your child may meet an offender while online at a friend's house or at the library. Most computers come preloaded with online and/or Internet software. Computer-sex offenders will sometimes provide potential victims with a computer account for communications with them.

These are sobering thoughts, to be sure, but there are a lot of weirdoes in the world. Something else to read is the "Online Safety" section of www.familypc.com's Web site. You'll find lots of tips and suggestions and an introduction to some of the specific solutions that I'll discuss here.

The best and most protected environment for children remains, as of this writing, AOL. They offer a number of parental controls and means of preventing your children from viewing the ugly underbelly of cyberspace. You can restrict younger children's e-mail accounts to only accept e-mails from specific correspondents, and you can reject all attachments, if that is a concern. You can limit them from viewing messages in all newsgroups, too. AOL provides numerous controls, and if you have AOL and intend to keep using it, then I urge you to go to the keyword "parental controls" to see what they offer. This won't do you any good if you promote your child's screen name to full "adult" status, which isn't something that you should do.

When my daughter had her AOL account, her friends all compared notes one day and found out who had adult-level access and who was still a kid in the eyes of their AOL account. There was much gnashing of teeth as we tried to come to terms with what she wanted versus what we were comfortable with. This is in a family that is very familiar with computers and understands the consequences. It was a difficult fight, and one of the reasons why I gave up on AOL eventually. You may have other reasons, too.

SURVIVAL TIP

Make sure that you are armed with information and understand what each of the various age-level access restrictions means before you make any changes for your child.

Interestingly, once my daughter moved off AOL, the issue about her "branding" of access vanished. She really didn't care that much; it was more a badge of pride than anything else. It wasn't that she was interested in doing the sorts of things that were available to the levels of control for the older kids. It was the notion of being considered "grown up" enough. I mention this in hopes you can understand this request from your children when it arises.

These controls are available only if you use the dial-up network of AOL itself. Once you have a continuous Internet connection, you can circumvent the AOL parental controls quite easily, just by bringing up the copy of Internet Explorer that comes with every copy of Windows. Why? Because when you run the AOL dial-up connection, you must connect to the Internet through the AOL software. All of your access goes through the AOL client, which has its own copy of the Web browser that is separate from the version of Internet Explorer on your Windows computer. When you supply another Internet connection mechanism, such as through a cable modem, you don't need the AOL dial-up network anymore (unless your cable provider goes south), and these controls are no longer in force.

If you want the high-speed Internet access that a cable or DSL line brings you, you have to be prepared to spend some time locking down your home network so that your kids have some protection when they use it. You also have to be confident in your abilities as a technologist to keep after what your children are doing in cyberspace. Make it clear to them that you are watching their every move and are willing to spend the time keeping track. It is a big investment, to be sure, but something that you must do if you really are concerned about where your children are surfing.

Consider several tactics:

+ Where to locate your computers in your home

+ Creating house rules about appropriate computer usage

+ How to monitor usage

+ How to block usage

Computer Locations

First, put all your computers in public places. If you are tempted to hide them away in your kids' bedrooms, don't. While having a public PC is no guarantee that they will always behave, it shows that you consider their actions public, not private.

I know this is a big issue for some parents, based on my discussions with neighbors and friends over the years. This is probably the single biggest step toward safe computing that you can take as a parent. If you already have computers in your children's bedrooms, you will probably have a major fight on your hands to remove them.

My daughter has been after me to have a computer in her bedroom, even though we have as many computers in our house as people. Why? Because some of her friends have their own computers in their rooms. So I tried a thought experiment with her: I told her she could have a computer in her room, but not with any Internet connection or any connection to the rest of the house's computers. "Why would I want that?" she asked me, thus verifying the importance to her of having access to the outside world.

That doesn't mean that older kids shouldn't have computers in their rooms. An 8- or 9-year old, however? No way. The dangers are too great.

If you have your computers in public places, from time to time you should "shoulder surf" by watching what they are doing. Ask questions, such as "what is sexygrl99's screen name, and where did you meet her?" Don't be afraid to get involved.

I'd go a step further: Spend some time surfing the Internet together, checking out sites, seeing what interests your kids have, and learning along with them. Get a feel for their natural curiosity and help direct it. You may not know where to look for information, but you can discover things together.

When you have some free time in the afternoon after they come home from school, sign on at work and IM them to say hi. AOL's Instant Messaging is the de facto communications tool for kids, and you might as well learn how to use it. You should also check out the online buddies that your kids have via their own IM sessions.

House Rules

Next, tell them that you'll be watching what they are doing, even when you are not around the house. Make it clear what the consequences of misbehavior are and exactly which kinds of sites are and aren't allowed. Tell them that plenty of people prey on children, and while you do trust your children, you still have to know where they are going, just like you have to know where they go in the physical world.

The www.childnet-int.org site has information about Internet safety, including their SMART program. You might want to adopt these policies as your own, after you discuss them with your spouse:

- Keep your personal details secret. Never use your parents' credit card without their permission, and never give away your name, address, or passwords—it's like handing out the keys to your home!

- Never meet someone you have contacted in cyberspace without your parent's or caregiver's permission, and then only when they can be present.

✦ Don't accept e-mails, open attachments, or download files from people or organizations you don't really know or trust—they may contain viruses or nasty messages.

✦ Remember that someone online may not be who they say they are. If you feel uncomfortable or worried in a chat room, simply get out of there!

✦ Tell your parent or caregiver if someone or something makes you feel uncomfortable or worried.

If you want to take this a step further, print copies of Larry Magid's contracts for safe surfing (http://www.safekids.com/contract.htm). There is one for parents and one for kids, and both should "sign" or at least discuss the issues and points raised in these documents.

NOTE

Whatever you end up doing, the important thing is to make sure you communicate your wishes and overall strategy to your children. Make it clear what happens when they disobey you or try to bend the rules. Even though we are talking technology here, your rules should be just as firm as the time they go to bed or when they do their homework.

Monitoring

Rules and discussions will get you only so far. The next step is to make sure that your kids are actually going where you agreed that they could go out on the Internet.

You can start your monitoring program by doing several things. First, examine the history files of your computer's Web browser. These files tell you which Web sites have been visited over the past several days. Kids can delete this information, so if you don't see any entries, you know they have tried to erase their tracks. It just takes a minute to bring up this information and scan it, and it should be pretty obvious by the site names of places if your kids have been where they shouldn't. You'll need to do this on every computer in your home.

You can also examine the cookies left by various Web sites. Typically, these are stored in a folder named "Cookies." Use the Find File command to look for this folder. A list of all the cookies on the machine can then be sorted by date or name, and while Amazon.com might not merit a further look, "babes.wetsexy-girls.com" does.

While you are poking around your computers, you should also examine any deleted files that may still be in the Trashcan or in the C:\Windows\Temp directory.

Next, you should also turn on the ability to save all sent messages in whatever e-mail software your children use: most, including AOL, Outlook/Outlook Express, and Eudora, have this ability. You should also check for any suspicious files in any deleted folders of your children's e-mail accounts.

Finally, check the newsgroups that your kids have subscribed to: again, a name like comp.graphics.misc is probably fine, but alt.mag.playboy isn't. Sometimes, finding these files can be difficult. With Outlook Express and Windows 2000, they are stored in C:\Documents and Settings\Administrator\Local Settings\Application Data\Identities.[2]

You should be able to bring up your e-mail software, log into your child's account, and see at a glance what newsgroups they have subscribed to, if any. Most kids don't use this corner of cyberspace, which is just as well because it can be a real snake pit.

If you want more monitoring, consider a keystroke-recording program that will keep track of everything typed into the computer. A number of them are available both free and for a fee. One that I have used is Online Recorder. (See Table 7-1 for similar programs.) These programs capture every keystroke to a log file, which you can access with a special password. Online Recorder can also record chat sessions and play them back if you are concerned about what your kids are discussing there. Again, you will have to buy a copy for all of your computers to be truly effective. Realize that these recorder programs can generate huge amounts of data in their log files. You might not need to review them periodically, but the mere mention that they are working can serve as a powerful deterrent.

Product Name, (Price)	Web Site (Win or Mac)
Online Recorder ($40)	www.online-recorder.com (Win)
KeyKey (Free)	http://www.yourbusted.com (Win)
Keystroke Recorder ($20 shareware)	http://www.campsoftware.com/ksr.htm (Mac)
WinWhatWhere (Free)	http://www.winwhatwhere.com (Win)
PC Activity Monitor Pro ($150), Stealth Keyboard Interceptor ($70)	http://www.softsecurity.com (Win)
Keylogger (Free)	http://www.cotse.com/sw/keylogwn.zip (Win)

Table 7-1.   Keystroke Recorder Programs

2   With Windows Me and Outlook Express, you can find these files at C:\Windows\Applications Data\Identities. If you have configured Outlook Express to have multiple identities or e-mail accounts, then you will have to search under each folder, each of which has some incomprehensible name like "{1238996781236-DF8986234-234896234}." I told you this wasn't always easy.

You can find other programs by looking at Google's directory at http://directory. google.com/Top/Computers/Security/Products_and_Tools/Keyloggers_and_Spyware/.

The disadvantage with recorder programs is the sheer overhead of maintaining them, and that you have to install them on every machine on your network. A far better approach, and one that is suited to the champion home network that you have created, is to use a network-based tool to monitor what your family is doing. Sadly, the products aren't there yet.

The ideal location for this monitoring would be a log file (created by your frhub) that you are e-mailed periodically to view where your family has been in cyberspace. Of the frhubs I recommend, the SonicWALL comes closest in this respect, and it still isn't quite where it could be. For example, it doesn't log newsgroup access, and it doesn't tell you much beyond the domain name of the site and the number of bytes of data received from that site.

To set this up if you have a SonicWALL, go to Log | Reports and click the Start Data Collection button. Let this run for a few days, and come back to this screen to view the data collected—a list of the sites visited.

Blocking

Monitoring can go only so far, and you may want to try to filter out or block entire portions of the Internet. This is fraught with problems, but because it is such a popular topic and plenty of methods are available, I'll discuss what your choices are.

NOTE No matter what you do, you can't block everything. The Internet was designed to get around problems, and people are clever in exploiting new methods to remove obstacles as soon as they appear.

Before we begin our discussion on blocking tools, remember to keep your password to yourself, and don't use one that your kids can easily guess. While you may be tempted to share your master AOL account or ISP account password with your kids, don't. It may be useful for them to make changes to your account, or to do some debugging if they have more experience than you do when it comes to computers, but it is almost always a bad idea for them to have the keys to your online kingdom. The better strategy is for you to sign in first and then supervise their actions.

SURVIVAL TIP The best way to block inappropriate content is to make sure it never reaches your home to begin with. The only solid method to do this is to use AOL's dial-up network and AOL client software, and to enable the various parental controls at your disposal.

If you want higher-speed Internet access, you can't use that method. You have several choices, yet all of them are a compromise:

1. You can purchase your Internet access from a filtered access provider.

These providers, like Earthlink or anyone else, will sell you an access account. The difference is that once you are connected on their network, they automatically block inappropriate content, so your kids can't find it, unless, of course, the service's blocking routines don't catch a particular site (which does happen). At least if you buy your Internet access from these operations, you have a fighting chance that the garbage stream into your home will be reduced somewhat.

You can find some of these providers if you search on Yahoo or on http://thelist.com for "filtered access." There are dozens of these vendors, but only some of them offer the services for higher-speed access, including http://www.safeplace.net, http://www.i4f.com, http://www.cleanfamily.com, http://www.clearsail.net, and http://home.integrityonline.com.

These providers have DSL and/or ISDN access accounts available, so you can install a high-speed line to your home. They also cost a bit more than their competitors. I have not tried any of them and would urge caution when exploring them. Some will be out of business at the time you read this book, which is not a good sign for this overall market sector. Still, if this issue is of concern for you, and you haven't yet purchased your high-speed Internet access, you might want to investigate these filtered access providers further. If you have a cable Internet provider in your neighborhood, I would be reluctant to choose one of these filtered access providers. You will spend more money and get less to show for it—all on the chance that they might be able to block the more objectionable sites.

2. You could unplug the cable or DSL modem when you aren't home.

While this is probably the simplest method, it is somewhat draconian and introduces the possibility that when you plug everything back together, something won't work. I don't particularly recommend this method, although if you are desperate, you can threaten to do so.

3. You could install a special Linux or other firewall that can restrict access during specific times of day.

If you are familiar with Linux, then by all means try this. You'll need to set the Web browsers of each of your PCs to connect to your Linux server as the proxy server, and prevent access around the Linux server. Windows XP also has features to enable this, although they are just as hard to set up. If all this sounds like Greek to you, then read on. This is neither the time nor the place to learn Linux, and you could mess up your home network so that you'll have the ultimate in blocked Internet access—a nonworking network.

4. **You can install blocking software on each of your PCs in your home.**

If you already have an Internet provider that you are happy with, and you don't want to switch, then you need to consider this approach. You might have heard about products like NetNanny and CyberSitter. These insert themselves in your PC such that when you try to connect to a blacklisted site, you can't get there. I don't recommend this approach either, mainly because these products just don't work. You can wade your way through a very long list of the various software products here (http://www.microWeb.com/pepsite/Software/filters.html), or you could read a review from *PC Magazine* to learn about just a few of them at http://www.zdnet.com/pcmag/features/utilities98/filtering/intro.html.

Two problems arise with these individual blocking programs. First, you have to install them on every PC you own. If you leave one computer unprotected, your kids can quickly find that one and use it to surf to inappropriate sites. The far more troubling problem is that you have to trust the makers of these blocking tools to block the kinds of sites that you find objectionable, and that process is far from perfect.

5. **You can install network-based blocking software.**

Your last choice is to install network-based blocking tools, and this is probably the best of the suggestions so far. Ideally, these things should live on the network, and this way you can set them up once and not have to worry about maintaining the same piece of software on multiple machines. Two frhub devices that I recommend can handle family filtering or blocking: the Netgear RP114 and the SonicWALL.

Even with these devices, you have the problems that the available blocking tools aren't going to catch everything and that your children can circumvent them.

If you have to buy a frhub anyway, these two devices are good ones for other reasons, so you might want to experiment with them.

To use the Netgear product, specify the keywords or Web site addresses that you want to block, along with a range of times that you want the blocking to take effect. Go to Advanced | Content Filter | Keyword, and enter the keywords and URLs that you want to keep away from your network. (In the illustration on the next page, you'll notice we have blocked the name of a popular magazine among teenaged boys.) You can also free up a particular computer that isn't subject to the blocking filter, by going to the Trusted tab on the screen.

CONTENT FILTER - KEYWORD

| E-mail | **Keyword** | Schedule | Trusted | Logs |

☑ Enable Keyword Blocking

Block Websites that contain these keywords or domain names :

playboy

[Delete Keyword]   [Clear List]

Keyword : [   ]

[Add Keyword]

[Apply] [Cancel]

In addition to these keywords, you can limit access based on the time of day. Click on the Schedule tab and you'll see something similar to the screen in the following illustration. You can block access everyday at all times or on particular days and times.

CONTENT FILTER - SCHEDULE

| E-mail | Keyword | **Schedule** | Trusted | Logs |

Block by content according to this schedule :

Days to Block :

☑ Everyday

☑ Sun ☑ Mon ☑ Tue ☑ Wed ☑ Thu ☑ Fri ☑ Sat

Time of Day to Block : (24-Hour Format)

☑ All day

Start : [0] (hour) [0] (min)   End : [0] (hour) [0] (min)

[Apply] [Cancel]

The SonicWALL operates with a special subscription service that you need to sign up for that is operated by CyberPatrol. Once a month this company updates its list of objectionable sites, you download this list into your SonicWALL, and it takes care of the blocking. You can also specify times of day that the blocking is in effect and add your own keywords or Web site addresses to the list. The screens for the SonicWALL are a bit more involved than the Netgear frhub, but basically accomplish the same thing.

Troubleshooting

The most likely problem to occur is that the blocking tool is blocking legitimate traffic. You'll want to know how to turn it off or how to uninstall it. Given the wide range of tools available, I can't give you exact details here, and some of the individual PC-oriented blockers are designed *not* to be easily uninstalled. With some of them, you'll need at least a password before you can remove all traces of them from your hard disk.

The major problem with blocking inappropriate sites is that you can never block all of them. There will always be new sites that aren't part of the blocker's databases and ways around the blocking utilities if your children learn about anonymous redirecting sites. (There are sites designed to get around just about any obstacle that can be created on the Internet.)

Even the best blocking programs will probably get in the way of your own Internet surfing, whether or not it is innocent and work related. For example, one household I know has two lawyers: She is a sex-crimes prosecutor, and he works for a number of tobacco and breast-implant vendors. Any blocking software they would install on their home computer would probably prevent both of them from using the Web to do research for their jobs and would have to be turned off when they want to go online.

Futures

Blocking software will improve, although it still won't be perfect. We are already seeing better blocking implementations at the frhub level, rather than geared toward individual PCs. Having a networkwide blocking utility is more useful and a better solution anyway, since you can set up a policy for your entire household rather than have to go from computer to computer and make sure that it is set up properly.

Still, the technological arms race between blockers and porn merchants will continue, and most likely the blockers will end up on the losing end of the stick.

Chapter 8

Fun and Games

Now that you have a home network, you might want to expand your horizons by adding something more fun than sharing a few files, printers, and that fast Internet connection. The good news is that the longer you have your home network, the more uses you'll find for it. What has been interesting for me is to see how quickly my family has taken to having the network around the home, using it in ways that had little to do with my reasons for putting it together in the first place. That's why I am still excited about using networks after many years: something new is always around the corner, some product or service that can leverage the few computers and bits of wire and applications that you already have put in place.

This chapter is meant to stimulate your thinking and to provide a few suggestions for ways in which you can enhance your home network and take advantage of many low-cost services and products to make your home life more productive. This is a rapidly expanding area and one that will see many changes over the next few years. I welcome your suggestions and recommendations about products and services that you have tried.

I'll cover the following topics in this chapter. Some of these are serious applications, some just for fun, but all are useful and can give you an idea of where to take your network beyond the basic sharing of files and an Internet connection.

Given the breadth of topics, I'll abandon my usual structure of problem/solution/ troubleshooting here and combine them under each topic's heading. Here are my Top Ten topics:

1. Playing games on your network

2. Keeping track of the time

3. Making movies

4. Getting e-mail when away from home

5. Hooking up your PC to your home stereo equipment

6. Internet appliances

7. Web-based calendar and contact services

8. Internet-based fax services

9. Home control

10. Internet phones

Games

I wanted to start this chapter off with a bang, to tell you about all the great games you can play on your network with your kids. After all, the family that computes together stays together. While many games make use of the Internet, I couldn't find one that I would recommend for home network uses.

Back in the olden days of computer networking, each copy of Novell's network operating system came with a game. It was primitive by today's standards, akin to PacMan or Pong for those of you old enough to remember the state of the art of games circa 1982. The game worked across the network and was often used by network administrators to make sure that their networks were operating up to spec. (Yeah, right.) Too bad there isn't anything like that today.

Windows Me and the home edition of XP both come with numerous games as part of the operating system: Spades, Hearts, Checkers, Backgammon, and Reversi all come with the ability to play someone else over the Internet and all over the world. It is quite exciting, when you think about it: your child could be playing someone in Sweden or Australia. Apart from these meager resources, you are on your own.

I don't recommend many network games, mainly because of their violent subject matter. I'll leave that for another book. A few games don't have weaponry as their focus, including a few racing-car simulations. See the HomePCNetwork site (http://www.homepcnetwork.com/gamesfree.htm).

Other places to check for gaming sites around the Internet include Billsgames.com and gamespot.com. However, any advice you get on the 'Net will be obsolete by the time you read this. Your best choice is to review the games that your kids' friends are playing and to make sure they are acceptable and appropriate for your own family. "Appropriateness" goes out the window when they visit their friends' homes and play games on their computers, of course. Being a parent can be tough work.

My not finding appropriate network-only games doesn't mean the end of gaming in your home. You can still have multiple family members playing the same game against each other by connecting to a game site on the Internet. Read further before proceeding.

If you do install some multiplayer games on your home network, you will have to make some modifications to your frhub to allow the game to communicate with its Internet servers. Depending on the frhub you purchased, you will have to bring up a browser, enter a "special applications" area of its configuration, and most likely open one or more ports for the games to begin. You'll need to know the port number or numbers associated with the game and the IP address of the computers that your kids will be using. With some frhubs like the Ugate, you can open up a port only for one particular computer. This means if you have several kids with their own computers who want to play the same game, they will have to play it one at a time and from a single PC.

NOTE

With some games, you'll need to install the IPX protocol as part of your Windows networking configuration. Follow the same instructions as in Chapter 2 for adding TCP/IP protocol, and then add IPX as well. Appendix A goes into more detail about doing this.

Keeping Track of the Time

One of the most annoying things about my computers has to do with their clocks. They aren't always accurate and tend to gain or lose seconds that can accumulate, running to some pretty big errors in timekeeping. Every PC has a special battery (typically the size of a watch battery) that powers the internal clock, and these batteries tend to wear out after a few years. Trying to replace them is a nightmare: if you thought opening up your PC to add a network adapter was tough, the battery replacement is another kettle of fish entirely. Some of the batteries have been soldered to the system board, making them virtually impossible to replace.

Lest you think I am some Type A micromanager, having the right time displayed on your PC is important. It becomes especially so when you begin to use your home network. If you are trying to find the most recent version of your files, without the proper timestamps you will quickly get confused when you compare the file stored on one computer with one on another.

NOTE

With some Internet games, having the right time is critical to enhanced game playing. If you are trying to make sense of your e-mail messages, it helps to have the right time stamped on them, too.

As mentioned in an earlier chapter, I send out periodic e-mail essays to a small mailing list of a few thousand people. The way I currently send out messages is to use a mailing list program that picks up the current date and time of the message I send to it and then broadcasts to the list. If the computer I use to send the message has the wrong timestamp, then every message to my list will have that wrong timestamp. It happened to me, and a few of my sharp-eyed correspondents picked up the mistake and asked me why the messages had the wrong date.

The solution is software and an Internet protocol that doesn't get much airplay because it is so simple to use: the Network Time Protocol (NTP). Yes, Virginia, there is a special protocol that has been invented to keep track of time around the world, and you, too, can use it. Like other Internet protocols, it has both a server piece and a client piece. The servers, located around the world, keep and are trusted to keep accurate time. The client piece is loaded on each PC on your network. This software sends out a request every so often—not too often, because you don't want to bother these servers too much, and in general your PC's clock is pretty accurate. You should send your request often enough (say once per day), however, that your own humble computers' clocks can be kept in synch with the world's best timepieces.

The good news about NTP clients is that once you set one of them up, you don't have to lift another finger to deal with it. This is the best kind of Internet application I know of, and while your teenagers won't be as excited about NTP as playing the latest Net-based multiplayer game, it does help you manage your home network. Best of all, most of the products are free.

First, you have to find an appropriate NTP server that is "near" you in the Internet sense of the word. It isn't difficult; numerous lists of these servers are maintained in various places. I suggest this Web page as a starting point—http://www.ntp.org—and then scroll down until you find a list of public NTP servers. Choose one of the level 2 servers located in your general geographic vicinity. If you have a Macintosh, you can skip this step, as Apple maintains its own NTP servers.

Once you have the NTP server name, you now have to find the place to enter it in your computer. The Macintosh, of course, is way ahead of Windows here. Built into Mac OS 8 and later versions is a place where you specify the NTP server name.

Go to Control Panels | Date And Time, and select the box next to Use A Network Time Server. Click on the Server Options screen, and you'll see a place to edit the server name and also how often to synchronize your clocks. If you don't see the Apple servers listed here, edit the list and add time.apple.com as your server if you live in North America. Click OK and that's all you need to do.

For all versions of Windows other than XP, you have your choice of software, since, unfortunately, the NTP client isn't part of the operating system yet. If you go to the ntp.org Web site, you can choose among dozens of Windows NTP clients. The one that I use is Automachron (http://www.oneguycoding.com/ automachron). Windows XP includes an NTP client, just like the Mac does.

Once you install the software, specify the time server you want it to connect to. There are some other configuration options, but you don't have to worry about them.

That's it. Once you get things configured, you are done. All the PCs on your home network should now display the same time, down to the second. As long as your Internet connection is up and running, you don't have to bother with this again. You can even use this time to set the non-computer clocks in your house, in case of power failure or during daylight saving time changeovers.

Making Movies

Keeping track of the time isn't all that exciting. True, you now have your home network periodically making use of the Internet in a new and interesting way that you can brag about to your friends and neighbors. Let's get down to something that all of us can see the effects of: using your computers to make home movies.

This isn't really a networking application; although once you finish your home movie, you can upload it to a Web site or send it via e-mail (if you can figure out how to shrink it so that it won't take years for your relatives to download). It is an enjoyable application, nonetheless.

The most fun that I have ever had with any of my computers was using my Mac to edit and produce digital video movies. Maybe it was because of my strong interest in photography. Maybe because the Apple iMovie software is one of the best pieces of software that I have ever used. (Given how many products I have touched, that is quite a compliment.) Maybe because making movies is a lot of fun.

If you are considering getting a new video camera, I strongly recommend one of the digital ones. You will pay a few hundred dollars extra for a digital model, but you will find that having a digital camera changes everything about how you make and finish your films.

Note that I am talking about a true video camcorder here, not one of the "toy" video cameras that hook up to your PC's USB port. These don't have anywhere near the resolution or abilities of the camcorders, and while they are fun for sending pictures of the baby to the grandparents, they don't really rate in terms of doing true digital movie production.

In my video life BiM (Before iMovie), my wife and I were typical about how we filmed home movies. We shot lots of hours of tape through the camera, mainly around various family events, and then watched the tapes an average of one time. Most of the time, the scenes went on for far too long for anyone, even the filmmakers, to view them without fidgeting. Then we would store the tapes and never see them again unless we had a spare day or week to wade through all the scenes to find the one or two moments captured on tape that were really interesting.

Soon after getting my Mac, I was deep into video production mode, mining all these great moments of yesteryear and condensing unwatchable hours of tape into just a few minutes of joy and fun. What was unwatchable at several hours is another thing entirely at a minute or so of highlights. While you could edit the tapes without a computer, having a program like iMovie makes it really workable to do this.

If you do decide to go this route, you will need a recent Mac that has a firewire connection. Most of the iMacs and the G3/G4 series come with such a connection, which is also called IEEE 1394 or i.Link, depending on whom you talk to. (There are two standard firewire cables with different pin connectors.) While some Windows PCs come with firewire ports (the Sony desktops and laptops in particular come to mind), you don't even want to consider using Windows for digital movie editing when you can see how much easier it is to do on a Mac.

These firewire Macs come with the right kind of cable to connect your camera and computer. (You can buy them at various computer supply houses as well, and if you do, you'll need a four-pin to six-pin configuration.) Next, you have to consider what kind of digital video camcorder you want to buy. If you have already shot a great deal of analog 8mm movies and like me have tapes galore that you have hardly ever watched but want to edit into something useful, then you have a simple decision: which Sony Digital 8 camera to buy.

Sony is the only major vendor that sells cameras with this format. Their Digital 8 cameras can view older analog 8mm tapes, in addition to creating new digital ones. The digital Sonys use the same 8mm tapes that you buy for your older analog camera—the difference is that when you use these tapes to record, you only get half the time that the tape is rated for. In other words, a two-hour 8mm tape will film only an hour's worth of digital movies.

If you don't have a significant 8mm video archive, consider other digital formats: some use smaller tapes called miniDV and therefore have smaller camcorders, for example. A great site to evaluate these products is Steve's Digicams (http://www.stevesdigicams.com). There you will find reviews of individual camcorders, explanations of the various technologies, and lots more help. Steve is very responsive to any e-mail questions you might have.

If your Mac didn't come with iMovie, you can purchase it directly from Apple's Web site and download it to your computer. A few years ago, Apple did something really stupid and didn't sell iMovie at all—you had to buy a Mac that came with the software bundled. Happily, this has changed, and if you own a Mac that has a firewire port, you can buy a separate copy of the software and have it running in minutes.

The process flow for making a movie is as follows. First, shoot your videos. Then hook up the camera to your Mac with the firewire cable, and bring up iMovie. Now play the scenes back from the camera, capturing them into your computer's hard disk. Once you have all your content transferred, you do your edits in iMovie, adding titles, sounds, backgrounds, and special effects. Don't forget to cut down those scenes into something that is snappy, tells a story, and so on. The important thing, though, is to have a ball doing whatever you want. One of the nicer things about iMovie is that you can take one of your audio CDs, or even an MP3 file, and use the music in your movies. (Just don't plan on selling your movie—that would violate the copyright laws.)

When you are finished with your project and ready to save it, put in a fresh tape in your camera, and then play the movie from iMovie back to the camera to record the finished product. If you want to create a VHS version to distribute to friends and relatives, hook up your camera to your video deck and make a copy onto VHS tape or tapes.

A book that explains the various inner workings of iMovie is *iMovie: The Missing Manual* by David Pogue (O'Reilly, 2001). It takes you step by step through what you need to know about making a movie and includes tips about using the software effectively.

The future for digital video will bring more cameras that combine the best features from video and still photography into one device. For example, you'll be able to store still images on one medium, video on another, and have control over the resolution of the image that you store in either fashion. Apple's iMovie software continues to improve, making it easier to create very professional-looking and -sounding movies from your camcorder. I know I haven't tapped even 10 percent of its features, and yet it still is a great piece of software engineering. Perhaps the Windows world will get around to this level in a few years, but in the meantime it is worth getting a Mac for editing movies and the opportunity to use this software.

Getting E-Mail when Away from Home

Now that you have this nice home network, you almost don't want to leave home and venture out into the cold, cruel world of the disconnected—the land of dial-up Internet access. Remember those days, when modems would take forever to synch up and would tie up your home phone lines? What, you have already gotten used to a high-speed Internet connection? I thought so.

You may still leave home to go to the grocery store or perhaps to take a family vacation. If you presently own a laptop, you can continue to get your e-mail when you travel. Of course, if you do own a laptop, you don't need me to tell you what a pain in the modem it is to try to use one in your average hotel. I can't believe that in the new millennium I am still writing about this problem.[1]

While I realize that vacations aren't for work, you or your spouse (or your children) might insist on being connected anyway. Therefore you might as well learn how to do this with the minimum of fuss, so that the rest of the family members who don't want to check their e-mail every two hours can go about their vacationing uninterrupted.

Hotels are getting better about hooking you up: If you remember to bring an Ethernet cable, you can connect to their broadband networks for about $10 a day, which is far better and cheaper than paying their exorbitant rates for using their telephone systems to dial up your Internet provider.

Another place to look is your airport. Once the bane of any Internet access, airports are becoming more hospitable toward the connected traveler. As mentioned in Chapter 1, MobileStar is hooking up various airports, Starbucks coffee bars, Hilton and Sheraton hotels, and other places with its wireless networking gear. You pay a monthly fee to subscribe to their service (see Table 8-1), and you'll need a wireless networking adapter for your laptop. Go to http://www.laptoptravel.com/wireless, and then click on Services to learn more about this and where you can find your wireless connecting points.

Plan prices include up to 500MB of data transferred per month. Prices do not include the airport usage surcharge of 50 cents per 24-hour period per airport.

If you can't convince anyone at your office to buy you a laptop, or you don't plan on buying one yourself, here are some tips on how to stay connected when you are on the road.

Some new services and products—coupled with better Internet access and Web browser ubiquity—have at least made it easier to get your e-mail when on the road. I haven't owned a laptop for years and instead use a series of rented or borrowed PCs around the world. I seldom

---

1   My first column for *PC Week,* way back in 1987, was on this subject!

Plan	Details
Star Plan 200	$15.95/month. Monthly subscription plan includes 200 monthly minutes, $0.10 per additional minute.
Star Plan 500	$34.95/month. Monthly subscription plan includes 500 monthly minutes, $0.08 per additional minute.
National Galaxy Plan	$59.95/month. Monthly subscription plan includes unlimited monthly minutes.

Table 8-1.   MobileStar Pricing Plans

have had problems getting connected, and the cost and trouble are far less than the typical hotel/laptop scenario.

At the airport, try Get2netcorp.com or LaptopLane.com. Both offer rental PCs at various locations around the terminals of many major U.S. airports. Get2Net has free workstations that are supported by advertising, but usually you have to stand while you are typing, which can get tiring. LaptopLane offers a small cubicle with a computer, telephone, printer, and fax machine: your own little office away from home, for a reasonable hourly fee (all your phone calls are included in the fee, which is a nice touch). Both setups have PCs that are directly connected to the Internet.

Get2Net's Web page (http://www.get2netcorp.com/flash/locations_main.html) is explicit about the particular locations of its terminals, down to the gate number they are near. LaptopLane's Web site (http://www.laptoplane.com/locations.asp) has a clickable map that provides details about where their "offices" are in the terminals, along with hours of operation and contact information.

These services are just at the airports. You have other opportunities to get connected once you leave the airport and head into almost any major metropolitan area in any country of the world. I am talking about cybercafes, copy shops, and public libraries. Among these three, you should be able to find a computer—sometimes for free, sometimes for a very reasonable hourly fee—and collect and send your e-mail. A few years ago, when I got rid of my laptop, I used to look up the locations of these places before I left for a trip. Now I don't even bother: I know that somewhere Out There is an Internet-connected PC that I can use.

Kinko's is my current favorite. For less than $20 an hour, I can have my choice of Windows or Mac and a reasonably fast Internet connection, not to mention world-class printing facilities if I have to put together a presentation as well as check my mail.

Using a cybercafe or a library can be cost-effective, since they offer better bandwidth at very reasonable prices. Many cafes have T-1 or other higher-speed connections to the Internet, better than you would usually get using a 56-Kbps modem in your hotel room. Their charges typically are under $10 per hour of access, which is much less than most hotels charge even for local phone calls of any duration.

Once you get to the cafe, you have several choices. If you want to create a new e-mail account to use when you travel, check out one of the several free e-mail services that are available (searching Yahoo for "Free E-mail" will uncover dozens). A few of these vendors such as Yahoo itself and Microsoft's Hotmail offer e-mail accounts that don't require any special client software: you merely connect to their sites with your Web browser, enter your user name and password, and proceed to your e-mail activities.

If you do decide to use these services when on the road, remember to clear your browser's cache and exit the program before leaving the computer. This is important when you are sharing a public machine, as some of these services can save your user information in memory, making it easy for the next person who uses the machine to gain access to your account.

If your mail server is running POP and SMTP, then you can use one of the various Web-based e-mail "collector" programs to grab your messages from your e-mail server and view them in your browser. Check out sites like mail.chek.com, www.MailandNews.com, and www.MailStart.com. Bring up whatever site in your browser, type in your e-mail ID and password, and in a few seconds these sites will retrieve your mail from your server. You can delete, reply, and save this mail as you would any other POP account—the difference is that these actions happen inside the browser's frame. MailandNews has the best interface of the lot and the one I prefer to use.

Note that all of these products work in the situation where your Internet provider blocks you from sending mail from outside their systems. This means that you can still send e-mail when you travel, and your messages look just like they originated from your home PC's e-mail account. That is a nice feature.

With these services you can leave your e-mail on your server so you can download it to your desktop when you later return home. Both claim not to store any identifying information such as your password, but it is also a good idea to clear the cache and exit the browser if you are accessing these systems on a shared or public machine.

A warning: Some of these services don't work if your POP server is behind a firewall, or if your provider has turned off the ability to get mail from outside their network. If you aren't using a POP mail system, you can't make use of these products—for example, they won't work with AOL.[2]

---

2   AOL has its own Web-based e-mail collector program available on their Web site.

Hooking Up Your PC to Your Home Stereo Equipment

It all started when we remodeled our house three years ago. We put in speaker wire to have our stereo (relocated to our kitchen) play speakers in both the kitchen and outdoors. That left our living room music-free. My wife disliked having a rack of audio gear in the living room and refused to grant design approval for installing a new system. What to do?

A few years ago, I thought about buying a 100- or 200-CD jukebox, hooking it up in the basement so that the components (other than the speakers) wouldn't be visible up in the living room. Jukeboxes are clunky mechanical things, however, and putting in all the CD information would be tedious. Plus, the information available on a remote control isn't a satisfactory user interface.

I didn't do anything, and our living room continued to be a silent haven in the house. Some days, I would bring the speakers out of the attic and set them up on their stands, disconnected, as I fantasized about listening to music.

Then came the rise of MP3 software players, which run on your PC and allow you to play a digitized version of your CD songs through your computer's sound card and speakers. Fooling around with a few of these products gave me the notion of *ripping* (the term means converting your CD audio music to MP3 digital files) my entire music library to my PC's hard disk. Before I set everything up, I did a quick test with an old sound card and miniature speakers, then another test with a friend's old amplifier and my own stereo speakers that came back out of the attic, and the music sounded wonderful.

Based on these tests, I bought a new 40-gigabyte Maxtor drive for this purpose (about $200 now). It came with disk partitioning and formatting software, along with a very handy utility to upgrade my aging PC's BIOS to handle its huge capacity.

I also got the latest sound card from Creative Labs, the Soundblaster Live!, which sells for around $100. This card has a variety of sonic software to control two or four speakers from the PC, including "environmental" effects that you would normally find on a typical surround-sound amplifier. More important, it has enough processing power to be able to play music while you are on your PC doing other things. Some of the older sound cards rely too much on the PC's own processor, so if you are scrolling or typing on the screen while you are trying to play any songs, the music is interrupted or the audio quality quickly drops.

I tried several ripping programs, but the one I liked was MusicMatch (http://www. musicmatch.com). It could convert a CD and set up a directory for each album with the appropriate titles easily. It is also a great MP3 player, allowing you to create playlists (stored lists of your songs) or search through your music library.

If you do decide to go this route and convert CDs into MP3s on your hard disk, you will find that the speed and vintage of your CD-ROM drive on your computer becomes important. The ideal situation is to just buy a new CD-ROM if you have an older model PC: the newer drives do a much better and faster job of ripping your songs. I found that even a one- or two-year-old model CD-ROM drive wasn't as fast as I had thought. Part of the problem is that the CD-ROM drives come with all sorts of fantastic labels: 24x, 48x, and so forth. These numbers are supposed to mean the speed at which they can spin your CDs, but they are more marketing than anything else. The true way to find out how fast they can work is to rip a couple of CDs and see how long it takes.

The better CD drives will rip songs at a rate that is faster than the amount of time it would take to play the music normally: sometimes they can rip at speeds up to a fifth of the total playing time. This tends to vary from CD to CD, and I don't know why. Maybe the way the music is recorded onto the CD has something to do with it. It could also be due to problems with ripping "enhanced" CDs (combination music CDs with some software on them). The problem is that Windows (and occasionally Macs) wants to run the software when the CD is loaded in the drive, but you don't want this software to run: you just want your music. If you can turn off the AutoPlay feature, this might help.

To rip your music, select an encoding rate for your MP3s. Basically, this determines the sonic quality that you will "record" onto your PC's hard disk. In MusicMatch, these can be found under Options | Settings | Recorder. If you intend to purchase the software, the company will provide an unlock key that will give you a higher encoding rate to use. The highest rates (such as 160 kilobits) will produce the best sounding MP3s, but will also take up more room on your hard disk. Which rate you choose will depend on the quality of your home stereo gear and how discriminating a listener you are. I suggest experimenting by taking a few of your favorite songs, choosing different encoding rates, and seeing if you can tell the difference.

Most of your CDs will make use of a special directory service called CD database (CDDB). Each music CD has encoded on it a special ID number, and when the MusicMatch software detects a CD in the drive, it goes out on the Internet, looks up the code, and determines which CD you have in the drive. If it doesn't find the CD because it is too new or too obscure, then you have to type in the song names and title yourself. Once again, we have another use for a continuous Internet connection.

Only one thing remained, which was how to connect the PC to the amplifier. For my tests, I was using a three-foot Y-cable that had a 1/8th minijack to fit inside my PC's sound card on one end and two RCA connectors for my amp. That wasn't going to be long enough, especially because I wanted to put the amp in the basement. Radio Shack had the answer: a 20-foot "headphone extension cord" that did the trick. Some other folks buy an RCA extension cable to make this work. It is a shame that these cables aren't available from Creative Labs or your usual PC suppliers yet, although MusicMatch sells them on their Web site.

NOTE

If you want to spend some money and get a neat piece of gear, check out the Gateway Connected Music Player or Turtle Beach's Audiotron music appliance. (They're the same device. Gateway sells a private labeled version of it, currently at a discount, if you purchase a PC from them.) This is a small device that connects both to your stereo and to your home Ethernet or PhoneLine network. It works in conjunction with the MP3 files that you have ripped and stored on your Windows hard disk (sorry, no Mac support yet). Be aware, however, that getting it configured on your home network isn't easy.

Once you get everything working, you now have lots of time on your hands to rip your entire CD music library into your PC's hard disk. It took me the better part of several months, when the mood would strike or when I had a few minutes to load in a new CD. If you are serious about this, it would pay to get a new CD-ROM drive and save time in doing the conversions.

The real power of having all your music on your hard disk is that you can become a DJ overnight, with no training and little preparation. All it takes is to select a bunch of your song files and load them into a playlist, which is a standard feature of MusicMatch and other MP3 players. You save this playlist file—basically a list of pointers to your music files around your hard disk—and thereafter you can bring up dozens of your songs and hours of music without ever having to get up from your sofa to change a CD. To me, this is probably the killer feature and well worth the hours invested in doing all the music conversion.

Another benefit of having your music on your PC is that now you can use your CDs elsewhere: in your car, in a portable CD player, at your friend's house, etc.

If I had another pair of speakers, I could drive them with another cable from the PC sound card to the amp, because the Soundblaster Live! card contains two sets of speaker output jacks. For now, the single pair is fine, and anyway I don't think I can get spousal design approval on adding any new speakers to my living room.

I've heard problems from many of you who have connected PCs to stereos but get a loud hum, interference, or some other substandard sound quality. Shorten the distance between the two, if you can, or try a better quality cable. You also should experiment with hooking up your PC's sound card to various input jacks on your stereo amplifier and see if the hum goes away. If this is really a problem, then try the Gateway/Turtle Beach Audiotron device.

Setting up the Audiotron isn't going to be easy. You have to be specific about how you configure your PC and where you store the song files on it. You have to make sure that it can grab a DHCP IP address from your DHCP server, or at least have the same IP subnet address that your Windows PC has. A few other quirks exist, like putting in your Windows user name and password, depending on the version of Windows you are running and how you have configured the networking features. Still, once you get it running, it is a pleasure to listen to. If you store your MP3 files on a Mac, you are out of luck: The unit only works with Windows PCs.

The Audiotron also comes with an optical TOSlink output, in case you have a stereo amplifier that has one of these jacks, so your music can take a completely digital path from your PC to your speakers. One of the advantages of using the Audiotron over MusicMatch or some other MP3 player is that it knows the makeup of the songs on a particular CD and can play them from beginning to end. For most of my CDs, this isn't important, as I only want to listen to one or two songs. For some of them, though, such as *Abbey Road,* I like to hear the songs in the order that the Beatles intended, and this can come in handy.

You can play MP3s on your home stereo in other ways. Quickly checking the www.MP3.com Web site (go to the Hardware/Home Stereo section), you'll find several devices that are basically small PCs that look like stereo components and can be connected to your audio gear, playing MP3s that you store on a writable CD. Table 8-2 lists some of these products. This is still a chaotic marketplace, with announcements about and revisions to various products. I haven't tested any of them yet and would urge you to see them in person before buying anything, to make sure that they fit your needs.

Some of these things aren't really what I have in mind. Having an ordinary Windows PC store and run my music tracks is better. If I find another ripper or player down the road, it is easy to replace and upgrade. I don't want any other audio components that I can't control from limited remotes—it is far better to have Windows programs that I can manipulate. So far I've converted about 60 discs and filled up several gigabytes of hard disk space. When the current hard drive gets filled, I'll just add a new one.

My living room has music again, my wife is happy that the electronics are hidden, and I can program in long playlists of music so I don't have to get up to change a CD. The sound is great.

Once you start filling up your hard disk with MP3s, you might want to widen your music horizons to other artists whose CDs you don't own. Napster and its offspring such as Aimster

Vendor	Approx. Price	Description
Audioramp.com iRad	$600	Streaming audio, hard disk to contain MP3s
Audiotron.net /Gateway.com Connected Music Player	$300	Ethernet and PhoneLine connection, reads files from your PC's hard disk
Dell Digital Audio Receiver	$200	Ethernet and PhoneLine connection, reads files from your PC's hard disk
Netplayradio.com	$200	Attaches to your PC's sound card, broadcasts music over specific FM channel that you pick up anywhere in your home

Table 8-2.   Audio Networking Devices

and GNUtella allow you to trade MP3 files with others over the Internet. The site that I like is My.Mp3.com, which allows you to download songs from many artists, some for free and some for a small fee. You can listen to samples from their oeuvre and then pay for the song and have it immediately available to you for your listening pleasure.

Given the amount of legal action surrounding Napster by the recording industry, I hesitate to write anything here for fear it will quickly become obsolete, but it is clear that MP3s are here to stay, and that more and more people will be using them as time goes on. One way to leverage your MP3s is to make use of a portable music player to carry all of your music around with you.

The idea is a good one, and several portable MP3 players now on the market start at about $250 and go up from there. If you think about the size of a portable CD player, you have the right idea, except the MP3 players weigh more. My favorite is still the Nomad Jukebox C from Creative Labs. While the software and battery life could use some improvements, it is still the best way to take your music on the road. Its sonic quality is first rate, and while it's a bit pricey, you can't beat the convenience.

The Nomad Jukebox C is the latest in a series of portable digital music devices from Creative. The company sells other less capable devices that don't have their own hard disks, so they can't really hold much in the way of music storage. To give you an idea, an entire CD's worth of music can take up 60 to 75MB of disk space. The Nomad C includes a 6GB hard drive inside the unit. That gives it plenty of room to store your music. Depending on the compression routines you use to convert files from CDs to various digital formats, you can hold more than 100 CDs worth of tunes. The Nomad supports a wide variety of file formats, including MP3s and Windows Media Formats.

You can carry the Nomad around, unlike a portable CD player, without having to worry about it skipping if it gets bumped or moved. It is the perfect accompaniment on the plane for road warriors who don't have the energy or the space to drag out your laptop and who don't want to watch some bad movie for the 18th time.

Loading your jukebox will take a series of steps. First, you have to convert your CDs to digital files. You can do this with the included software, called Creative PlayCenter, although my favorite still remains the MusicMatch Jukebox software. Then you have to transfer the files from your PC to the Nomad's hard disk, via a USB cable and software. The process isn't complex, but it will take a while to move all this data. (It took me about two minutes to move 25MB of music or five songs from my Windows Me 200-MHz Dell to the player.)

Creative has done a decent engineering job. Earlier versions of the Nomad player had plenty of bugs and took forever to transfer music. These problems seem to be fixed with the more recent versions of the PlayCenter software. Once you buy a Nomad, you can easily download updates from its Web site, something you should do in any event when you get your player.

The controls for the Nomad are fairly simple to operate. It comes with a small LCD display and a series of buttons whose functions will be obvious to anyone who has ever operated a stereo or portable CD player. You can search for music by just about any parameter, such as artist or album name or song title. It's also a snap to set up playlists of favorite songs either on the unit itself or by typing in the information from your PC's keyboard in the PlayCenter software, and then transferring the list into the player.

One of Nomad's latest enhancements is its ability to use PlayCenter to transfer the contents of organized audio file folders to the Nomad itself. What is particularly nice for those of you who have already ripped lots of audio CDs is that you can retain your folder information and organization from your PC to the Jukebox.

One item that is big on my wish list is better battery life. The Nomad uses rechargeable batteries, and they don't last longer than a couple of hours of continuous play before you have to recharge them for several hours. More important, the battery life indicator on the unit could use some work as well: it drops quickly from, say, 67 percent available life to practically nothing.

The Nomad isn't the only MP3 portable player on the market. More than a dozen different ones are available, although most don't include their own hard drive, so their storage is fairly limited. Good places to look for reviews of these products include *MaximumPC* magazine (start at http://www.maximumpc.com/reviews/mp3players.html). The folks at Mp3.com also have assembled some guidelines about portable players and offer useful advice (http://hardware.mp3.com/hardware/guide/portables).

As I mentioned with the Nomad, another format for digital music that Microsoft has developed is called Windows Media. Built into Windows is Microsoft's audio and video player, Windows Media Player. Microsoft has also developed a companion Web site (http://www.windowsmedia.com). It is worth looking at to see where the future lies for digital music.

Windows Media, for those of you who have been under a rock, is Microsoft's answer to Real's player to let you listen and view multimedia content. The current version does much more than play audio and video clips. It has become a way of life, a user interface, a Web site, and a mechanism for searching for audio (and video) entertainment. While it pains me to say this, I think the world is better off with it than without it. It does a better job integrating into my applications and my desktop, and has the best user interface of similar products. In short, it is a tour de force.

Forget about Napster. This is the way we all will be finding our music from here on out. Granted, we'll have to pay for songs (versus sharing and stealing them), but eventually the music companies will figure this out and attach a low-enough price tag on per-song downloads. With Windows Media's Web site, you can search for streaming audio from your favorite radio stations, although the software isn't quite as wonderful as I'd like. It couldn't find my wife's favorite station, and once I did locate WFUV's stream, it wasn't easy to add it to my favorites list.

You can see why I like the windowsmedia.com site and software so much by comparing it with its competitors. Take, for example, the latest music search tool from AltaVista: it is dog ugly, disorganized, and difficult. You get, instead of a nicely formatted page showing you a picture of the album, a song list, and brief bio, the usual spew from a search engine with hundreds of irrelevant hits and barely enough information to figure out whether the link is worthy of your clickstream.

There is more to the Windows Media story than nice searches, too. As I mentioned earlier, the Nomad MP3 player can play WMF sound files in addition to MP3s. You can use the Windows Media Player to organize your music and download it to the Nomad quite nicely. (Although it isn't possible to transfer any of those 30-second clips from the 'Net. I believe this is because of the copy protection scheme employed by Microsoft). The number of WMF music files is a mere trifle when compared to MP3s, but so what?

Granted, Microsoft isn't going at this alone. Windows Media makes use of technologies from various other parties, but does so in a well-integrated way. This began when IE was brought into the operating system for Windows 95.5 (the updates issued after 1997). Now Windows Media Player can use this technology to present the appropriate Web pages "inside" its player interface, the same look and feel that anyone using IE would get if they connected to the windowsmedia.com Web site. It's an ingenious plan. In the meantime, the rest of us can enjoy searching for our favorite songs.

The future for digital music is hard to predict, but one thing is certain: we will continue to see rapid advances and major changes in how we listen to, store, and purchase music. I eagerly anticipate some of these changes and hope you experiment with some of the products I've mentioned in this section.

Internet Appliances

As in the digital music world, you can hook up to your home network a number of devices that aren't quite PCs and have some computing functions. In the case of the music appliances, they are used to organize and play your songs across your network. In the case of PC appliances, they are used to do some of the things that you would normally use a PC for: browse the Internet, send and receive e-mail and Instant Messages, and play audio/video streams from faraway radio and TV stations. I've used several of these products, and all of them aren't satisfying for one reason or another. While I don't recommend any of them, I want to give you an idea of where they stand in case you come across them.

The notion of an Internet appliance has many meanings to the vendors selling them, but what it means to me is something simple yet capable. Three products in this category are the New Internet Computer (NIC), 3Com's Audrey, and Compaq's iPaq. Since introducing the

Audrey, 3Com has discontinued it. The other two are still being sold, and all three fail on both the simplicity to use them and their capabilities when compared with a "real" PC.

The three devices have three different designs, centered on three different ideas: a Web browser, the MSN service, and a Palm Pilot. None of the three ideas really works as a PC replacement, or even as a PC competitor. You'll find if you buy one of these things that your family will grow tired of trying to do their computing tasks within the limitations of each device. If you have one of these units and a PC in your house, your PCs will be more useful and more in demand.

The NIC (http://thinknic.com) is a small form-factor 266-MHz PC that runs Linux from its built-in CD drive. It comes with speakers, a modem, and an Ethernet connection, along with some simple instructions on how to connect it to the Internet. It is a $200 machine (plus a monitor) that is designed to run the Netscape browser and little else. 3Com's Audrey comes with a modem and a USB port to connect to either a printer or, with a 3Com USB network adapter, to your home network. It has a 7.5-inch color touch screen and an infrared wireless keyboard. For some odd reason, all of Audrey's keys are labeled in lowercase—that threw me and anyone else who has learned to type in the last 75 years. Compaq's iPAQ IA-1 (http://athome. compaq.com/showroom/static/ipaq/iabridge.asp) comes with several USB ports, a 10-inch color screen, an infrared wireless keyboard, and a modem. It does not have any ability to attach to your network. They also sell an iPAQ IA-2, which has a larger display but essentially the same setup.

Of the three, the NIC is probably the best device for someone with a home network. However, it is the best of a bad lot.

I really was pulling for the NIC. An inexpensive, Microsoft-free machine has lots of appeal. The problem is that while the NIC is easy to set up, it doesn't deliver.

The NIC is great at viewing plain text Web pages or those with static images. Its processor and graphics components deliver pages quickly, and better than a 300-MHz Windows machine. The world of the Web isn't like that anymore. We have animations, video, audio, and hundreds of other things that complicate the surfing experience, not to mention AOL Instant Messenger, Napster, and other things that require their own non-Web client software.

As a result, many of the Web sites that I visited didn't display properly, or else like Shockwave.com weren't supported at all. In the interests of keeping it simple, the NIC folks have also kept their baby stupid. You can display (but not edit or store) Microsoft Word files using a built-in translator and also see Acrobat documents. That's about it. MyFreeDesk.com was the only one of the Web-based browser suites I found that could work with the NIC, among several that I tested.

Many of the things I wanted to do with it were difficult, and some were impossible, even though the device was running a relatively recent version of Netscape. Some of the pages were displayed with fonts too small to read, so I assumed I could change their size. That menu choice isn't available. Bringing up more than one window was tricky, too. Don't waste time looking on the hard disk for a place to store your content, because you won't find it—the NIC doesn't have any local storage, other than a small amount of room to keep track of your bookmarks.

NOTE

When I saw the speakers, I had great hopes for the NIC. However, you can't use the built-in CD drive to play audio CDs (or run anything else, for that matter). It is locked shut all the time and used to run the machine's firmware. If you want to listen to music, you'll have to find a streaming server out on the Net.

Speaking of firmware, the NIC has a great idea in terms of using a CD in this fashion. This means when the folks at NIC come up with an upgrade, you just pop out the old CD and put in a new CD. That's the theory, anyway. I tried to download the new firmware from the Internet and burn it on my own CD, but I couldn't get it right. I ended up on the phone with NIC support to obtain a new CD and then to press a few keys to run it and update my machine. This isn't for your average consumer.

If you want to do e-mail, you won't find Netscape Messenger (the companion e-mail client that comes with the Navigator browser): it isn't there. You'll have to settle for reading and writing your e-mail inside the browser, using something like Hotmail or Netscape's own Web-based version or some other service provider.

The NIC folks have tried. They have added the AOL IM client on the latest update of software, along with some card games. Still, these are barely acceptable versions. You can't cheat at Solitaire—no way to Undo. The NIC isn't my father's computer. My dad does Windows. When he finally wanted to get with the Internet generation, we went shopping for a WebTV. He couldn't navigate the tiny menus, and reading text on the TV screen wasn't for him. We left the store and he bought a PC shortly thereafter. I think it was the right move, even though he does call me for help every now and then.

The useful thing about the NIC is the built-in Ethernet. You can set up the NIC to grab an address from your home DHCP server, and you are on the Internet and surfing away within minutes. This means that you have the freedom to choose whatever Internet provider you wish, and NIC comes with a free provider in case you don't currently have one. The other two units aren't as flexible, as you'll see in a minute.

The iPAQ is a step down from the NIC. It is designed to work with various parts of the Microsoft Internet: it runs a version of Windows CE, connects up to the MSN home page, uses Hotmail as its e-mail provider and MSN Messenger for instant messages, and so forth. However, once you set up your account info, you can't easily change it if you made a mistake or want to transfer the device to others in your extended family. It has a terrible gizmo that you use instead of a mouse to move the pointer around the screen, but since it comes with USB ports, you can hook up a real PC mouse quite easily.

The iPAQ is so tied to Microsoft's Internet services that you shouldn't consider it unless you plan on using MSN, et al. for your Internet access. Those of you who have home networks and don't want to get near MSN will do best forgetting about this device. (To make matters confusing, Compaq sells several different kinds of computers under the iPAQ line, including a few Pocket PC digital assistant–style devices that are quite capable.)

Audrey was designed to work with the Palm portion of the 3Com empire: you can synch up your contacts and schedule with your Palm Pilot, for example. Indeed, the Palm is the design nexus for the machine. Just about anything that you can do with your Palm you can do with Audrey, which is probably why the machine was discontinued by 3Com: the Palm is a better and cheaper product. Audrey has a touch screen with a nifty clear stylus that sits on top of the unit like an antenna, which immediately won my daughter's praise.

Both the iPAQ and Audrey are designed as single-tasking devices. Those of you who can handle more than one thing concurrently will be as frustrated as I was in trying to do more. The argument here is simple is as simple does, but I don't buy it. Humans are multitasking beings. We want to be able to do more than one thing at a time on our computers.

Both units are fine for viewing the occasional Web page and doing light e-mail duties. Anything more demanding than that, though, will be a stretch and will be frustrating, especially on the tiny screens provided. The one thing that the NIC has going for it is a real VGA monitor that you can hook up to it. You can play Real audio streams on Audrey and Windows Media streams on the iPAQ, and the sound quality is great. Too bad neither of them comes with a CD drive to play music.

The iPAQ is a picture frame until it dials up MSN. By that I mean you get a very nice single photograph displayed on screen (as a screen saver) when it isn't connected. To do anything else requires you to tie up your phone line. That isn't good. Even with the USB ports, you can't connect it to an Ethernet line, at least not yet. Audrey has some brains when disconnected: you can view your schedule and compose e-mail. With the iPAQ, you can't even compose a message unless you are online. That is acceptable with a broadband or other continuous Internet connection, but not in a dial-up machine.

Both units come with a flashing warning light that signifies you've got e-mail. Neither works well; sometimes the light wouldn't flash for several hours, depending on how I was connected. Audrey, showing its 3Com/Palm heritage, had an extra coolness factor here: you can annotate your e-mails with recorded messages (that are saved as WAV files) and "scribbles" using the touch screen (saved as GIFs). With the iPAQ, you have to stick with plain ol' text. Neither unit worked when it came to viewing HTML e-mail.

Audrey's documentation reminds me of early Macintosh—lots of detail in places that you don't need it and limited info in places you do. The iPAQ has one manual that goes into correct posture and location of the unit, something I thought 99 percent of its users would either be scared away by or ignore completely. Audrey's manual is not geared for new computer users.

If you have a hard time coming up with the server names and other info for setting up your Internet connection, think of what fun beginners will have with this section. At least the iPAQ is simple in this regard: its operating manual is a pamphlet that is easy to follow.

All I can say after using these devices is that I still think getting a cheap PC or iMac for the beginning user is your best bet. Especially if you are the de facto technical support person in your household, trying to debug these units remotely won't be easy, unless you get a second copy of the user manuals or buy a second unit for your own home. For example, it took me a while to find Audrey's volume switch (on the back) to quiet her down. Listening to beginners describe which of the cute little buttons they pressed did what will be an amusing exercise in family communications.

The future for these PC toy-like appliances is mixed. Audrey came and went in less than a year, perhaps the victim of the dotcom crash, perhaps the victim of bad planning by 3Com, perhaps just because people with Palms didn't want to buy yet another non-PC device to synchronize their contacts to. The NIC seems to be holding its own, and perhaps other vendors will get the point that people who have home networks want to use devices that rely on the network more rather than less. Compaq needs to enable Ethernet connections with its iPAQs before they can become truly useful and to break the Microsoft connection for those of us who want to choose our own Internet provider. Other companies, such as Sony, have begun to sell computer-like appliances.

Web-Based Calendaring and Contacts Services

The usual scenario for the Internet appliance commercial is to show the device sitting in some upscale kitchen, while the wife is surfing around looking for a new recipe. The electronic version of *Leave It to Beaver* might be more of an advertiser's dream than reality. A better use for these appliances, and indeed any Internet-connected PC, is to store a common family calendar and contacts list out on the 'Net.

There are many reasons why you would want to take advantage of these services. If you have a continuous Internet connection from your home, these providers are now another extension of your home network and can house your data securely and conveniently. You don't have to worry should something happen to one of your desktops where this information formerly resided: the service provider will make sure that the information is backed up. What could happen? Your kids could accidentally delete all your relatives' addresses one day, or your computer's hard drive could crash. It's reassuring to think that you could have some protection for your data in this scenario.

Perhaps the biggest advantage is a simple one: You, your spouse, and your children can coordinate your calendars without everyone leaving notes on the refrigerator door or kitchen bulletin board.

My family began this experiment gingerly, by using a single copy of Outlook kept on a computer that was in the kitchen. We used Outlook to keep track of my work travel schedule, along with the family activities. It has a great user interface, and everyone in the family is used to it, including the Chief Scheduler, my wife. The problem is, however, that Outlook is then tied to a single computer, the one in the kitchen. It was a good idea, but if one of us wasn't in the kitchen when we wanted to make an appointment or check our calendar, we had to run down there and look.

After careful discussion with the Family Software Standards Committee, we decided to upgrade to My.Yahoo.com, and things got interesting. Now I could make appointments from my office or on the road, and my wife could see them when I made them, not when I remembered (typically the day before) to tell her about them.

The results so far have been mostly favorable, although every so often my wife wishes for the Outlook version. (I know there are tools to synchronize the two, but they are more complex than either of us would like.) Lately my daughter was heard to complain, "Can't we just have a normal paper calendar like everyone else? Why does everything we do have to be on the computer?" For the most part, we all use the Yahoo calendar and it works well.

Yahoo isn't the only one that provides Internet-based calendar services. There are dozens of vendors, as shown in Table 8-3. Besides calendars, you get a free e-mail address, a place to store your contacts and files.

Some of these products work in conjunction with other desktop or digital assistants' contact and calendaring products, so you can keep your online version in synch with the version on your Palm or in Outlook. Some only allow you to upload the information to their services, as shown in the table.

I continue to use My Yahoo for calendaring. I like JungleMate for the contact management, and MyDocsOnline for its file storage features. All but MyDocsOnline are free for some minimal feature set. Why not try them and see for yourself which one or ones you like? Typically, fees start only when you want to purchase more than the minimum number of megabytes of file storage. MyDocsOnline used to be free but now costs about $3 a month for the basic service.

Internet-Based Fax Services

If you bought a PC within the last five years, chances are good it came with a fax modem and fax software. This is both a blessing and a curse. Generally, setting up your PC to receive faxes works well, but sending any fax from your PC that isn't already an electronic document is hard to do.

Fax is old technology. Yet the uses for fax seem to be growing. Given that just about every PC comes with a fax modem and you can buy a fax machine for about $100, they continue to proliferate. While I think that faxing is a waste of paper and resources, the reality

Provider	Desktop Contact Software Supported	PDA Supported	Features (Boldface indicates recommended service)	Synchronization Support
JungleMate.com	Organizer, Access, Excel	None	**Contacts**, calendar, e-mail, file storage	Upload only
Myphonebook.com	Goldmine	None	Contacts	Upload only
Scheduleonline.com	Outlook, Palm	Palm	Contacts, calendar, e-mail, file storage	Two-way
My.Palm.net	Outlook, Notes, Organizer, ACT, Goldmine, Palm	Palm, Pocket PC	Contacts, calendar	Two-way
Magicaldesk.com	Palm	Palm VII only	Contacts, calendar, e-mail, file storage	Two-way
My.Yahoo.com	Outlook, ACT, Palm	Palm, Pocket PC	Contacts, **calendar**, e-mail, file storage	Two-way
Visto.com	Outlook, Outlook Express, Palm	Palm	Contacts, calendar, e-mail, file storage	Two-way
MyDocsOnline.com	None	Various cell phones, Palm	**File storage**	None

Table 8-3. Internet Calendar and Contact Management Services

of the situation is that you might want to use fax technologies that can save on paper and also leverage your nascent home network.

I mentioned early in this book that sharing a fax modem on your network isn't for most of us. Another idea that is worth exploring is the notion of using your e-mail account to send and receive faxes.

The idea is a simple one. You sign up with one of several Internet fax service providers, some of whom offer free versions of their service. They give you a random phone number somewhere in the continental United States that is your very own fax line. If someone sends a fax to this number, it gets routed over the Internet to your e-mail address, where the fax arrives as an attachment to your e-mail message. You can view the attachment using some special software that the service provider gives or sells you.

The advantage here is that you can get a fax without having to tie up one of your phone lines with a "real" fax machine. You also don't get phone calls in the middle of the night or at other inconvenient times. If you do travel, you can get a fax when you are on the road, provided you use one of the techniques mentioned earlier to collect your e-mail when you travel.

The service provider that I recommend is eFax.com, which offers free and fee-based services. The free service doesn't give you the opportunity to pick a fax phone number that is near your own voice phone area code; you get a number "located" somewhere else in the country. That may be unnerving for some of your fax correspondents, who could wonder where you "are," based on the area code. (Mine is located in western Massachusetts, nowhere near my Long Island home and office.) For the most part, it is a great idea. If you want to pay more, you can pick your area code and also use eFax to send faxes as well as receive them.

Since eFax is free, every family member can have their private fax line directing faxes to their e-mail box. If you do need to send a fax from your computer, you can either use the fax modem that came with the PC, or use a common fax machine for this purpose.

Most of the free providers have discontinued their services. The others typically require you to download a piece of software, or to format an e-mail message with an appropriate header that contains the phone number of the fax recipient.

Some Internet fax vendors require special viewing software to see your received faxes, some don't. Some require special software to send your fax, while others use e-mail or Web browsers. Table 8-4 reviews some of the choices for Internet faxing. Some vendors, such as Ureach.com, offer a combined voice/fax/messaging mailbox: you get one number for all your communications needs, and when voice callers dial this number, they get an answering machine that will record their message. When a fax machine calls this number, they get a fax tone answering the line. You can sort out all these messages using your Web browser.

Home Control

One of the more practical aspects of having a home network is to use your computers to control and monitor actual home functions, such as lighting, temperature, and physical security. These "smart home" functions have been talked about and demonstrated for years by various vendors, and a number of demonstration projects have popped up all over America to showcase these technologies.

Company	Receiving Fax Technology	Sending Fax Technology	Typical Prices
Callwave.com	No viewer required	Web-based, sends confirmation of fax via e-mail	Free with ads displayed in faxes, need to requalify periodically
eFax.com	Viewer required, toll-free and local fax number options	Windows software, Web form, and e-mail gateway (for $5/month fee)	Free (fees for toll-free/local and sending options)
Faxaway.com	Not available	E-mail gateway and Windows driver	Per page costs
j2.com	No viewer required	E-mail gateway and Windows driver	Free (or per-page costs) and $15 set up, $12.50 monthly, voice-mail options as well
Messageasap.com	No viewer required, faxes forwarded to e-mail	Web-based	Free, voice and e-mail integration also
Onebox.com	No viewer required	Not available	Free with ads, receive voice-mail and e-mail
Protus.com	No viewer required	E-mail gateway, others	$4 monthly for various Canadian numbers (more for toll-free numbers)
TPC.int	Not available	E-mail and Web-based, sends confirmation of fax via e-mail	Free to limited locations
UReach.com	Toll-free, no viewer required (Web-based)	Web-based	$5 monthly for voice/e-mail/fax integration

Table 8-4. Internet Fax Technologies

Before you get involved in this area, you might want to take a look at a few of these projects to get an idea of what is involved. As always, it depends on how skilled you are and how much money you want to spend. Yet the basics can be accomplished with very little expertise, money, and time, with the right kinds of technologies.

The JP Davis public-relations company has coordinated a variety of smart home vendors in the Portland, Oregon, area in a project that is a three-story, two-bedroom, two-bath townhouse with an office and garage on the first floor (http://www.jpdavis.com/smarthome). The entire home is wired for Ethernet, and you can control the automation functions of the home via a Web browser care of technology from Home Automation, Inc. The home also includes a robotic lawn mower!

Typical of many new communities are the homes in Alliance, Texas (http://www. alliancetexas.com/heritage/index2.html). They are being built with Internet connections. Each home has at least four rooms completely wired with data, telephone, and two video coax runs, all connecting to a master panel in the basement to allow for easier networking. Each street has plenty of fiber to facilitate high-speed Internet access.

A contractor in North Carolina (http://www.ees1.com/Demo2.html) does have a smart home available to the public. It is focused more on whole-house multizone audio and lighting/heating controls, but doesn't include any data networking features.

A number of computer vendors have set up their own demonstration homes near their main corporate headquarters, including Microsoft and Cisco. While these homes aren't open to the public, you can view lots of information about the kinds of technologies and toys that have been assembled by these vendors to showcase their own products and approaches to home automation. Try these sites: http://www.cisco.com/warp/public/779/consumer/internet_home.html and http://www.microsoft.com/homenet.

The home control universe separates into two basic categories. On the high end are whole-house wiring systems that are great for new construction but lousy for renovations. They create a wire center in your basement where everything other than the electrical wires comes together and fans out throughout the house. As you can imagine, these systems are fantastically expensive. The companies that sell these systems (like Home Director) are counting on the fact that because you are about to pay several hundred thousand dollars for your new home, you won't notice the tens of thousands that are tacked on for setting up all this wiring.

The other end of the market is for do-it-yourselfers who have more time than money and are willing to integrate a variety of products together to do what they want to do. A number of vendors offer bits and pieces of X-10 gear that you can integrate on your own. X-10 is a power-line networking standard that is decades old and popular with the Radio Shack set. It covers a simple series of protocols that operates over your internal AC electrical wiring and is used to control lights and other appliances. These vendors offer integration with your Windows PCs (http://www.alwaysthinking.com has Macintosh X-10 controller products) to control the various X-10 endpoints. The gear requires you to replace wall switches for lights and to add modules to lamps and other appliances. BeAtHome also offers products that work with a Web browser to control home functions.

Since these products operate over your electrical wiring, you don't have to worry about cabling your home. You attach an X-10 controller to your PC's serial port. Since your PC is already plugged into the wall, it bridges the X-10 network with the computer, and you can begin to control when your lights go on, and so forth, according to a schedule you program into your computer. It is all great fun.

Here are Web sites where you can get more information about their products:

http://www.x10.com

http://www.homecontrols.com

http://www.marrickltd.com

http://www.beathome.com

http://www.mousehouse.net

I have tried a few of these X-10 products, and they work reasonably well, as long as you don't have that big a house, say less than 8,000 square feet. (For these larger mansions, some products can amplify the signal that is sent through your electrical wiring.) You have to invest some time to get everything integrated and working according to your own needs and home configuration.

Last but not least, a number of individuals have posted descriptions of their own home automation projects on the Web. At http://my.ohio.voyager.net/~dhoehnen/ha/list.html you'll find a page of links maintained by Dan Hoehnen that has a comprehensive listing of products and other home automation resources.

The Internet Telephone

One of the basic technologies that we all take for granted is the telephone. This ordinary device is undergoing lots of changes as the Internet grows. Specifically, I am talking about using the Internet to carry your long-distance voice conversations and cutting the cost of long-distance calls accordingly.

You can use the Internet as a long-distance provider in several ways. One of the easiest is to sign up with a long-distance carrier who will route your calls over a TCP/IP network. There is nothing for you to install, and as far as you are concerned, you dial your faraway friends' phone numbers the same old way as before: your bills are just lower.

Perhaps this isn't cheap enough for you—you'd like to have unlimited and free long-distance calls. Once the domain of hackers, this is now readily possible. Indeed, Microsoft MSN Explorer and Yahoo's Messenger both come with phone dialing applications included, and more are on the way.

You can hook up "phone appliances" to your home phone line, and instead of placing a voice call, they dial up an Internet service provider and route your voice communications over the Internet. These appliances require that all of your conversations take place with others who own the device, which is cumbersome to say the least.

CAUTION

Overall, I don't recommend any phone appliance. The voice quality is second-rate compared with a "real" long-distance connection, they are far too fussy to set up and maintain, and once the novelty wears off of talking to people from your computer, they aren't as convenient as picking up the phone. If you are pained to pay for long-distance calls and you have the patience to deal with their quirks, you might want to try either Dialpad or Net2Phone, and see if your ears can deal with either of them.

The Future of Home Networking

All good things must come to an end, and our tour of home networking is complete.

We have come a long way since the beginning of this book, and I hope it has been as rewarding for you hooking up all this gear as it has been for me to tell you about it. The future for home networking will be a bright one. In ways that we can't even imagine, lots of new products will take more advantage of having multiple computers connected together and to the Internet.

A few years ago there wasn't any easy way to connect your PCs at home, other than stringing Ethernet cabling around the house. Now we have PhoneLine and wireless solutions that are relatively inexpensive and reliable, and more vendors are building-in support for both of these technologies. Look at how many music players sport both Ethernet and PhoneLine connectors on them, how print servers are coming down in price and supporting PhoneLine networks, and how many places around the globe you can connect via a wireless network card in your laptop. This is just the beginning.

A new wireless technology is in the works that promises even more fantastic opportunities. Called Bluetooth (after a Scandinavian king, of all things, because some of the developers hail from Sweden), it will allow wireless connections over 10 to 20 feet. Already Bluetooth cell phone headsets are available, so you can walk around your home or office and not need wires to talk on your phone, making you truly mobile. Bluetooth will be included in a wide array of devices because the chips to enable this network are extremely cheap. Expect them to be used in various digital assistants and in home appliances where power and distance aren't a problem.

While Bluetooth enables low-power short-distance networks, there are plenty of developments on the higher end of the spectrum as well. Given that Apple includes gigabit

Ethernet now in their higher-end Macs, expect to see more of this available to a wider range of PCs, including Windows, and expect to see more home-related networking gear that will handle these extra-high-speed technologies.

I also anticipate greater use of and expanded features for security tools and services, particularly as hackers become more interested in taking advantage of home networks and their continuous Internet connections. While this always will be an arms race between the protectors and the violators, products will continue to improve and be easier to use and ubiquitous.

Finally, with more broadband Internet home connections appearing, there will be a wider array of services that will appeal to home users, expanding on the basic contact/calendaring/file storage features and extending the desktop further into the virtual realm of cyberspace.

These are exciting times to be using a home network, and I hope you share my interest and excitement, and continue to enhance your own network. Once you triumph over the problems and setbacks, you will have many trouble-free years of connectivity in front of you. Good luck and best wishes.

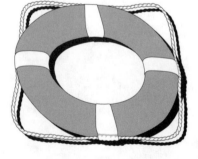

Appendix A

Tips for Fixing Windows Network Problems

By Carey Holzman

ecause of the tens of thousands of different hardware and software configurations possible, as well as differences in quality and compatibility from one manufacturer to another, getting a network to function can be quite a challenge. It can be even more so if you expect Windows to determine all these factors automatically.

Although Windows Me advertises itself as offering free and easy home networking, many real-world users are finding this a difficult-to-realize reality. It has been my experience, working with hundreds of Windows Me networks, that certain steps may be needed. Microsoft may consider some of those steps unconventional. Sometimes, however, nobody understands why a problem existed in the first place. Some of these steps are equivalent to kicking a jukebox to make it work, without the resulting physical damage that actual kicking can cause. These tips are not intended as a "how-to" guide, but rather as a guide to repairing a non-functional network.

Problems

As a certified computer technician for over 11 years, I have experienced the nuances and quirks of nearly every consumer-based Microsoft operating system. It is my goal to share with you virtually every common problem and its solution with regard to networking with Microsoft Windows, and especially Win Me.

Let's get started. First, see if you can find your specific problem listed in Tips 2 through 22. If not, please start at Tip 1.

SURVIVAL TIP

If you are connecting one computer directly to another (without using a hub, switch, or router) using a single cable, you *must* use a crossover cable. You *cannot* use a regular Ethernet cable. For more information about these kinds of cables, see Tips 11 and 12.

Tip 1: How to Reset Your Networking Configuration

1. For all Windows Me PCs, download and install the networking patch (whether you think you need it or not—it won't hurt anything) from Microsoft at http://support.microsoft.com/support/kb/articles/Q272/9/91.ASP.

2. Go into your control panel, and double-click the Network icon. Make sure you have the following items installed:

   ✦ Client for Microsoft Networks

   ✦ Your network adapter

   ✦ TCP/IP

   ✦ IPX/SPX

   ✦ File and Printer Sharing for Microsoft Networks

3. If IPX/SPX is not listed, install it now. If IPX/SPX and/or NetBEUI are not listed as available protocols, please see Tip 2.

4. Double-click on Client For Microsoft Networks. Make sure the Log On To Windows NT Domain check box is clear. Select Logon And Restore Network Connections. Click OK.

5. Double-click on your network adapter, and click the Bindings tab. Make sure both TCP/IP and IPX/SPX are listed and that both are selected. Click OK.

6. Double-click on TCP/IP, click on the Bindings tab, and clear File And Printer Sharing. Click on the Advanced tab, and for the Allow Binding To ATM option, select No. Select the Set This Protocol To Be The Default Protocol box at the bottom of the window. Click OK.

7. Double-click on IPX/SPX and, on the NetBIOS tab, clear the I Want To Enable NetBIOS Over IPX/SPX box (unless you are connecting to a Windows 2000 PC, in which case you will want this box to remain selected). Click on the Bindings tab, and make sure that both Client For Microsoft Networks and File And Printer Sharing are selected. Then click OK.

8. Double-click on File And Printer Sharing For Microsoft Networks. Click once on Browse Master, and make sure its value is set to Automatic. Click once on LM Announce, and make sure its value is set to No. Click OK.

9. Below the Add button, you'll see a line that says "Primary Network Logon." Click the down arrow in the window below that and select Windows Logon.

10. Below that, you'll see a File And Print Sharing button; click it. Make sure that "I want to be able to give others access to my files" is selected and that "I want to be able to allow others to print to my printer(s)" is also selected. Click OK.

11. Click on the Identification tab, and change your workgroup name to **WORKGROUP**. (Use all capital letters; the workgroup name can be case sensitive on some PCs.)

12. Click on the Access Control tab, and make sure that Share-Level Access Control is selected.

13. After you have rebooted, select the resources you want to share on each PC. To share the C: drive, double-click the My Computer icon, right-click on the C: drive, click on the Sharing tab, select Shared As, and click OK. Repeat this process for sharing Printers (right-click on the printer you want to share) or individual directories (right-click on the yellow folder you wish to share). Optional password protection can be found here as well.

14. Make sure you do steps 2 through 13 on all Windows 95 and Windows 98 PCs on your network.

15. When you reboot, you should be able to double-click My Network Places, double-click Entire Network, and click View The Entire Contents Of This Folder (on the left side of the window). If the left side now says, "Hide The Contents Of This Folder," then you did it correctly. You should see the name WORKGROUP here; this should *not* be an empty window. If this window is empty or displays any form of error, please continue with these steps, and then locate the error and the prescribed fix, listed later in this appendix.

16. Choose Tools | Folder Options and click on the View tab. Make sure that Automatically Search For Network Folders And Printers is selected. If it is not, select it and click Apply. Next, click OK.

17. Close all windows.

18. Click Start | Run, type **REGEDIT**, and press ENTER.

19. Click the plus (+) symbol next to Hkey_Current_User, click the + symbol next to Software, click the + symbol next to Microsoft, click the + symbol next to Windows, click the + symbol next to Current Version, click the + symbol next to Explorer, click the + symbol next to NetCrawl, and then click on the yellow folder next to Printers.

20. Select each item listed in the window to the right by clicking on it once, and then press DELETE. *Do not remove the first item labeled "(Default) value not set."* Repeat this process until the window on the right is empty except for "(Default) value not set."

21. Just below the yellow Printers folder, you should see another yellow folder labeled "Shares"; click once on the yellow folder. Repeat the same process used in step 20.

22. Click Registry (at the top of the window) and click Exit.

23. Reboot the PC.

The network should now work. If it does not, see the common problems and their resolutions listed next.

Tip 2: NetBEUI and/or IPX/SPX Are Not Listed as Available Network Protocols

1. Click Start | Run, type **MSCONFIG**, and press ENTER.

2. Click the Extract File button.

3. For the name of the file you want to restore, type **NETBW.INF**.

4. Restore the file from your Windows Millennium CD. (If your CD is your D: drive, type **D:\WIN9X.**)

5. Save File In: C:\WINDOWS\INF.

6. Once the file is restored, repeat this process with NETTRANS.INF (during step 3), and then once more with RPCLTC5.DLL (during step 3), except extract this last file to C:\WINDOWS\SYSTEM (during step 5).

7. Back in your network properties, click Add | Protocol | Add, and click the Have Disk button. Click the Browse button, and go to C:\Windows\Inf. On the left you should see NETTRANS.INF; click once on it and click OK. NetBEUI and/or IPX/SPX should now be listed as available protocol options in your network properties.

Tip 3: You Double-Click on "My Network Places" | "Entire Network" and Get the Error "Cannot Browse Network"

Microsoft has acknowledged a potential problem with Windows Me attempting to contact the master browser for the workgroup over one protocol, instead of over both protocols. Contact their technical support to receive a patch for this. See this Microsoft Knowledge Base article: http://support.microsoft.com/support/kb/articles/Q284/0/84.ASP.

There is, however, an alternative to this support patch:

1. In the control panel of the computer that will be on most often, double-click the Network icon, double-click File And Printer Sharing For Microsoft Networks, and set Browse Master to Enabled.

2. On all the other PCs on the network, set the preceding setting to Disabled, so that only *one* PC is running with Browse Master enabled.

Tip 4: You Get a Script Error When You Double-Click "My Network Places"

1. You must have the Microsoft utility Tweak UI installed and configured to replace the first icon that appears on the desktop. See this Knowledge Base article: http://support.microsoft.com/support/kb/articles/Q190/6/43.ASP.

2. Change this option back to its default setting, My Documents.

Tip 5: You Can See the Workgroup Listed in "My Network Places," but After Double-Clicking It, You See an Empty Window

Apply the same steps as in Tip 3, or use the following procedure.

See if you can search for the PCs by their name by clicking on Start, Search, For files and folders, and select the option 'Computers' listed under "Search for other items", found on the bottom left of this window. Also, if you know each PC's IP address, you can try to ping each PC by clicking Start, Run, type COMMAND, press Enter and at the DOS prompt, type PING followed by the IP address of the PC you wish to ping. If a response, or 'pong' comes back from the ping, or if the PC's are found using the search method, the problem might be that during the setup of the Home Networking wizard, Microsoft somehow renames your workgroup as "Mshome" (the default value) *even if* you have specified your own name. Here is the fix:

1. Click Start | Run, type **REGEDIT**, and press ENTER.

2. Find "Mshome" (which should be in My Computer\HKEY_LOCAL_MACHINE\ System\CurrentControlSet\Services\VxD\VNETSUP).

3. Right-click on Workgroup (in the right panel), select 'Modify' and then, under 'Value Data' change -> Modify-Change the workgroup name to match the same workgroup name on all the other PC's.

4. If that does not work, you might also try adding these lines to your registry:

   ```
   [HKEY_LOCAL_MACHINE\SOFTWARE\Microsoft\Windows\CurrentVersion\Network\RealMode Net]
   "preferredredir"="nwredir"
   "Autologon"="1"
   "transport"="*nwlink,*netbeui,"
   "netcard"=""
   ```

(Remember to back up your registry before modifying it.)

Tip 6: Windows Family Logon Is Missing from Your Network Control Panel

The file you will need to extract is NETFAM.INF:

1. Click Start | Run, type **MSCONFIG**, and press ENTER.

2. Click the Extract File button.

3. For the name of the file you want to restore, type **NETFAM.INF**.

4. Restore the file from your Windows Millennium CD. (If your CD is your D: drive, type **D:\WIN9X.**)

5. Save File In C:\WINDOWS\INF.

6. Back in your network properties, click Add | Client | Add, and "Microsoft Family Logon" should appear.

Tip 7: Your Network Keeps Disconnecting, or You Get Many Collisions

Plug-and-play has, more than likely, set the IRQ or other memory address and is sharing it with another device. Both devices cannot be active at the same time.

1. Set the Network card manually using the software that comes with the card, or download the software from the manufacturer's Web site.

2. Use an IRQ and memory address that is not currently in use, and go into your computer's BIOS. Under Plug And Play, select Manual, and turn off the IRQ that you assigned to the network card.

Tip 8: While Transferring Large Files from PC to PC, the Network Speed Drops and the Process Slows

Try limiting the Windows VCACHE setting to 32MB regardless of the amount of RAM on the system. Download and install Cacheman (http://www.outertech.com). This application lets you change the VCACHE settings easily. Set maximum and minimum disk cache to 32768 and Chunksize to 512.

Tip 9: Your Network Is Slow

In some cases when the driver is installed properly and no errors are reported in Device Manager, some users may experience delays with transferring files or have problems browsing the network. If the protocols and the File and Print Sharing are set up properly, try changing the Transmit setting in the card.

Go to Control Panel | Network. Highlight the network card driver in the list and click Properties. Click on the Advanced tab. Highlight "Transmit Threshold," and change the value option to Store And Forward. (This setting will solve most problems; you can also try other values.) Click OK. Click OK again. Windows may ask for the installation files and ask you to restart the computer. Click Yes to restart.

View this page for more information about speeding up your network adapter: http://www.911networks.com/network_slow.htm

Not all network cards may have changing the Transmit setting as an option.

NOTE

Tip 10: You Map a Network Drive to a Drive Letter Assignment, You Receive No Error Message, but You Don't See the Mapped Drive

More than likely you have the Microsoft utility Tweak UI installed. It has an option on the My Computer tab to enable or disable certain drive letters. Ensure you enable the drive letter you are mapping.

Tip 11: What a Crossover Cable Is

A cable's job is to send and receive data. If pins 1 and 2 send data, and pins 3 and 6 receive data, when you plug this cable directly from one PC into another PC, the PCs will each try to send data on pins 1 and 2 at the same time. Neither PC will receive any data. A crossover cable reverses the wiring on one end of the cable so that the send wires on one side become the receive wires on the other side. A hub, switch, or router does this for you without special wiring.

Tip 12: Where and for How Much You Can Get a Crossover Cable

Crossover cables can be found anywhere computer networking supplies are sold, like CompUSA, Fry's Electronics, Best Buy. They typically run $5–$20, depending on length.

Tip 13: You Change the Access Privileges to Share Level or User Level, and After You Shut Down the PC and Log In, the Change Doesn't Take Effect

Try making the change in Safe mode and then restarting in Normal mode. Be sure to click OK after making the change.

To start Windows Me in Safe mode:

1. Click Start | Shut Down | Restart | OK.

2. Hold down the CTRL key until the Windows Startup menu appears.

3. Enter the number for Safe mode and press ENTER.

Tip 14: Your Mapped Drive Letters All Appear as Open Windows When You Start Up Your Computer

1. This can be caused by Norton Internet Security software. See this link for more information: http://service1.symantec.com/SUPPORT/nip.nsf/docid/2000040412261536&src=w.

2. Alternatively, you can delete the offending drive letters in the contents of this registry setting: HKEY_CURRENT_USER\Software\Microsoft\Windows\CurrentVersion\Explorer\MountPoints_WantUI.

SURVIVAL TIP

The last part of the registry key may have a different name on your PC, but whatever that first yellow folder is called, check its contents. Remove the drive letters you don't want to see. Remember to back up your registry before modifying it!

Tip 15: Attempting to Update Windows Me, You See the Message "Your Organization Has Decided to Provide Software Updates Internally Rather than Through Windows Update. To Download Updates for Your Windows Computer, Please See Your Network Administrator."

It appears that this error message is given if the file wupdinfo.dll is either missing or damaged. To restore it, follow these steps:

1. Click on Start | Search | Files Or Folders.

2. Type **wupdinfo.dll** into the Named field.

3. Make sure that it is looking in your C: drive and click Search Now.

4. If it finds this file, right-click and Rename it to **wupdinfo.old**. If you do not find it, then continue with the next step.

5. Close the Search window.

6. Now click on Start | Run, type **MSCONFIG** in the blank, and click OK.

7. This will open your System Configuration utility. Click on Extract File on the General tab, and then type **wupdinfo.dll** in the blank. Then click Start.

8. Click the down arrow to the right of the Restore From box, and this should display the path to your install files. If it doesn't, browse to their location (or the CD containing them).

9. Click the Browse button to the right of the Save Files In box, and browse to C:\Windows\system.

10. Click OK to accept the location to extract the file.

11. Click OK to accept the Backup folder to store the old file.

12. When the file has been extracted successfully, click on Start | Run, type in **regsvr32 wupdinfo.dll**, and click OK. (This will register that file.)

This should resolve the error on your next visit to the Windows Update site.

Microsoft has acknowledged the existence of this problem, and you can read more about it at http://support.microsoft.com/support/kb/articles/q283/2/88.asp.

This error can also occur if the file MFC42.DLL is also damaged or missing.

Tip 16: Your Firewall Software Tells You that Explorer.exe Is Trying to Connect to 239.255.255.250 Port 1900

1. Uninstall Universal Plug and Play.

2. See if these Microsoft Knowledge Base articles help:
   http://support.microsoft.com/support/kb/articles/Q262/4/58.asp and
   http://support.microsoft.com/support/kb/articles/Q276/5/07.asp.

Tip 17: Internet Explorer Doesn't Find Any Web Pages

1. Go to Control Panel | Internet Options | Connections | LAN Settings, and clear all of the boxes.

2. Re-create the Winsock2 registry entries:

   a. Uninstall ICS (if installed).

   b. Uninstall Dial-Up Networking. Do *not* reboot.

   c. Delete registry key HLM\System\CurrentControlSet\Services\Winsock2.

   d. Reinstall Dial-Up Networking. Reboot.

   e. Reinstall ICS (if desired).

Thanks to Microsoft MVP Steve Winograd for this tip.

Tip 18: Attempting to Install Internet Connection Sharing, You Get the Message "Netconn Has Caused an Error in Netconn.exe"

1. Try finding Netconn.exe in your C:\Windows directory and double-clicking it.

2. If the error still occurs, delete Netconn.exe.

3. Click Start | Run, type **MSCONFIG**, and press ENTER.

4. Click the Extract File button.

5. Type in **NETCONN.EXE** as the file you would like to extract, and click the Start button.

6. For Restore From, type the path (example: D:\Win9x) to your Win Me installation files.

7. For Save File In, type **C:\Windows** and click OK.

8. Back up your registry and move a copy of the keys to be deleted to your desktop before removing them from the registry.

9. Delete HKEY_LOCAL_MACHINE\System\CurrentControlSet\Services\ICSharing (entire folder).

10. Delete HKEY_LOCAL_MACHINE\System\CCS\Services\RemoteAccess\ LocalNameResolution (all keys).

11. Extract ics.inf, icshare.inf, and icsharep.inf to C:\Windows\Inf following steps 3-7, above. Then reboot the PC and re-attempt to install Internet Connection Sharing.

Tip 19: Netconn.exe Is Still Causing a Crash

1. Click Start | Settings | Control Panel | Add/Remove Programs, click the Windows Setup tab, and remove ICS. Do not reboot.

2. Click Start | Run, type **Regedit**, and press ENTER.

3. From HKEY_LOCAL_MACHINE\System\CurrentControlSet\Services\ remove the ICSharing key.

4. Under Class, note the number of folders under the NETTRANS key. Don't close the window, just go to the next step.

5. Under Network properties, add the protocol called NetBEUI, and remove all instances of TCP/IP.

6. Click OK. Do *not* reboot.

7. Return to Regedit and press F5 to refresh the screen.

8. Remove all folders under the NETTRANS key that *were* there before. Do not remove the new keys. They might be at the end or in the middle. Don't remove the new NetBEUI folders.

9. Back in Network properties, add the TCP/IP protocol.

10. Be sure that File And Printer Sharing is not present (this is a must), and delete the NetBEUI protocols.

11. Click Start | Settings | Control Panel | Add/Remove Programs, and click on the Windows Setup tab, choose Communications, and select ICS. Click OK and click OK again.

ICS should run perfectly. Now, at your discretion, you may open network properties and add File and Printer Sharing.

Tip 20: Installing and Configuring Internet Connection Sharing

Microsoft MVP Steve Winograd has written an excellent step-by-step process that you can find at http://www.practicallynetworked.com/sharing/ics/icsmeinstall.htm.

Tip 21: You Never Assigned a Password for the Resource IPC$, so You Can't Access the Resources on Your Win 2000 PC from Your Win Me PC

Create a user account on the Windows 2000 machine with the same user name and password that you now use to log onto Windows Me. Instead, you can log onto Windows Me with the same user name and password that you now use to log onto Windows 2000. On most home LANs, where security is not an issue, I find it easiest to log in as

Administrator on all PCs. Also, see if your guest account on the Windows 2000 computer is disabled. If so, then enable it and check the access rights on the shared folder.

Thanks to Microsoft MVP Steve Winograd for this tip.

Tip 22: Your Modem Logs On and Then Seems to Stop Sending/Receiving Data. Attempting to Browse Web Pages, You See the Error "Page Cannot Be Displayed." When Trying to Send/Receive E-Mail, You See "Server NOT Found," and When Pinging Web Name Addresses and IP Addresses, You See "Unknown Host"

1. Go to Control Panel | Internet Options | Connections.

2. If there's a LAN Settings button, click it, and then clear all the boxes on that screen.

3. Uninstall Dial-Up Networking. Don't reboot.

4. Delete registry key HLM\System\CurrentControlSet\Services\Winsock2.

5. Reinstall Dial-Up Networking.

6. Reboot.

Other Reasons Why Your Network May Function Incorrectly

1. Make sure you have loaded the latest drivers for your network card.

2. Try changing the slot the network card is plugged into on the motherboard, and be sure it is seated firmly in the socket. Many motherboards have PCI slots designated as "masters" or "slaves," and some motherboards even have "combo" slots, which can be either. Your network card should be in a "bus master" slot. You'll need to contact your PC manufacturer or refer to your motherboard manual to determine which slots are bus mastering. If your computer only has one PCI slot, it may not necessarily be a bus master. Some models of PCs will not support PCI network cards.

3. Ensure your cables are good.

4. Make sure your hub, switch, or router is working.

5. Replace your network card as a last resort.

6. Beware of interference. Ensure your network cables are not routed next to or alongside power lines such as power outlets, light fixtures, fans, or other sources of strong electromagnetic interference.

7. Ensure you are using category 5 cabling and that no wires are exposed or crimped.

8. Some network interface card manufacturers say that their products are incompatible with 586 Cyrix processors on 486 motherboards. Cyrix doesn't employ a plug-and-play BIOS, so there is no way for Cyrix users to configure the card's I/O and interrupt settings. Cyrix 686 CPUs may need their bus speed decreased from 75 MHz to 66M Hz (or even lower).

9. Because the many network interface cards sold are plug-and-play, it depends on your PCs BIOS for its IRQ and memory I/O allocation. Please ensure that your BIOS is set up to automatically configure plug-and-play devices.

10. Make sure your network card is *not* sharing an IRQ or I/O address with another device. If your BIOS allows you to select a particular IRQ or memory I/O address for a card, be sure to pick values that are not already used by other devices in your computer.

11. Motherboards with some VIA chipsets (most AMD CPUs and some Intel CPUs) require the latest version of the "4-in-1" drivers to be downloaded and installed. Visit http://www.via.com.tw to find those drivers.

12. Even if your network card worked in Windows 95 or 98 without any problems, that does not automatically mean that the card is compatible with Windows Me. I have been told Windows Me prefers cards that support Network Driver Interface Specification (NDIS) 4 or NDIS 5. You can check what version of NDIS your card is using by running Regedit and examining the contents of this key: LOCAL MACHINE>System>Current ControlSet>Services>Class>Net>0000>Ndi>Interfaces.

13. Check to see if your network card is on the Hardware Compatibility List that Microsoft certifies for each operating system, at http://www.microsoft.com/hcl/default.asp.

14. Visit my Web page at http://cps.everwork.com for a list of updated problems and solutions discovered since the publication of this book. Feel free to e-mail me directly if you are still having difficulties. My e-mail address is Carey@Budweiser.com.

Carey Holzman is a 33-year-old resident of Phoenix, Arizona. He has been interested in computers since the early '80s, when he bought his first TRS 80 Model I computer. Since 1996, he has run his own small business, Computer Performance Specialists, which focuses on fixing, upgrading and repairing PCs, as well as installing network and telephone wiring for home and business users.

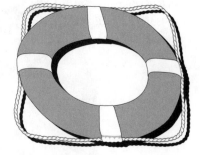

Appendix B

Securing Your Desktop from Automatic File Associations

By Tony Ryan

The ever-helpful Windows operating system automatically associates certain types of files with specific programs, so that you don't have to find the program and can just click on the particular file to bring it up on your PC. Unfortunately, virus creators can take advantage of this.

If you catch such a virus, it enters your computer looking like an ordinary data file, automatically proceeds to run, and then cause its dirty work.

One way to secure all of your desktops is to break the association with particular file types, especially those that are seldom used by most of us. This way, even if you do catch a virus, it won't automatically start doing any damage, and your antivirus screening tools have a fighting chance to eliminate it before any harm is done. Here is how to turn off this automatic feature using Windows 2000/Me/XP.

1. Right-click My Computer, and choose Explore.

2. Choose Tools | Folder Options. (For Windows 95, go to View | Options; for Windows 98, go to View | Folder Options.)

3. Click the File Types tab.

4. In the list provided, click the file extension type, and then click the Delete button (or the Remove button for Windows 95/98).

5. When prompted, click Yes.

Repeat this procedure for all of the file extension types shown in Table B-1. These are the ones most prone to security risks (that is, viruses delivered via e-mail or floppy). The table lists their function and the application typically associated with the extension. If these extension types aren't listed, then you are relatively safe.

The VB Script files are currently a popular means of creating viruses, and if home users need to open a VBS file, they should specifically know why they need to do so.

Except in rare cases, the only MS Office template files home users need are those that they "naturally" customize through using the MS Office products—if a template file came by e-mail to me, I'd delete it immediately.

Extension	Function	Associated Application
.VBS	Visual Basic Script	Script Host
.DOT	MS Word template	MS Word
.MPT	MS Project template	MS Project
.XLT	MS Excel template	MS Excel
.XLM	MS Excel macro	MS Excel
.TAR	TAR compressed file	PKZIP, WinZip, etc.
.GZ	GNUZip compressed file	PKZIP, WinZip, etc.
.UU	UUEncode file	Compression or e-mail programs
..	"Double Extended" file	Usually only as an e-mail attachment

Table B-1.   Potentially Dangerous File Extensions

The UNIX compressed files, or any compressed files, pose a simple threat: unless you scan them and/or can see their contents prior to extraction, you don't know what you're getting and should be cautious. (See http://www.gzip.org for information on GZ files, and http://helpdesk.uvic.ca/how-to/exchange/internet/coding/tar.html for information on TAR files.) The UU files are another easy door for a newsgroup-based virus, although most newsgroups are good about scanning. (See http://helpdesk.uvic.ca/how-to/exchange/internet/coding/uu.html for more information on UU files and decoder programs.)

Finally, a double extended file (that is, a file in the format *filename.ext.ext*) is understood and probably safe to a Linux or UNIX user, but can be trouble to a Windows user because many people will assume the file is something safe and open it, only to find out that it contains a virus.

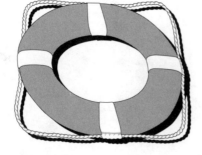

Appendix C

A Case Study in New Home Wiring for Data, Voice, and Cable

By Pat and Brownell Chalstrom

This appendix describes the wiring we installed at our new house in Annapolis, Maryland, in the spring of 2001.

We had four objectives to support our various communications needs:

✦ Internal data networking among a half dozen computers and devices

✦ Telephone for at least two outside lines

✦ Cable TV to most rooms in the house

✦ External high-speed Internet, either DSL or cable (we did not consider satellite)

Stereo distribution was not an objective, although some speaker wire was installed, with no active components, to allow the living room stereo to be played in the kitchen.

The house is new construction with three bedrooms and two and one-half baths in an established neighborhood. Comcast, the cable TV provider, recently did an infrastructure upgrade and now supports Cable Internet with the @Home service. We chose this service, because it is cheaper than Verizon's DSL and seems to provide better, faster service. We have been pleased so far, but with the rapidly changing broadband marketplace, we felt it was important to deploy systems that would make it easy to switch over to some other broadband access method. We believe we accomplished this.

We considered wireless for internal data networking and for voice, but rejected both. We felt the cost of the wiring in new construction was low enough to offset the uncertainties of wireless. We did look at the new generation of multiset phones from Panasonic and Siemens, but decided it was a little early to commit to that approach. If for no other reason than resale purposes, we felt it was important to completely wire the house for phone.

The functionality we achieved is as follows. A computer can be plugged into any data port in the house and be connected to all other computers in the house, as well as to the Internet. A simple, analog phone (or fax machine or computer) can be plugged into any phone jack in the house and be connected to either or both of our two phone lines. (We have expansion capability for two more phone numbers, for a total of four.) A TV can be plugged into a cable TV jack anywhere in the house and access the basic cable service we have (not digital cable).

The total cost for all this came to about $4500, which included the wire and labor to run it, and all the equipment and network performance testing before drywall installation. (Performance testing is very important—more on this shortly.) This cost may sound high, but we have 14 data jacks, 12 phone jacks, and 10 cable TV connections, plus a LAN and broadband Internet connection. It would be hard to deliver all this with the flexibility we have for much less money.

We ran Cat5e for the data and voice, and RG-6 for the cable. We were lucky to receive an invaluable article about home wiring from Brownell's brother Harry, who is in the construction industry. Entitled *High-Tech Home Wiring* by Joe Stoddard from the May 2000 issue of *The Journal of Light Construction* (http://www.jlconline.com), it explains all the different types of wiring and the pitfalls to avoid. We showed the article to the contractor doing all the other electrical work on the house and, fortunately for us, he admitted that he had neither the expertise nor equipment to do this type of cabling.

So we contracted with a commercial computer networking company to do the work, with which we were pleased. Even though their first-string team was terrific, the knowledge gained from the magazine article helped us monitor the work. Then, as often happens in construction, they sent in a second-string team to do some of the work. Their work was not acceptable. Fortunately, Pat was on the job site and asked them to stop the work.

The problem was the second-string team's lack of experience. Commercial wiring contractors are accustomed to installing cabling in offices, not homes. They usually must be reminded to do things a lot cleaner and neater. More of the work has to be hidden and put in walls than required in their industrial installations. The team was unaccustomed to stapling wire to studs, which is common in residential wood construction. They also were unprepared to drill holes through studs, and they were unable to install conduit. They were unaware of the need for plates to be installed to protect the cabling from being damaged by nails and screws. A trim carpenter installing baseboard could also ruin the network cabling. We had the residential electrician install metal plates for all the network cabling, as he did for the electrical cabling.

The networking and electrical contractors had to work together in other ways; thankfully, the two we had on the job got along very well. Providing power to the network devices is an example of this collaboration. City permits do not allow networking contractors to run electrical wire. They had to coordinate with the electrician to get power where they needed it—mostly at the wiring hub.

The networking contractor obtained his permits separately from the electrical contractor. This created the need for two inspections before the drywall could go up; luckily, the same city inspector did both in one visit.

The networking contractor used a network performance testing tool to test the installation. This piece of equipment costs around $7000, and residential electricians rarely have access to it. Network performance testing after running the cable but before putting in drywall decreases the chance of ripping out walls later to fix wiring problems. That's why a lot of commercial wiring is run outside of walls in cable troughs. We ran complete loopback tests on every cable that was run in the house and received 30 pages of performance output.

At the recommendation of the computer networking contractor, we chose Leviton for all the equipment, both at the "hub" of the networks and for the faceplates. Leviton is a leading manufacturer of lighting switches and other home electrical equipment, and has entered the home automation market. They have an excellent brochure (http://www.leviton.com/lin/pdf/ productcat/structured_media_systems.pdf) describing their approach and products.

It is critical to have a good schematic for all the wiring that is to be done. On size-reduced copies of the architectural floor plans we diagrammed where we wanted each faceplate and all the hub equipment. On this schematic we numbered each wire run and labeled each end of the cable with the corresponding number. We put faceplates, with three or six connectors, where we needed them. Most faceplates have a data port, a voice port, and a cable TV port together. The faceplate plastic for data network ports is blue, and for phone ports, white. For consistency's sake, all faceplates have phone on the top, data in the middle, and cable TV on the bottom.

Each cable is a dedicated direct run from the faceplate to the wiring hub in the basement, and all are Cat5e 8-wire, whether intended for data or voice. (We used blue-covered wire for data, and white for phone, but the actual copper cable is the same inside.) Using all the same wiring provides maximum flexibility, so any jack in the house can be used for phone or data. Switching a phone jack to the use of data, or vice versa, requires reconfiguration at the wiring hub, but no new wiring. We chose to use Cat5e rather than Cat5, so we may run Gigabit Ethernet some day, though currently we use only 10 Mbps.

The wiring hub consists mostly of Leviton parts, found in the catalog mentioned earlier. The exact Leviton parts used are

Two 18-port structured media panels	47603-18P
3x8 Video amplifier	47690-38B
AC Power Module	47605-DP
Enclosure SMC-420	47605-42W

Leviton resells a 4-port Ethernet hub, but we decided to use one device for the LAN and the external Internet connection. We bought an SMC Barricade Broadband Router that connects directly to our Comcast cable modem, has a 10/100 Mbps switch, and has a firewall built in. (It even has dial backup and a print server.) It also supports all the network address translation necessary to allow the one IP address supplied by Comcast to be shared by all the computers. It is small enough to fit into the Leviton enclosure. More PCs are supported by fanning out to a hub.

Figure C-1 shows the logical connection of all the parts. All the house wiring runs down to the wiring hub in the basement, where it is punched-down into the appropriate part of the

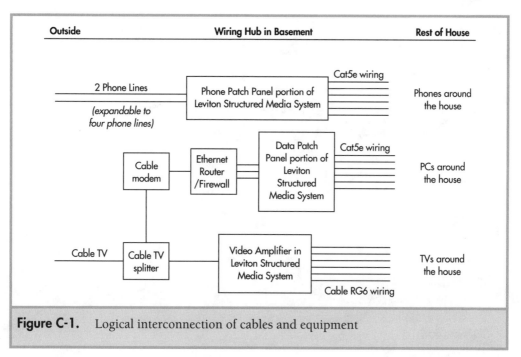

Figure C-1. Logical interconnection of cables and equipment

Leviton equipment. Short RJ-11 cables patch voice wires to the outside phone lines. Short RJ-45 cables make the connection between data wiring and the router. The cable TV wires all plug into the single 8-port video amplifier.

Overall we are very happy with the design and the installation. It is probably overkill for the growth we will experience in its use, but you never know. We are already looking into IP devices that can sit next to the stereo and play music from the Internet.

The most valuable lesson we learned from our experience is that running and terminating Cat5e cable is so different from running electrical cable, that it is crucial to have someone on the job with experience in data networking. We were glad we made the decision to bring in such a contractor early on in the process, and also that we were able to closely supervise our contractors while the work was in progress.

The Chalstroms can be contacted via their Web site, naturally, www.chalstrom.com.

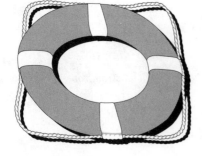

Index

✦ **I**

INTERNATIONAL CONTACT INFORMATION

AUSTRALIA
McGraw-Hill Book Company Australia Pty. Ltd.
TEL +61-2-9417-9899
FAX +61-2-9417-5687
http://www.mcgraw-hill.com.au
books-it_sydney@mcgraw-hill.com

CANADA
McGraw-Hill Ryerson Ltd.
TEL +905-430-5000
FAX +905-430-5020
http://www.mcgrawhill.ca

**GREECE, MIDDLE EAST,
NORTHERN AFRICA**
McGraw-Hill Hellas
TEL +30-1-656-0990-3-4
FAX +30-1-654-5525

MEXICO (Also serving Latin America)
McGraw-Hill Interamericana Editores S.A. de C.V.
TEL +525-117-1583
FAX +525-117-1589
http://www.mcgraw-hill.com.mx
fernando_castellanos@mcgraw-hill.com

SINGAPORE (Serving Asia)
McGraw-Hill Book Company
TEL +65-863-1580
FAX +65-862-3354
http://www.mcgraw-hill.com.sg
mghasia@mcgraw-hill.com

SOUTH AFRICA
McGraw-Hill South Africa
TEL +27-11-622-7512
FAX +27-11-622-9045
robyn_swanepoel@mcgraw-hill.com

**UNITED KINGDOM & EUROPE
(Excluding Southern Europe)**
McGraw-Hill Education Europe
TEL +44-1-628-502500
FAX +44-1-628-770224
http://www.mcgraw-hill.co.uk
computing_neurope@mcgraw-hill.com

ALL OTHER INQUIRIES Contact:
Osborne/McGraw-Hill
TEL +1-510-549-6600
FAX +1-510-883-7600
http://www.osborne.com
omg_international@mcgraw-hill.com

Symantec
Security Check™

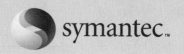

Symantec Security Check™ is a FREE online service that helps ensure a safe, productive Internet experience. Symantec Security Check identifies system vulnerabilities that could put personal information at risk—or even allow your PC or Mac® to be attacked by hackers or viruses. Symantec Security Check conducts two system check-up's, one to check for Internet threats, the other to check for virus infections.

 Scan for Security Risks—Test your computer's exposure to online security threats and learn how to make your computer more secure.

 Scan for Viruses — Examine your computer using Symantec's award-winning virus detection technology to determine if it is infected by any known virus or Trojan horse.

Currently, over 4.5 million people have used this valuable tool and the numbers continue to grow.*

Check your PC for security threats at
www.symantec.com/securitycheck

Symantec Corporation, a world leader in Internet security technology, provides a broad range of security solutions to individuals and enterprises. The company is a leading provider of virus protection, vulnerability assessment, intrusion prevention, Internet content and e-m filtering, remote management technologies an security services around the world. Symantec's Norton brand of products include such names as Norton AntiVirus,™ Norton Utilities,™ Norton Internet Security,™ and Norton™ Personal Firewa

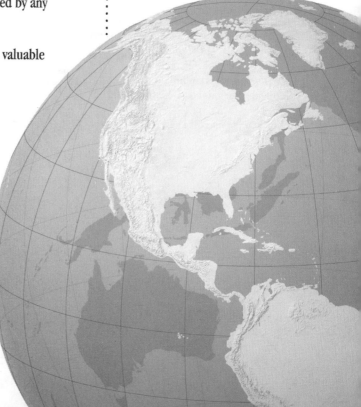